RICHARD S. SCOTT, M.D.
1719 KELTON AVE.
LOS ANGELES, CA. 90024

RECEIVED
NOV 10 1981
R. S. S.

9/6

3M

W9-BUA-519

OPERATION SUNRISE

The Secret Surrender

OPERATION SUNRISE

The Secret Surrender

BY

RICHARD S. SCOTT, M.D.
1719 KELTON AVE.
LOS ANGELES, CA 90024

BRADLEY F. SMITH

AND

ELENA AGAROSSI

Basic Books, Inc., Publishers

NEW YORK

Library of Congress Cataloging in Publication Data

Smith, Bradley F.
  Operation Sunrise.

  Bibliography: p. 222
  Includes index.
    1. Operation Sunrise. 2. World War, 1939–1945—
Diplomatic history. I. Agarossi, Elena, joint author.
II. Title.
D748.S55   940.54′21   78–73767
ISBN:0–465–05290–8

Copyright © 1979 by Basic Books, Inc.
Printed in the United States of America
DESIGNED BY VINCENT TORRE
10 9 8 7 6 5 4 3 2 1

Contents

Acknowledgments

IN THE COURSE of this project we have accumulated a number of individual and collective debts of gratitude. Archivists and librarians at many institutions aided us, especially Agnes F. Peterson, Hoover Institution, Stanford University; William Cunliffe (Modern Military Branch) and Patricia Dowling (Diplomatic Branch), National Archives; Donald Schewe, Franklin D. Roosevelt Library; Don W. Wilson, Dwight D. Eisenhower Library; James Miller and James Hastings, Federal Records Center, Suitland, Maryland; and Alexander P. Clark and Nancy Bressler, Princeton University.

A special thanks is due the director of the Woodrow Wilson International Center for Scholars, James H. Billington, who helped us gain access to the Allen Dulles Papers at Princeton.

John Toland and Professor Renzo De Felice read portions of the manuscript and made helpful suggestions, while our editors, Martin Kessler and Libby F. Bruch, gave valuable finish to the final product.

We gratefully acknowledge permission to reproduce material from the Allen Dulles Collection, Princeton University; the Henry Stimson Collection, Yale University; and the John Toland Collection, the Library of Congress.

Foundation support was provided by the Woodrow Wilson International Center for Scholars (this project was initiated while Elena Agarossi was a fellow at the Center in 1974) and by the Consiglio Nazional delle Ricerche. Chapters 2, 5, the first half of chapter 6, and the last half of chapter 7 were the primary responsibility of Elena Agarossi, while the remaining portions of the text were mainly authored by Bradley F. Smith.

While expressing our appreciation to all the organizations and individuals who assisted us, we wish to emphasize that the generosity was theirs, but the ultimate responsibility is exclusively ours.

Aptos, California, and
Rome, Italy
November 1978

OPERATION SUNRISE

The Secret Surrender

Introduction:
First Light

OPERATION SUNRISE was a covert mission executed near the close of the Second World War in Europe by America's major intelligence organization, the Office of Strategic Services (OSS). In an effort to arrange the surrender of Axis forces in northern Italy, the OSS chief in Bern, Allen Dulles, met secretly with a number of German officials headed by the SS and police chief of northern Italy, SS Obergruppenführer Karl Wolff, in March–April, 1945. The talks and dickering between the SS and the OSS were long and complicated, so much so that they occasioned serious squabbles among Anglo-American leaders and even more bitter controversy between the Western powers and the Soviet Union. In the end, Dulles managed to get his special surrender, but it did not come until 2 May 1945, just five days before the general capitulation at Rheims brought the complete demise of the Third Reich.

What caused peace to be established in Italy five days earlier or later, thirty years ago, is obviously not now a matter of vital importance, but many of the issues involved in the affair go much deeper than that. Among them is the fact that although the Rheims surrender of 7 May simply formalized the total military defeat of Nazi Germany, the surrender of 2 May was the culmination of a long discussion process in which political considerations occupied the minds of the major participants. Wolff and Dulles were certainly not in full political agreement, but they did share some common concerns, including a fear of Communism and a desire to effect an orderly transition from German to Anglo-American authority in northern Italy. The political coloration of the talks, when coupled with the secrecy that surrounded them, has raised serious questions about the fidelity of the Western powers to the principles of Allied unity and unconditional surrender. These questions, in turn, have given Operation Sunrise a vigorous life in the writings and controversy of the postwar world. Political espionage can be interesting reading—especially in the era of James Bond—and Sunrise has produced its share of fictional and nonfictional adventure stories since 1945. But especially following Allen Dulles's appointment as chief of the CIA in the 1950s, the questions surrounding what happened during his dealings with the SS in the spring of 1945 became more serious. Dulles himself, after his retirement from the agency, wrote a book about Sunrise which gave the impression that this affair was the archetype of what he thought a covert operation could accomplish.[1] But a number of revisionist historians, sharply critical of American cold war policy, also zeroed in on the Bern affair, and they contended (much as Molotov and Stalin had done in the spring of 1945) that it was little more than an Anglo-American effort to double-cross the Soviet Union by making a separate peace with Hitler's Germany.[2]

Four years ago, when large numbers of Anglo-American wartime documents were opened to research, the time seemed ripe for us to reexamine Sunrise. Since 1974 was the year of Watergate, it was also an appropriate moment to use federal declassification procedures to obtain important records which were still stamped "top secret." The process of locating materials and getting the necessary permissions was long and taxing but also very rewarding. This book is based almost completely on documents until now classified, which were released due to our efforts; we were also the first historians allowed access to the Dulles papers. With public denunciations of cover-up ringing in their ears, even CIA officials were more willing to listen when we pleaded that secrecy requirements should be relaxed. Not all of our documentary prayers were answered—we were not able to gain entrance to the central files of the CIA—but the agency did release most documents we found in various other archives. The CIA declassified ninety-six pages of text from the surreptitious monitoring that U.S. Army intelligence men had done in Karl Wolff's cell after he was made an Allied prisoner in June, 1945.[3] When combined with the SS man's postwar written statements, and his numerous declarations to the Nuremberg war-crimes investigators, these records throw a new light on Wolff's willingness to take the lead in dealing with the OSS. Important though these materials are, we scored an even more dramatic success when the agency finally bowed to our repeated requests and released a large file containing the Sunrise messages which had passed between Allen Dulles and the OSS officials attached to Allied Mediterranean headquarters at Caserta, Italy, from March to May, 1945.[4] Since this is the only group of OSS field intelligence dispatches which has ever been declassified by the CIA, it will be valuable for those trying to understand many aspects of Allied wartime intelligence operations. But for the history of Operation Sunrise, this material is nothing short of priceless. Throughout the Bern affair, Dulles reported to the OSS headquarters in Washington and

Caserta (with copies to OSS headquarters in London, and at SHAEF), and all of those dispatches plus the replies from the military and OSS authorities in Caserta are in this file. For the first time it is possible to trace Dulles's actions precisely, and also to catch glimpses of his thought patterns and motivation. To supplement, and to serve as a partial corrective for this material, Princeton University generously allowed us to examine the private files which Dulles used as sources when he prepared his own apologia in 1965–1966.[5]

But the importance of the original Sunrise dispatches extends far beyond the direct light which they throw on the OSS representative himself. Heretofore historians have tended to approach the Bern incident as if it were a three-cornered relationship consisting of Wolff, Dulles, and the American government in Washington. The original Dulles dispatches now show that this view was far too simple, because much of the direction that the OSS man received came not from Washington, but from the Caserta headquarters of the Allied military commander in the Mediterranean theater, Field Marshal Harold Alexander. Thus we were forced to examine the records of Alexander's headquarters in order to see why the Caserta authorities acted the way they did,[6] and this in turn made us take a long look at one of the most neglected aspects of the history of World War II, the political-military labyrinth that was the Italian campaign.

Yet even Caserta could not be the end, only a very important way station on the journey, because in addition to immediate circumstances in Italy, Alexander and his aides made their decisions on the basis of the instructions they received from their superiors. Since Alexander was a British field marshal, many of those messages came from the prime minister, the British Chiefs of Staff, and the Foreign Office in London, and as might readily be anticipated, the available records of those officials indicate that in the spring of 1945, British authorities were watching the American-German talks in Bern with lively, if nervous, interest.[7] The United Kingdom was desperately trying to hold on to a special British "presence" in the Mediterranean, but its relative weakness vis-à-vis the United States and the Soviet Union was becoming increasingly apparent. Consequently London wanted to guide Alexander's hand on Sunrise in such a way that British interests would be protected, but it was also anxious (with a few momentary, if significant, lapses) to keep in close touch with the Americans who had become the senior members of the Atlantic partnership. So, in addition to those from London to Caserta, messages about Sunrise flowed back and forth between the British and American capitals. More such communications moved along the Caserta-Washington line, because Alexander received his broad policy directives from the Combined Chiefs of Staff, who were headquartered in the

American capital. The westward focus of Sunrise messages were rounded out by the dispatches that Dulles exchanged with his OSS superiors in the Pentagon.[8]

Due to the triple stream of information pouring into Washington, as well as the intrinsic importance of the Bern affair, many of America's top wartime agencies and officials were drawn into decision making for Sunrise. By combing through the Washington records, we uncovered new data which allowed us to correct many of the factual errors about America's Sunrise policy that have been included in earlier accounts, and, more important, these documents gave us a rare inside view of the decision-making process in Washington. We discovered that few, if any, of the revisionist contentions about Sunrise and the general characteristics of American wartime policy were borne out by the records of the policy makers involved with the Bern incident. There was, for example, no sign of significant influence from the State Department planners, who, revisionists contend, were at this time preparing a bid to establish a worldwide system of American capitalistic influence in the postwar world. The State Department played a very modest part in the whole affair, and the direct role of presidents Roosevelt and Truman was only slightly more important. The main policy line was set by the military authorities, especially the Joint Chiefs of Staff and Secretary of War Henry L. Stimson.[9] Not only did they chart the broad course to be pursued by Alexander and the OSS chiefs, they also shaped Washington's policy toward America's allies. The crucial Sunrise communications to the British and Russian governments, which were dispatched over the name of the secretary of state, were actually drafted in the War Department, on occasion by Secretary of War Stimson himself. Similarly, a number of the last "Roosevelt" cables to Stalin—messages often cited as indicative of the president's thinking on the eve of his death—were in fact written by the chairman of the Joint Chiefs of Staff, Admiral Leahy, with little or no supervision by the president.[10]

The Washington Sunrise records also fail to bear out the revisionist contention that in 1945 the American leaders were primarily concerned with controlling and isolating the Soviet Union. Relations with Russia did occupy a central place in the thoughts of the military spokesmen who were directing American policy and, like everyone else involved in Sunrise including the British, Dulles, and especially Karl Wolff, Stimson and the American generals showed some nervousness about Russian plans and the possible threat of Communist expansion. But there is no indication that their main interest was to gain a march on the Russians in order to open the door for the spread of capitalism. The American military leaders were primarily concerned with preventing troubles with Russia so that the completion of their *wartime* tasks would not be more difficult. They had been charged with the supreme duty of ending the war as quickly and cheaply as possible and all their wartime planning rested on the belief that friendly cooperation with the Soviet Union was essential if they were to discharge this duty effectively. In 1945 they still saw relations with Russia in this light, not only because they believed that Soviet power would be significant in the last stage of smashing the Third Reich and in slaying the Nazi dragon during the early months of the occupation of Germany, but also because they wanted Soviet bases and Soviet military support in the war against Japan. Because they were not in possession of clear presidential policy guidelines on postwar relations with the Russians, the future role of Germany, or the long-range economic and military interests of the United States, the Service chiefs had little choice but to make their Sunrise decisions on the basis of wartime policy considerations.

Stimson and the generals wanted a quick end to Nazi power and Sunrise seemed to offer hope of that, but they also believed that they needed good military-political relations with Russia, and Soviet hostility to Sunrise posed a serious threat to that. How to cash in on Sunrise's peace prospects and at the same time maintain friendly ties with the Soviet Union was the crucial problem that they posed for themselves. That some officials in the lower echelons of the American government were at that very moment toying with plans for the postwar world and possible restraints on the Soviet Union is a fact pregnant with meaning for the cold war future, but in those hectic days of March, April, and May, 1945, the members of the Supreme Command had their eyes turned in a different direction. They were struggling mightily to make Operation Sunrise help them reach their most basic wartime goal: the attainment of a rapid and total victory over Nazism through cooperation with the Soviet Union. Blundering here, squabbling there, they backed their way toward the end of hostilities, with eyes fixed on the issues of war rather than those of the coming postwar world.

Thus, examining the Bern affair can give us not only a good spy story and a glimpse of some of the significant byways in the cold war controversies, it is also an especially enlightening chance to view the Western leadership in action during the vitally important days of the end of the war in Europe. To obtain the maximum benefit from this opportunity, however, we must set Sunrise down in the context of the time, and then carefully unravel the threads which made up this labyrinth of darkness and light.

CHAPTER 1

Creators of a Sunrise

AMERICA entered World War II with the largest industrial war potential on earth, an army the size of Sweden's, and much of the United States Navy resting on the bottom of Pearl Harbor. Of course America was not alone. She had cobelligerents: two modest ones in her struggle against Japan (China and the remnants of the British Empire), and two formidable allies in the war with Hitler (the Soviet Union and Great Britain). But in December, 1941, Allied military forces showed few bright prospects anywhere. Chiang Kai-shek's armies had been battered by the Japanese for four years, and the Anglo-American units in Asia were also soon routed and most of them overrun. In Europe, Britain had little to show for two years of combat except impressive retreats and the achievement of having at least survived the Nazi Blitzkrieg. Further east, Hitler's Wehrmacht was slicing up European Russia in a savage campaign that annihilated soldiers and civilians with equal ruthlessness. Not until December, 1941, the very moment when the United States declared war on Germany and Japan, did the Red Army finally make a stand which temporarily contained the German forces west of Moscow.

Gloomy Allied military conditions existed everywhere, and the political outlook was not much brighter. Not only were the Axis powers armed to the teeth and flushed with victory, but as far as the Allies could see, Germany, Italy, and Japan appeared to be politically united and to have fully coordinated their military operations. The appearance of Axis unity was an illusion, but compared with the divisions and chaos among the Allies in December, 1941, the Tokyo-Rome-Berlin Axis seemed to be one line, straight and true. Everywhere one looked within the Allied camp, there was real or potential trouble. On the surface, the British and Americans worked smoothly together, but underneath, Washington was deeply suspicious of British

8

imperialism, and for their part, many leaders in London did not relish the prospect of Britain disappearing into the warm embrace of an all-powerful United States. The conflicts, rivalries, and tensions between the Soviet Union and the Western capitalist states were legion, and the turns and twists of 1930s diplomacy had done nothing to increase mutual confidence between East and West. Far across the world, Chiang's regime was holed up in Chungking, crying for aid and eyeing everyone—Communists, Americans, Russians, British, and Japanese—with icy suspicion. Beyond these general problems, there stretched broad fields of specific inter-Allied territorial dispute, economic rivalry, and conflicting claims to zones of interest; they were issues which plague every coalition that manages to hold together until the moment of victory.[1]

Whatever president had been in the White House in late 1941, the same harsh and fundamental problems would have had to be faced. The United States government needed to limit the initial Axis advance while preserving the unity of American public opinion and strengthening the bonds among the Allied Big Four. Only if the care and feeding of public opinion was put in the foreground would American war production be maximized; only if the Allied coalition was knit tightly together would there be enough manpower available to win a decisive victory with American material. That much was fixed and given.

But the immediate past experience of the actual Commander and Chief, Franklin D. Roosevelt, gave things something of a special twist. Roosevelt had just escaped from years of bitter conflict with the isolationists over whether the United States was in such grave danger that aid had to be extended to Britain, China, and Russia. Pearl Harbor stilled that debate. Virtually every American was ready to fight Germany, Italy, and Japan and to aid the Allies in December, 1941, simply because the members of the Axis had shown themselves to be so treacherous, evil, and dangerous. However, Roosevelt realized that this consensus did not mean all Americans trusted him or his policies; partisan political struggles and the isolationist controversies had cut too deep for that. Nor did it mean that Americans had abandoned their suspicion of the outside world. They had not become instant internationalists and they had not suddenly found a clear set of objectives in foreign affairs. The foreign policy debates prior to Pearl Harbor had been little concerned with economic interests or zones of influence; they had revolved around whether there was an immediate danger to American security. That had been the issue, and that was what was settled by Pearl Harbor.

Obviously then, FDR saw that the best way to maintain American unity was to leave public opinion right where it was by emphasizing patriotism and the cause of democracy as counterweights to Axis aggression. The president was willing to back this up with vague bits of idealism, such as the Four Freedoms and the Atlantic Charter, but he assiduously avoided articulating specific political objectives or war aims. He wanted no repetition of the strident debate which had occurred over Wilson's Fourteen Points during the First World War. Roosevelt's war program rested on the spirit of "Remember Pearl Harbor!" and he did all in his power to keep American attention focused on the military, not the political, side of war.

But depoliticizing the conflict at home was only one aspect of the president's problem. In order to be successful, he also had to convince his Allies that they should stand shoulder to shoulder despite their many differences, and that they should not discuss divisive political issues. The Alliance had to be maintained in an atmosphere of political silence because intergovernmental wrangling might threaten the unity of the Big Four and, equally important, might cause serious fissures in American public opinion. Roosevelt never tired of stressing to Churchill, Stalin, and even to Chiang, that debate on political questions should be delayed as much as possible until victory had been won. A postwar United Nations Organization, keyed to controlling aggression, could then act as the supreme political problem-solver. But so long as the war continued, FDR believed that on most critical issues his hands were tied. Questions such as the stationing of American troops in postwar Europe or a possible partition of Poland could not be dealt with openly because they were controversial at home, and American political strife had to be avoided at all cost. Instead of frank discussion and clear political deals, Roosevelt sought to bind the Allies together through promises of military assistance, such as Lend Lease and a Second Front. In addition, FDR stressed the importance of interallied pledges not to negotiate with the enemy. Seen from this perspective, the policy of unconditional surrender was not an off-the-cuff political blunder; rather it was an important step in Roosevelt's campaign to minimize the war's political dimensions.

But all of this would have seemed merely clever footwork if Roosevelt had not developed a system for masking the political aspects of military operations. As Clausewitz noted long ago, where one commits military forces, whose troops go there, and what they do to the civilian population on the spot are all political choices of the first magnitude. Not only do they affect military operations, they also largely determine the relative power positions of both victors and vanquished. The old aphorisms, "To the victor belong the spoils" and "Possession is nine-tenths of the law," sum up why command decisions are inherently political. If Franklin Roosevelt was to successfully defuse political controversy, he had to develop a method for making operational choices which appeared to be apolitical.

Roosevelt accomplished this by reserving to himself and his top military officers virtually all decision-making powers related to the conduct of the war. Not only did he exclude Congress from tampering with strategy and military administration, he almost completely froze out the civilian executive agencies such as the State Department. The practical direction and strategic conduct of the war was given over to the Joint Chiefs of Staff, a body created in the first weeks of 1942, which acted as counterpart of the British "Chiefs of Staff Committee." The Joint Chiefs of Staff thus became the American representatives on the Combined Chiefs of Staff, the supreme Anglo-American military agency. The Joint Chiefs of Staff was made up of the Chief of Staff of the Army, General George C. Marshall, the Chief of Naval Operations and Commander in Chief of the Fleet, Admiral Ernest J. King, and the Commanding General of the Army Air Forces, Lieutenant General Henry H. Arnold. In March, 1942, a fourth member was added, Admiral William D. Leahy, the newly appointed Chief of Staff to the President, who acted as a *trait d'union* between the president and the Joint Chiefs.

It should be noted that the members of the Joint Chiefs of Staff were not civilian officials of the Army and Navy departments, nor were they even the respective Cabinet members. Roosevelt went around the civilian, and politically oriented, Cabinet government structure, in order to establish a body for military coordination run by the generals and admirals. The individual members of the Joint Chiefs of Staff, such as General Marshall, were still formally subordinate to their respective Cabinet superiors—in Marshall's case, Secretary of War Henry Stimson—but as the war went on, the focal point for important military decisions steadily moved out of the hands of the Cabinet and into those of the Joint Chiefs.

In effect, FDR gave the generals and admirals an agency through which to coordinate their operations. To get any significant military action approved and organized, common action between the various military and naval branches was essential, and the Joint Chiefs of Staff was the only unit through which this could be accomplished. Having given them a workable coordination agency, FDR told the military leaders to go out and win the war.

Of course Roosevelt never gave any subordinate carte blanche. Ever conscious of the importance of public opinion and the power of the word, he made certain that the generals and admirals were guided by a broad principle, in this case, "military necessity." What this phrase meant in practice was that the Joint Chiefs were to plan operations taking into account only those factors which military specialists usually weigh when making command decisions. They were to destroy the maximum enemy forces and war-making capacity at the minimum cost in American men and material.

OPERATION SUNRISE

One of the major effects of this system was that it put the primary emphasis on responsiveness to immediate events and militated against long-term operational planning. Even though detailed production and logistical plans were made, the movement of armies, much of the strategy, and nearly all of the tactics had to be continually adjusted to the battle situation. If military necessity meant anything at all, it had to mean that the field commanders should make the basic decisions on how best to exploit the battle situations which they faced, while the Chiefs determined which of the theaters, and zones within them, offered the most favorable prospects for a speedy and inexpensive victory. Here and there, long-term planning, and even a dash of overt political calculation, left their mark, but short-term improvisation was the transcendent principle of the wartime American system.

The Joint Chiefs of Staff, then, were told to produce a quick victory, but at the same time they were directed to heed the law of military parsimony. They had to produce their triumphs with the lowest possible cost in American lives. Roosevelt obviously knew that he had to avoid the war weariness associated with a prolonged conflict and he was even more sharply aware that public enthusiasm for the war depended on a short casualty roll. The Joint Chiefs therefore made their professional military decisions ever mindful that the supreme "Chief" wanted speed and special attention to holding down losses.

The major effect of this presidential pressure was to make the Chiefs and their military planners emphasize production and technology rather than raw manpower. Much of the great military/industrial leap forward occasioned by World War II arose directly from this intense desire to finish the war quickly, and, in American terms, cheaply. The firepower and mechanization of the United States forces drastically increased after 1941, as every possible device from massed artillery to saturation bombing was employed to more rapidly obliterate the enemy.

When America's production and her technology-swathed manpower were coupled with British military force, they gave new life to the Western alliance. By 1942, the existence of this developing colossus, paralleled by the remarkable recovery and advance of the Red Army, enabled the Allies to pass over to the offensive in the East and West. The Russian advance in the winter of 1941-1942, and the Allied landings in North Africa in November, 1942, marked a turn in the initiative, if not a full turn of the tide. There were still reverses for the Allies, such as the German offensive toward the Caucasus in the summer of 1942, and the counterattack of the Afrika Korps on the Tunisian-Algerian border in December, but the period in which the Allies had little choice but to hold on, or fall back, was clearly over.

However, with the acquisition of new offensive opportunities, the Western Allies also confronted new challenges in their attempt to depoliticize warfare. As long as they had been fighting a defensive war, the international political choices were few. They mainly reassured those neutrals who could not be enticed to intervene, and simultaneously passed pledges of loyalty and support back and forth to each other. As soon as the Anglo-Americans began to contemplate where to strike their own blows, however, and especially when they actually entered foreign countries, the political realities of warfare came tumbling down upon them. When Eisenhower landed in Morocco and Algeria in November, 1942, none of the American officials in control—not Roosevelt, not the Joint Chiefs, and not Eisenhower—were sensitized to the political hazards that existed there. Eisenhower naively assumed that the best way to accelerate his advance, in the spirit of military necessity, was to recognize, and cooperate with, the Vichy French officials whom he found there. That these men were representatives of the French government which worked closely with Hitler did not deter Eisenhower, but it did unleash a storm of political protest in the United States.

Roosevelt dealt with the resulting domestic political crisis by means of a three-point response. It was at this point—after little consultation with anyone—that he proclaimed the policy of unconditional surrender. At first glance this might seem to have settled the matter. The government of the United States, and then those of the other Allies, pledged themselves not to repeat the mistake of 1918: In World War II there would be no muddled armistice with Adolf Hitler. But actually the problems in North Africa had not been occasioned by deals made with Germans, but by those with the Vichy French Admiral Darlan. Vichy France had not officially joined the Axis, and the United States was not at war with the Vichy government at the time of the landings. The heads of the French regime, Laval and Petain, had cooperated closely with Hitler, and only a blind person could fail to see that Vichy was a German satellite, but no simple formula like that calling for unconditional surrender of Germany, Italy, and Japan could meet situations such as that which had been encountered in North Africa.

Roosevelt's intermediate-level answer to Darlan-type crises was to give more effective guidance to the Joint Chiefs of Staff. Through Admiral Leahy, he set about raising the political consciousness of the men who controlled the strategic direction of the war. Although never totally success-ful—it was not possible for men like General "Hap" Arnold to acquire a very broad international vision—none of the Joint Chiefs' subsequent blunders was quite as serious as the 1942 North African fiasco. If they did not become strikingly perceptive in the last three years of the war, at least the Joint Chiefs did become somewhat more cautious.

OPERATION SUNRISE

At the level of actual combat operations, Roosevelt made his third attempt to circumscribe and control the political aspects of offensive warfare. Special representatives—in Eisenhower's case, Ambassador Robert Murphy—were assigned to the theater commanders to provide political guidance. Men like Murphy, and Britain's Harold Macmillan, were supposed to read the minds of FDR and Churchill respectively, and then help turn the generals away from courses of action involving serious political hazards. This system may have helped to prevent some monumental blunders, but it also increased confusion and hesitancy in operational decision making. The next major political issue which emerged after the North African campaign was the fall of Mussolini in July, 1943. This time the Allied leaders—both Eisenhower and those in London and Washington—did avoid a full-scale Darlanish political controversy. Nevertheless, they still produced a muddled and politically compromising deal with Badoglio which failed effectively to exploit the opportunities offered by the Duce's fall.[2]

Through all of this patching and hauling, Franklin Roosevelt managed to cover up most of the political consequences of offensive, as well as defensive, warfare between 1942 and 1945. But there was one major exception, rising like a political sore thumb in his panorama of pure and unsullied military operations. Neither the president nor the generals were prepared to give up the military advantages which might accrue from propaganda, espionage, and covert operations. All of these methods were fraught with political risks, but ideological warfare was an old, and to Americans, a well-accepted practice, while the glamor and prestige of espionage and covert operations had risen to new heights in the 1930s and 1940s. Although somewhat nervous about all this, the generals knew that intelligence gathering was necessary and that propaganda and covert operations might help bring a quicker victory.[3] Roosevelt shared their view and in addition had a soft spot for what he saw as clever innovations. Like all recent American chief executives, Roosevelt also seems to have relished the sport of international intelligence and deception. When an old friend, General William Donovan, approached him in 1941 with the suggestion that in the event of war, the United States should form an intelligence agency which would use the weapons of espionage and covert politics to hasten victory, FDR was very receptive to the idea.

The United States would surely have developed a special intelligence organization to supplement military and naval intelligence during World War II in any case, but its actual form was largely due to the determination and initiative of Donovan.[4] The general, who was actually a New York lawyer pressed into wartime service, enjoyed a measured respect from the military authorities because of his intellect and his heroic army service in the

First World War. He also had FDR's confidence and was in possession of what to Americans seemed a catchy idea. Through close personal connections in London, Donovan was familiar with the major organizational innovations in intelligence and covert operations which the British government had made during the first two years of hostilities. To meet the needs of a complex and ruthless conflict, the old British Foreign Intelligence Branch (MI6) was reorganized and renamed the Secret Intelligence Service (SIS). In addition, London's counterintelligence organization (MI5) had been expanded, and two new agencies created: the Political Warfare Executive (PWE) in the propaganda field, and the Special Operations Executive (SOE) charged with the task of carrying out sabotage and assisting guerrilla warfare. The British government hoped that SOE, supplemented by PWE and SIS, would, to use Churchill's picturesque language, "set Europe ablaze."

All this organizational activity made a deep impression on General Donovan. Understanding the enormous and largely uncontrollable power of full-scale economic war, the general was not convinced that having total war run amok was necessarily in the interest of the moderate and conservative economic groups who like to think of themselves as the leaders of American society. In Donovan's view it would be better to avoid an all-out slugging match and win the contest with brains, maneuvers, and the weapons of politics. What he wanted, and ultimately obtained, was an American organization which could hasten victory by combining intelligence operations (like the SIS) and propaganda efforts (paralleling the PWE) with a covert political warfare branch (similar to the SOE).

Donovan obtained part of the loaf in the summer of 1941 when he was designated coordinator of information (COI). Directly subordinate to the president, he had the task of collecting and analyzing security information drawn from all sources, including those of the army, navy, and State Department. A year later, after the United States entered the war, this organization was expanded, renamed the Office of Strategic Services (OSS), and placed under the general direction of the Joint Chiefs of Staff. The OSS had three constituent subunits patterned after British models: the Secret Information Branch (SI), the Special Operations Branch (SO), and the Morale Branch (MO)—the latter specializing in covert ("black") propaganda. The responsibility for disseminating official ("white") propaganda was not assigned to the OSS, however, but went to another new agency, the Office of War Information.

The OSS was thus a composite copy of the British intelligence and political warfare organizations. The only significant difference in structure was that Donovan had put all of the functions—except white propaganda—under one roof, while the British kept each specialized activity in its own organizational

RICHARD S. SCOTT, M.D.
1719 KELTON AVE.
LOS ANGELES, CA 90024

hut. Little wonder then, that when the time came to train the first OSS agents, Donovan simply sent them across to the British to learn espionage techniques, clandestine communications, and the use of secret codes. Just as understandably, this initial dependence made the OSS men look like schoolboys, and Donovan was forced to spend much of his time and energy during the war trying to counter the impression that his men were only amateur secret agents who were dominated and overshadowed by their British masters.

The taint of amateurism which clung to the OSS made American military leaders suspicious of the organization and also inclined them not to share their own intelligence secrets with it. This was more than a question of mere bureaucratic jealousy, although there was a generous supply of that. The military and naval chiefs held in their hands the decisive intelligence-gathering weapon of World War II, namely cryptographic analysis. The "Magic" units of the American Navy had cracked the Japanese codes, and the British "Ultra" team had done the same with the German ciphers. Donovan's cloak-and-dagger men never had a chance in an intelligence competition with these wonder weapons. The machines, not OSS agents, cranked out a steady flow of vital top-level information on the enemy's aims and operations; since the military, not the OSS, controlled the information obtained by cryptographic analysis, the prestige of Donovan's organization sank considerably. In addition, the military and naval authorities were reluctant to pass their intelligence finds on to the OSS because most of their important information came directly, or indirectly, from Magic or Ultra, and they would not circulate this material. In consequence, OSS officials spent endless time doing superficial intelligence analysis based on low-level information gathered from the organization's own sources and whatever scraps could be obtained from the army and navy. Although individual OSS representatives made intelligence coups, as Allen Dulles did on the German V-2 rocket program, there was little possibility that OSS research and analysis would reach conclusions vital to those making command decisions. Understandably, the Joint Chiefs of Staff do not seem to have taken this activity very seriously.

The military's chilly reserve was made even colder by the unusual personnel policies that Donovan used in his organization. The men who held top administrative posts for the agency were, like Donovan and his close friends David Bruce and Allen Dulles, corporate attorneys, business executives, and bankers. Solid and conservative, many of them Republicans from the wealthiest families in the country, they were the kind of men who would be a reassuring presence in official Washington and would not be threatening to the military high command. But at the operational level, Donovan chose agents with little regard for social standing or ideology. Individuals were selected to be OSS operatives because they seemed "calculatingly reckless"[5] and held promise of having "disciplined daring" when "trained for aggressive action." Consequently men from every walk of life, and from every political persuasion, served as OSS intelligence agents and as liaison officers with the various resistance movements of Europe and Asia. Conservative, liberal, and communist OSS men went about the business of assisting partisan groups and fighting the enemy, while frequently squabbling with each other. Inevitably this produced a great deal of confusion regarding the aims of the OSS and of the American government, and just as inevitably, the Joint Chiefs of Staff looked askance at this quarrelsome band which had been let loose in enemy-occupied Europe bearing the stamp of United States government approval. The American Army was uneasy about all kinds of irregular and partisan warfare—professional military men do not think that "franc-tireur" is a nice word—but that the United States was aiding and supporting resistance movements with an organization as unprofessional and politically muddled as the OSS made the military high command's attitude range from cool to icy.

It is difficult to avoid the conclusion that if the military authorities had had their way, the size and scope of the OSS would have been sharply curtailed. The OSS maintained itself chiefly because Franklin Roosevelt supported it to the end. Perhaps like Donovan, the president had lingering doubts whether a knock-down total war would advance the cause of the older and simpler America which he loved. The White House never abandoned the hope that some lucky break might be exploited by the OSS to produce a lightning victory, which might, parenthetically, save America from leaping completely into an age of brutal mass power.

Thus the OSS remained part of America's war machine, but it was not a central part; the Joint Chiefs of Staff did not extend it full confidence, and the OSS leaders were not privy to the thinking of the military high command. In World War II America, there was little room either for long-term planning or full-scale political warfare by the OSS, because the military was allowed to call the tune. From first day to last, the Joint Chiefs of Staff, and the principle of military necessity, held the center of the parade ground.

Across the Atlantic, things sounded rather differently, or at least they were played on different instruments and in another key. British ties to the United States were extremely close during the Second World War, but the policies of the two countries were not identical. When the British accepted the preservation of the Empire and the importance of the balance of power as cardinal principles in their self-interest, it was obvious that the United Kingdom could not fight a war totally bereft of immediate political calculation. In addition, the economic burden which two world wars had laid on the British required them to make every effort to protect and advance their economy. Still, in the minds of the men of the War Cabinet, and especially in that of Winston Churchill, there hovered the even more fundamental realization that British power had been seriously weakened both by World War I and by the events of 1939 to 1942. The United Kingdom was mortally vulnerable to Nazi Germany, and much of her position in Asia had been seized by the Japanese. To Churchill and the majority of his colleagues, the moral was painfully clear: Britain's continuation as a great power, and perhaps her very survival, depended on a quick, cheap victory, and on cooperation with, and support from, the United States. The prime minister grasped that the best way to affect such cooperation, and obtain the support which Britain sorely needed, was to adapt British methods, and to some extent British objectives, to American realities. Consequently, mixed Anglo-American military commands were established in the various combat theaters and the British and American commanders, as well as their staffs, were governed by the fundamental rule of "military necessity." On a higher level, as already indicated, the members of the Chiefs of Staff Committee were joined by their counterparts of the Joint Chiefs of Staff, to form the Combined Chiefs of Staff. The latter group, significantly situated in Washington rather than London, took over the task of turning "military necessity" into flesh by issuing operational directives to the field commanders and coping with sensitive political-military problems as they arose. Beyond the level of the Combined Chiefs of Staff, difficulties could only be dealt with by summit agreement between Churchill and Roosevelt.[6] By accepting this system, the prime minister put cooperation with the United States in the forefront of Britain's policy and left his country's special political and economic interests to be dealt with as best they could in the nooks and crannies of military necessity and by summit diplomacy.

Of course the merging of the British and American command systems did nothing to improve their speed or efficiency. Few political or long-term plans were agreed to. Basic policies should have been established jointly by the president and the prime minister, but occasional summit meetings and the exchange of personal telegrams were a far cry from systematic planning. The Combined Chiefs of Staff who were supposed to take summit decisions and hammer them into workable policies found themselves scampering after events, improvising military-political policies as they went along. Then, not only did they have to deal with the field commanders, while reconciling as best they could the special interests of the British and the Americans, on occasion the Chiefs also discovered that the president or the prime minister had gone behind their backs and given special orders to individual generals or admirals. Roosevelt was cautious about hopping down to the operational level, but the pixielike Churchill delighted in sneaking past the whole command structure in order to push one of his pet schemes onto a lowly British officer. Surely through all of this, there were moments when members of the Combined Chiefs must have felt that the Axis armies were the least of their problems.

For all its shortcomings, however, the Combined Chiefs of Staff system did succeed in its primary task—a war against the European Axis was won by combined military forces. The system worked slowly, often inefficiently, but in the end the purely military side of it worked. That the Chiefs did not fare so well with the long-term political effects of the war is obvious. Not only did they fail to establish clear political goals, but in conformity with FDR's wishes, they delayed every political decision for as long as possible. The American representatives set the tone for the Combined Chiefs of Staff and their focus was riveted on VE Day and VJ Day, with perhaps a few months of occupation duty thereafter. They were prepared to hold all possible controversies in abeyance until those magic days finally came; what happened next was not their problem. Not a farsighted or very edifying approach, perhaps, but one that inevitably followed from the system which the United States used to fight and win World War II.

That grave postwar problems were stored up in this "victory first" approach is now a well-worn cliché, but perhaps the most significant political effect of the Combined Chiefs' system was that its very existence widened the gap between the Soviet Union and the West. Since the Combined Chiefs were the instrumentality through which the British and Americans not only coordinated their operations but disposed of many political questions, Soviet exclusion from this system left them militarily and politically isolated. The separation of Soviet operational military planning from that done by the Anglo-Americans was not mortally significant because the Eastern and Western Allies were actually fighting on two nearly independent fronts. But the exclusion of Russia from the Combined Chiefs of Staff meant that she stood outside of the organization in which the Western powers made most of their important day-to-day political decisions. The Soviets only had direct contact with the Western decision-making process at the summit level, while the British and Americans continuously worked together ever more intimately inside the Combined Chiefs structure. On occasion, the Soviets tried to lessen their political isolation by advocating the establishment of organizations with representation of the three powers. For example, during the early stages of the Allied occupation of Italy, the Soviet Union called for the formation of a tripartite political commission, but the Anglo-Americans sidestepped this proposal by forming an Allied Control

Commission, which was actually run by the British and American military authorities. The Combined Chiefs of Staff established the policy guidelines, and the Control Commission implemented them under the ever-present principle of military necessity. All the Soviets received in consolation was participation in an Allied Advisory Commission for Italy, a token consultative group without significant influence. The net effect was that the Anglo-American military had their way and, in the process, the first precedent for creating zones of influence in territories occupied by the Allies was established.[7]

By and large, then, from 1941 to 1945, the Soviet Union was the outsider and the long-established suspicions of East and West were reinforced by the exclusions inherent in the Chiefs system. On occasion the gaps were narrowed by meetings of the Big Three and more frequently by cable communications that passed back and forth between Stalin and the Western leaders. It is also true that contact with the Russians was maintained through active Anglo-American embassies in Moscow and the Soviet embassies in London and Washington. But this line of communication did not connect the Soviets with the people directly involved in the significant Western decision-making system. These were State Department and Foreign Office liaisons, while the Anglo-American generals and admirals were the ones producing most of the military and political action. A less publicized but often more important communication line ran between the British and American Military Missions in Moscow and the representatives of the Red General Staff. Through this channel clear and specific information concerning the resolutions and intentions of the Combined Chiefs was frequently passed to the Soviets.[8] But at its best, this too was a coordination instrument, and the Anglo-American decision-making system still functioned independently from that of the Soviet Union.

When one considers this organizational gap along with all the other well-known sources of tension between East and West which had developed by 1945, it is much easier to understand crises such as the one which arose over Operation Sunrise.[9] The Soviet Union played no part in planning or executing this operation, or any other project carried out under the direction of the Combined Chiefs of Staff. Sunrise was a German initiative and an Anglo-American response; the Soviets were outsiders and they felt it. Therefore the first step which should be taken in trying to understand why it took place is to examine the factors which were uppermost in the minds of the people directing Anglo-American military policy in late 1944 and early 1945, which is to say that to grasp the basic elements of the Bern affair, there is no point in making one's first observation in the direction of Moscow. Operation

Sunrise did not come into being in a red sky, it was created by the Combined Chiefs' vision of the European situation as the war entered its final phase.

By January-February, 1945, the focus of the Western military leaders was fixed on crossing the Rhine to engage the German army in a final battle of annihilation. The long years in which the Anglo-American forces skirmished in the shadow of Soviet ground power had finally come to an end. For three and a half years the Soviets had met and battered the bulk of the German army while the Western powers nibbled on the enemy flanks and made generous use of their superiority on the sea and in the air. Even the D-Day invasion, dramatic technical achievement that it was, did not immediately alter the imbalance between the Eastern and Western fronts. First in August-September, 1944, with the breakout from Normandy and the race toward the German frontier, did the British and Americans begin to achieve parity with the Russians in the deadly game of tying down and destroying German ground forces. Even then, the era of humiliating reverses was not over, because the battle of the Bulge seemed to indicate that the Western powers were still vulnerable amateurs while the Red Army relentlessly pursued its appointed task of smashing the forces of the Third Reich.

Once the German thrust in the Bulge had been checked and careful appraisals of German losses had been made, however, the British, and especially the American, generals were convinced that the decisive moment had come. The Bulge fiasco had expended Germany's last strategic reserve, her supply and production situation was critical, and the effects of the long years of total war and Allied bombing were beginning to show. The Western powers still confronted one significant natural barrier, the Rhine river, in contrast to the open and gently rolling country which stood before the Red Army. But with an enormous force of men and material, as well as nearly total control of the air, and the surety of a strong Russian push from the East, the Western high command had no doubt that within the limits of conventional warfare, it needed merely to advance and meet the enemy in order to win.

For the combat commanders on the spot, such as Bradley and Patton, this was enough, and they set about destroying the German forces west of the river in preparation for a broad assault on the Rhine line. The Combined Chiefs also put their main energy into preparing the advance to the Rhine, but here and there doubts and uncertainties arose about what would happen as German resistance weakened. One lurking fear was that in a final Götterdämmerung the unscrupulous Nazi leaders might use Anglo-American POWs as hostages in a desperate attempt to bargain or to blunt the Allied advance. The Western leaders knew that in a battle of reprisals over POWs they were extremely vulnerable.[10] The Soviet Union had shown that it cared not a jot for Russian soldiers who were in German hands and Stalin would surely not have been deterred by a Nazi threat to slaughter the lot of them. For his part, Hitler had demonstrated that he could massacre millions of people when it suited his purposes. If it came to a showdown, would reprisal killing of POWs deter Hitler, and if so, what American or British leader would shoulder the responsibility of liquidating captured German soldiers? Even if someone could be found to assume the burden, would the American and British public continue to support a military advance, and a policy of unconditional surrender, that were being paid for by the systematic butchery of the POWs held by the Germans?

There was little that the Combined Chiefs could do about these possible threats to Allied POWs except to hope fervently and cling to the Geneva convention. No matter how rapid the Western advance, the Anglo-American military leaders knew that they were not safely home on the POW issue until the Nazi system finally collapsed. From this vantage point, offensive gains were gratifying, but the Combined Chiefs also looked longingly for signs of Nazi disintegration. Only a complete rout, or a capitulation, could produce a quick end to the war with few casualties and no threat to the POWs.

While the Allies coped with their fears regarding POWs with hope and nervous silence, they were forced to deal more directly with a second danger that lurked in the shadow of a Nazi demise. Nazi propagandists and some Allied planners agreed that the Third Reich would not disappear quietly. Rather, partisan warfare and the establishment of "redoubts," where fanatical Nazis could fight on to the end, might make total Allied victory painful and its full realization impossible. Goebbels's dire warnings that the Allies would encounter fanatical popular Werwolf resistance once they entered Germany had shown themselves to be hollow, but the Western leaders were still troubled by the possibility that redoubts, especially in the Alps, might serve as magnets for elite formations such as those of the SS. Obviously the Combined Chiefs did not relish the prospect of protracted costly campaigns to destroy these fanatics. This was not a significant problem for the Russians, since the terrain of north-central Germany offered little shelter from Allied air and artillery power. The Alps presented the most serious redoubt danger, and that area lay directly in the path of the American forces coming from the West and of the Anglo-American forces advancing slowly in Italy. The primary responsibility for dealing with possible redoubts thus fell to the United States.

The American military records for the spring of 1945 are laced with worried comments and appraisals of the redoubt threat. Intelligence sources were carefully combed to determine whether there was any real substance to

German propaganda boasts that the Alpine corner was being transformed into an impregnable fortress. Both agents' reports and aerial surveillance were used to gauge the flow of men and supplies into the area. In early March, Allen Dulles drew Washington's attention to a number of indications that the Nazi's redoubt claims were greatly exaggerated, and by late March Dulles thought it likely that isolated pockets of resistance rather than one compact and efficient fortress would remain in the Alps.[11] By early April the top American military leaders had also concluded that Nazi redoubt rumors "lack[ed] substance." On 2 April, General Marshall sent FDR a summary of military-intelligence conclusions regarding the end of the war in Europe. This eight page report titled "Probable Developments in the Third Reich" declared that although the redoubt area "lends itself to defence and is also highly suitable for guerilla operations" only pockets of resistance, not a coordinated fortress defense, should be anticipated. The Alpine zone was characterized by Marshall as "a food deficit area" and one with "only a few armaments works." Since "no reliable information" had reached the War Department indicating "unduly large storage of supplies" or the construction of fortifications in the Alps, the General dismissed the redoubt threat as one of minor importance.[12]

Closer to the areas of combat, however, the redoubt fear showed more life and vitality. Although the German commanders on the Italian front did not give it much credence—"a playful fantasy" Field Marshal Kesselring characterized it after the war[13]—their Anglo-American counterparts dreaded the prospect of fighting their way into the Italian and Austrian Alps. To Field Marshal Alexander and his staff, a long, bloody, senseless struggle for an Alpine redoubt seemed but a natural concluding act for an Italian campaign which had consisted of one bloody, indecisive battle after another.

For all the doubts and reservations which he showed on occasion, Allen Dulles was also unable to shake off the fear that a last dreadful showdown was being prepared in the Alps. When the SS/SD began to take negotiation soundings in Bern late in February and early in March, 1945, Dulles quickly overcame his initial skepticism and tried to turn these contacts to account. In a report to his OSS superiors on 3 March, Dulles justified his dealings with the SS on the ground that it might be possible thereby to "drive a wedge in the SD and thus reduce the effectiveness of enemy plans for the German 'reduit' [redoubt]." Dulles believed that aborting the supposed Alpine fortress plans was so important that all scruples should be thrown to the winds. Declaring that he had "no conscience about double-crossing types like Himmler and Kaltenbrunner,"[14] Dulles maintained contacts with SS officials throughout March and April, and he continued to justify his action partly on the grounds that he was trying to disrupt Nazi redoubt plans.[15]

OPERATION SUNRISE

General Eisenhower, who bore the direct responsibility for the conduct of Anglo-American operations in Europe during the spring of 1945, also revealed that he was troubled by the prospect of a redoubt. On 14 April 1945, six weeks after the Allies had crossed the Rhine in force, and only two weeks before Hitler's suicide in Berlin, Eisenhower sent an emergency cable to the Combined Chiefs of Staff regarding procedures to be followed in dealing with the end of hostilities. Citing alleged Nazi plans for last-ditch resistance in a number of areas, especially the "National Redoubt" in the mountains of western Austria, Eisenhower made the amazing request that in the event of a Nazi collapse the Combined Chiefs should withhold any public declaration of VE day. Eisenhower predicted "that the storming of the final citadels of Nazi resistance may well call for acts of endurance and heroism . . . comparable to the peak battles of the war." Therefore, he concluded "that a premature declaration of VE Day might well have a serious adverse effect on the morale of the troops." No announcement of victory should be made, the general contended, until Allied "forces have occupied the key positions in the so-called National Redoubt of Western Austria, thereby preventing long drawn out operations on a considerable scale."[16] Obviously Eisenhower's recommendation that a VE Day announcement be muzzled—one of his many lapses into political naïveté—was not followed by the Combined Chiefs, but the dispatch of 14 April indicates that the redoubt fear was far from dead among Allied combat leaders, especially those immediately in touch with operations.

Yet it would be a mistake to overemphasize these indications of fear and uneasiness among the Anglo-American military commanders. With due allowance for the apprehensions related to Allied POWs and a Nazi redoubt, the dominant mood was one of confidence. VE Day was close, and whatever twists and turns the Nazis might produce, it was coming. Beyond that, the Allied military chiefs were not prepared to cast their eyes clearly in any direction. Here and there individual officers were ready to let their estimate of the postwar power situation intrude on operations. During the notorious raid on Dresden in February, 1945, for example, the pilots of the lead planes were instructed that if they found themselves in trouble they were to try to reach Allied lines, but if that failed, they were to crash in German territory. Under no circumstances were these aircraft to come down inside Soviet lines.[17] The fact that the planes had sophisticated new targeting equipment on board was the obvious reason for the instructions. It is also clear that RAF planners no longer held Germany to be a military threat and were keying their postwar planning to the reality of Soviet military power. Other similar, if muted, indicators that some of the Western generals were noting probable postwar power alignments surfaced in the spring of 1945. But considerations relating to East-West or Anglo-American power ratios were not allowed to come into the open, and they only exerted the most marginal influence on operations, if indeed they had any effect at all.

The ruling theme continued to be "military necessity" and VE Day the transcendent goal. The events of early March, 1945 seemed but confirmations of the system and of the wisdom of the Combined Chiefs of Staff. On 7 March, through an incredible combination of German blunders, American daring, and a generous helping of luck, the U.S. Ninth Armored Division seized a bridge over the Rhine at Remagen. Immediately, Eisenhower and the Combined Chiefs decided to exploit the break, and they threw the main weight of their attack to the right wing. Instead of advancing on a balanced broad front across the face of Germany, they nominally continued a general advance, while in fact giving priority to the American dash toward Bavaria, Austria, and the Alpine Redoubt.

All the balmiest dreams of the Combined Chiefs seemed about to become reality. The seizure of the Remagen Bridge opened the way for a rapid advance to the southeast, nullifying the worst dangers of a redoubt. How rapidly the Soviets advanced had become a matter of secondary importance; what Hitler did about Allied POWs and redoubt plans was still troubling, but not terrifying. The Combined Chiefs of Staff had turned the corner, and with George Patton soon out in front, the race toward VE Day was on.

CHAPTER 2

The Italian Setting

WHILE the Western front was in full gallop, the Allied forces in Italy trudged slowly forward, bleeding their way up the peninsula. March 1945 was the eighteenth month in which the Western armies had been fighting in mainland Italy, yet they had managed to advance only about 350 air miles, an average of less than 18 such miles per month. Even this modest gain had been purchased at the price of nearly 300,000 Allied casualties. By cleverly exploiting the defensive features of the terrain, the Germans had turned every crossroad and village into the scene of a pitched battle. German artillery battled Allied air and artillery power; the infantry on both sides was decimated, and Italy had been laid waste from Salerno to Pistoia.

The disastrous Italian campaign resulted not only from the military necessity principle which stressed short-term and reactive planning, it also arose from the frequently divergent political priorities of the British and American governments. The entire Allied strategy in the Mediterranean, including the Italian campaign, was the product of compromises between the Combined Chiefs' determination to concentrate energies for a cross-channel invasion of western Europe, and Britain's desire to employ forces in the Mediterranean which would otherwise remain inactive until the completion of preparations for a Second Front. The London government was looking for military opportunities within a context of political opportunism. If the lines of communication to the Mediterranean were opened, British influence, and eventually British hegemony, could be restored. Predictably, American military and political leaders were suspicious of what they considered British "imperialist aims," but they accepted the military argument that until sufficient troops had been massed to cross the channel, surplus forces might be used effectively east of Gibraltar. They nonetheless refused to commit themselves to a continuation of long-term operations there. To the Americans, the Mediterranean was an exercise ground; the battlefront would be across the English Channel.[1]

Therefore the Anglo-American penetration of the Mediterranean was made in a series of badly coordinated steps and shuffles. In July, 1942, the American military authorities yielded to British pressure, as well as some of Franklin Roosevelt's adventuresome enthusiasm, and reluctantly began preparing for Operation Torch, the invasion of northwest Africa. Four months later, the landings were made in Morocco and Algeria, trapping the Afrika Korps between the Torch forces driving eastward and the British Eighth Army, pressing westward from El Alamein. Only when the African campaign was fairly well advanced did Churchill succeed, at Casablanca in January, 1943, in convincing the Americans that once Rommel's forces had been destroyed, the Allies should push on with an invasion of Sicily. In early May, the remnants of the Afrika Korps surrendered in Tunisia, and two months later, on 10 July, the Anglo-Americans landed in Sicily.

As the Allied military forces advanced, a political battle over what to do next raged behind the scenes. At the Washington conference of May, 1943, the British reluctantly bowed to American insistence that the cross-channel invasion be given top priority. Churchill and the British Chiefs also accepted a timetable in which the attack was scheduled for May, 1944, and the withdrawal of a few divisions from the Mediterranean to be used on D Day was set for November, 1943. But Churchill was not willing to abandon his dream that a separate peace could be arranged with Italy. He still hoped that Allied military action would prompt the Italians to change sides and actively support the war against Nazi Germany. An invasion of the peninsula, with a full-scale advance as far as Rome, might topple the Fascist regime.[2]

However, the Americans remained cool to Britain's Mediterranean plans and ambitions. The Joint Chiefs cautiously conceded that a limited invasion of the mainland might be possible, but insisted that its sole purpose should be to protect lines of communication and acquire airfields from which targets in central and northwestern Europe could be bombed. The cross-channel invasion still had to have top priority and the Americans were particularly wary of any suggestion that the Western powers attempt to seize control of large areas of the Italian mainland. An American planning paper presented at Casablanca went so far as to contend that the Allies should not try to occupy the bulk of Italy, even if the Germans withdrew to the Alps.[3]

A compromise, as muddled as the problem itself, finally emerged from the Anglo-American wrangling. True to the principle of military necessity, the question of whether to invade the mainland with limited forces was left to the Supreme Allied Commander in the Mediterranean, Dwight Eisenhower. In the heady days of the Sicilian campaign, Eisenhower recommended that once Sicily had fallen, an attack should be made on southern Italy. The Combined Chiefs, echoed by the Anglo-American governments, then approved this recommendation. So it came to pass that plans were made to halfheartedly invade Italy.[4] The Americans had succeeded in relegating the attack to a secondary operation, but had not stopped it. The British had succeeded in getting it approved, but had been denied the military forces which would have made it strikingly successful or politically profitable. Therefore when fate offered the Allies a bountiful opportunity, they were ill prepared to grasp it.

On 25 July, before Sicily was completely in Anglo-American hands, Benito Mussolini fell victim to a political coup and was forced to resign. The new government, headed by General Pietro Badoglio, tried to negotiate a secret peace with the Allies, while avoiding counteraction by the Germans. But there were neither grounds for negotiation nor was there a secret to keep. The Allies wanted an unconditional surrender, and were prepared to let the country be occupied by the Germans, losing all Italy's war-making capacity in the process rather than accept anything less. Since the Allies refused to deal and did not invade the country in force, Badoglio was paralyzed. The disintegration of the Italian army and the Fascist Party then gave the initiative to the Nazis. Some German officers, such as Erwin Rommel, wanted to stand clear of the labyrinth by writing off most of the peninsula and building a German defense line at the Apennines, but Hitler was determined to hold Italy at all costs. Allied confusion and indecision allowed the Führer to disregard his cautious advisors and occupy the whole country. Hitler subsequently told Mussolini that "one could hardly have believed that the English would exploit the situation in such a timorous and irresolute fashion."[5] But the Führer was too generous to the Allies, who had merely stood by rather than "exploit the situation" at all. German troops were allowed to occupy the strategic positions without opposition, and the German high command hastily poured in new divisions. The already demoralized Italian soldiers were left without direction by the Badoglio government, and most were routinely disarmed by the Germans. Those who resisted were killed, and the majority of the rest, approximately 600,000 men, were rounded up and sent to Germany, where, in internment camps, they served as a significant labor force for the Nazi war machine during the rest of the war.

Only after the Germans had been granted two months to consolidate did the Anglo-Americans finally make their modest invasions of Italy. On 2 September, an Allied force crossed the Strait of Messina and seven days later a more ambitious landing was made near Salerno. But the latter force immediately ran into stiff German resistance which dashed any hope of a rapid advance to the north. In an effort to flank the defensive strongholds and force a German withdrawal, a third landing was made at Anzio south of Rome in January, 1944. But Anzio, like Salerno, turned into a stalemated hell with no room to maneuver. Here and there the Germans gave ground, but they also inflicted heavy casualties. In the horror and waste of such battles as the notorious one at Cassino, the Allies received lessons in the futility of military half measures. They could not move forward rapidly, yet the strength of the German forces made it dangerous to stand where they were. What no one, either British or American, had wanted had become a grim reality; the Allies were locked into a dreary war of attrition.

They were also stuck with the task of governing the areas of Italy which they had managed to conquer—territories that were devastated by this slow but destructive campaign. Since Sicily and southern Italy were the first European territories to come into the hands of the Allies, they became the testing ground for Anglo-American occupation policies. If the Allies had faced up to their responsibilities as victorious rulers, such experimentation need not have produced serious difficulty. But without a clear Allied agreement to fight in Italy, there could be no easy understanding on how the country was to be governed. Consequently the Anglo-American military did as little as possible and tried to create an impression that they were not really there, and in any event would be gone tomorrow.

The zones directly behind the lines were administered through an Allied Military Government of Occupied Territories (AMGOT, later AMG), and as the front advanced, the rear areas were turned over to the administration of the Badoglio government, under the supervision of an Allied Control Commission (ACC). But the Italian people were unwilling to become merely cargo for an Allied moving and storage company. From the time of the first landings in Sicily, they welcomed the Anglo-Americans as liberators, and in July they joyfully greeted the fall of Mussolini, hoping that this would mean the end of the war. In July-August 1943, the Fascist Party dissolved almost instantly, and in the areas occupied by the Allies, no sign of resurgent Fascism was ever seen. As the Western forces advanced, the Fascist organizations which had been reestablished during the German occupation again vanished, and the people who were most compromised by their dealings with the Nazis moved north with them.

Behind Allied lines, the anti-Fascist parties which had been forced to maintain a more or less clandestine opposition since Mussolini officially dissolved them in 1926 now reorganized themselves and appeared in public once more. They quickly joined together in an organization called the *Comitato di Liberazione Nationale* (CLN), united in opposition to the Badoglio government and the monarchy. To the CLN, both the king and

Badoglio bore the stain of long association with fascism and responsibility for the dissolution of the Italian army. Consequently the CLN called for the abdication of the king, and the formation of a new government, based on the political parties which it represented.

The political activity of the CLN was highly unwelcome to the Allied military authorities, who were trying to stand upright on a shaky base of Anglo-American compromises. The first directives which the Combined Chiefs of Staff issued to the authorities of Allied military government included a provision stating that once the Fascist Party was dissolved, "no political activity whatsoever shall be countenanced." AMGOT was further told that although political prisoners would be released, they were to be "cautioned that political activity on their part, during the period of military government, will not be tolerated."[6] These political bans were gradually relaxed, but it was done slowly and reluctantly.

The Combined Chiefs of Staff were also unwilling to assume responsibility for the disastrous social and economic effects which the war had poured down on the civilian population. The most that the CCS would grant was a directive declaring that "the administration shall be benevolent with respect to the civilian population [in] so far as [this is] consistent with strict military requirements."[7] Even this provision went too far for some British officials who thought the word "benevolent" overly generous to former "enemy" civilians.[8] Officers of Allied military government were directed to pay heed to the condition of Italian civilians only when the danger of "civil unrest" threatened lines of communication, or when disease endangered the health of the troops. Therefore the prevention of "disease and unrest" became the touchstone of the army's civilian relief program, and no serious effort was made to rehabilitate economic life.[9]

The Allied unwillingness to face the realities of a long-term Italian campaign thereby prevented them from seriously harnessing the peninsula's resources for war, or making significant efforts to democratize the country. Here and there relief was doled out and an industry or two was put back on its feet. A few divisions of the Royal Italian army were reorganized and used in the fight against the Germans, and AMGOT also made some modest political concessions. After the fall of Rome in June, 1944, Badoglio was dropped and a new government installed under the direction of Ivanoe Bonomi, a long-time anti-Fascist, chosen by the CLN. But from the beginning of the campaign until its end, the Allies were content to act on a short-term basis while hoping to finish the conflict before the economy collapsed or political discontent exploded.[10]

This stance of masterly, but repressive, inactivity, was viable because the American estimate of wartime power realities was basically correct—Italy's resources were not vital for an Allied victory, and Germany would be defeated in central Europe, rather than in the Mediterranean. The Anglo-American effort to keep Italy on ice was also successful because the Italian people felt that even a bad occupation by the Western powers was preferable to any system run by the Germans. On the surface, one might have supposed that the political structure erected by the Nazis in central and northern Italy would have had a measure of popular appeal. After all, in the German-occupied territory there was an Italian government, run by Mussolini, who had been freed from his prison by the Germans in September, 1943. This Neo-Fascist regime, the Italian Social Republic (RSI), emphasized its republicanism in an effort to capitalize on the broad popular disillusionment with the Italian monarchy. The RSI, with its capitol at Salò, was recognized as autonomous by the Nazis and was even designated an ally of the Greater German Reich. The most that the Western powers would concede to the Royal Italian government in the south, on the other hand, was the polite fiction of "cobelligerent" status.

The central and northern portions of the country also had some economic advantages. They were the most highly developed and prosperous regions of the country and, until the ponderous Allied assault finally reached them in 1944-1945, they were less damaged by the war. The Germans exploited the resources of the region, and life was hard and drab for the population, but economic conditions were often less chaotic than in the south. Near the end of the war, Mussolini even made some fumbling efforts to attract popular support by giving the workers a measure of control and profit in the factories.

Yet neither favorable conditions nor paper concessions succeeded in garnering more than a limited following for the Neo-Fascist regime. In the north a few people supported the RSI out of a sense of allegiance to the Duce or because of nationalistic feelings, but the bulk of the population was cool or hostile, and virtually no one in the Allied-occupied areas revealed any sympathy toward, much less a preference for, the RSI. The simple reality was recognized by all that not only was the RSI tied to a losing cause, but Mussolini's regime was just a paper facade behind which the Germans ruled and brutalized much of the country. Power was not in the hands of the Neo-Fascists, but in those of the Germans. The immediate battle zone was under the control of the commander of Army Group South, Field Marshal Albert Kesselring. The rear military areas were officially subordinated to the German army territorial commander, General Toussaint, and the German ambassador to the RSI and *Bevollmächtiger des Grossdeutschen Reich*, Rudolf Rahn. But as in all German-occupied territories, much of the real power was held by the SS and the German police. SS-Obergruppenführer

Karl Wolff controlled most of the repressive instruments—the regular German police, the Gestapo, the intelligence and counterintelligence forces of the SD, and the units engaged against the partisans.

Hitler paid lip service to his undying friendship for Mussolini by providing the RSI with a nicer puppet theater than the one given to Quisling, but Italy was subjected to the same methods that the Nazis used in all occupied countries: deportations, forced labor, torture, and mass killings. The population responded by expanding the clandestine anti-Fascist and anti-Nazi movement which had begun to organize in every town and village after the imposition of the German occupation. Cadres of those who refused to accept the Nazi-Fascist regime had fled into the mountains at the beginning and formed the nuclei of the partisan organization. As the Germans tightened the screw, these men were joined by others trying to escape military call-up or compulsory labor service. The resulting partisan bands were scattered and poorly organized in central Italy, where the terrain was not conducive to guerrilla operations. But in the north, where the German occupation lasted longest and the mountains were a protective ally, the size of the bands, and the scale of their operations, steadily increased. A clandestine counterpart to the CLN was soon created for the areas still held by the Germans. This organization, the *Comitato di Liberazione Nazionale Alta Italia* (CLNAI) had its secret headquarters in German-occupied Milan.

Faced with a tough and increasingly well-organized opponent, the brutality of the Germans made the worst of a bad situation, because every repressive measure called forth increased resistance. In trying to deal with the partisans, the Germans also shredded the veil around Mussolini's RSI.[11] The forces of the Salò regime became primarily police and antipartisan organizations. The *Guardia Nazionale Republicana*, composed of the Fascist Militia and the Carabinieri, was flanked by a new party unit, the Black Brigade, which soon made its name infamous in the partisan struggles. The Germans also employed most of the men of the RSI's four combat divisions in antipartisan operations. Partners with the SD and the Gestapo, serving under the direction of Wolff and other SS men, the police and military forces of the Salò government soon had a reputation for being little more than collaborationist murderers and slave catchers.

The effort of the RSI to pass itself off as the champion of Italian nationalism, under German protection, also turned out to be hollow. The Germans removed the Italian provinces of Venezia Giulia and Alto Adige from the administration of Salò and turned them over to two Nazi Gauleiters, Rainer and Hofer. These two men owed no allegiance to Mussolini, being directly responsible to Hitler and Bormann. This action was initially disguised as a military measure and the two areas were designated "operations zones" *(Operations-zonen: Adriatisches Küstenland und Alpenvor-land).* But by exploiting the nationalistic pressures of the Austrian and Slavic minorities in the two provinces, the Germans were obviously preparing to push their border southward by outright annexation. Not only was this a violation of Italian sovereignty, it touched on the rawest of Italian nationalistic nerves. The two provinces had been pursued by Italian nationalists ever since the Risorgimento and had finally been gained at great cost during World War I. When Mussolini acquiesced in the exclusion of Italian administration from Venezia Giulia and Alto Adige, he forfeited most of the RSI's claim that it was a protector of Italian national interests.[12]

Thus, though one might point to theoretical similarities between German-occupied central-northern Italy, and the sections of the south controlled by the Allies, Italian public opinion was not deceived. The Nazis and Anglo-Americans might both regard Italy as an occupied country, and both might manipulate the nominal Italian governments in their respective zones, but the Germans were cornered and losing the war; they had to seize Italian resources and they had a highly developed and ruthless exploitive system with which to do it. The German occupation was a harsh and bloody nightmare, while the Anglo-American tyranny was tempered both by slovenliness and democratic good intentions. Given this choice, the vast majority of Italians followed the Anglo-American lead and waited, worked, and fought for an Allied victory.

In the spring and summer of 1944, it looked as if neither the Italian people nor the Anglo-Americans would have to wait long for the end of the war. Monte Cassino finally fell to the Allies on 18 May, and soon after, a link-up occurred between the forces in the Anzio beachhead and those driving up from the south. The combined Anglo-American army smashed into Rome on 4 June, just two days before D Day brought the long-awaited cross-channel invasion to the Normandy beaches. In midsummer the Allied forces in Italy moved rapidly forward because the Germans were unable to establish an effective defense line in the relatively open country of central Italy. On 12 August, after hard fighting, even Florence fell to the Western armies.

For a moment it looked like the dream long pursued by the British was about to be realized.[13] Reeling under a series of defeats, the German high command wrestled with whether to abandon most of Italy and construct a new defense on the Alpine line. Even Hitler seems to have wavered on whether a prolonged defense in Italy was feasible or worth the cost.[14] But the German commanders on the spot, led by Kesselring, believed that the Allied attack was nearly spent and that when the battle moved into the Apennine mountains, the Germans would be able to hold. Citing the advantages that would accrue to Germany if the agricultural and industrial assets of northern

Italy were retained, the German field commanders persuaded Hitler that an extended stand could be made in the fortified positions of the "Gothic line."[15]

The estimate of the situation made by Kesselring and his colleagues was sound; the Allied offensive force in Italy was much weaker than it appeared in the summer campaign. The opening of the second front in Normandy had already deprived the Italian theater of troops, and the invasion of southern France (Operation Anvil), which was made on 15 August, pulled more forces from Italy. Henceforth Overlord and Anvil, not the Italian campaign, would gobble up most of the Anglo-American reserve forces.

At this point, the full consequences of the American insistence that Normandy have top priority finally made themselves felt. Churchill and the British Chiefs had vainly pleaded with the Americans at Teheran in December, 1943, not to take forces from Italy for use in Anvil. Repeatedly, the British urged the Americans to concentrate men and material in Italy so that a push could be made northeast, through Trieste and the Lublin gap toward Vienna. But the American Joint Chiefs believed they had again caught a whiff of British imperialism and condemned what they called "the commitment of Mediterranean resources to large scale operations in northern Italy and into the Balkans."[16] The American chiefs supported Eisenhower's recommendation that Anvil would assist the second front so significantly that the interests of the Italian theater should be sacrificed to it. Seven divisions were removed from Italy; the Americans had their way, and Anvil went forward.

Whether Churchill was correct in his contention that the Allies were close to a decisive victory in Italy in the summer of 1944 will be debated at least as long as the question of whether Operation Anvil was of significant assistance to the Allied offensive in France. These questions cannot be seriously explored, much less resolved, in these pages. Here the significant consideration is the effect that the decision had on the Allied advance in Italy. The two commanders on the spot, Generals Wilson (Commander in Chief, Mediterranean Theater) and Alexander (commander of the Italian campaign), had bitterly protested against the transfer of forces to Anvil. Once the decision had been made, and the assault was launched in southern France, however, they were briefly caught up in the rosy optimism which gripped the Allied command in the late summer and early fall of 1944.[17] In the second week of July, the Anglo-Americans had broken though the German defenses in Normandy, headed toward Paris. By mid-August the Anvil forces were dashing up the Rhone, sweeping the German occupation forces before them. Alexander and Wilson, grasping the larger hope, persevered with their northern Italian offensive, believing that even with reduced forces, a little more effort might trigger the general Nazi collapse which seemed so imminent. As August gave way to September and October, however, the rain became heavier, the mud thicker, the hills higher, and German resistance ever more bitter. Once again, the Allies found themselves in a bloody stalemate, spending men for handfuls of meaningless ground.

Only a large infusion of new forces could have gotten Alexander's forces moving again, and true to the now familiar scenario, Churchill tried to persuade Roosevelt to make the men available. But the American president was no longer interested in compromises or half measures. "Diversion of any forces to Italy would withhold from France vitally needed fresh troops, while committing such forces to the high attrition of an indecisive winter campaign in northern Italy." Roosevelt wrote to Churchill on 16 October, "We cannot withhold from the main effort forces which are needed in the battle of Germany. . . ."[18] The Anglo-American duels over Mediterranean strategy were thereby over. No more fresh troops would be going to the battle in Italy, which was relegated to the task that the Americans had wanted it to perform from the beginning: a secondary operation pinning down as many German forces as possible. Ironically the Allies only established this policy firmly at the very moment when Anglo-American intelligence officers concluded that the primary reason the Germans were remaining in Italy during the winter of 1944–45 was to contain as many Allied forces as possible![19] All the belligerent governments had reconciled themselves to a stalemate south of the Alps. If there was going to be an Allied victory in Italy, Wilson and Alexander would somehow have to make use of the opportunities at hand to produce it themselves.

In addition to their own battered forces, one of the few possible sources of assistance open to the two generals lay with the Italian people, especially those in the partisan movement. Until the spring of 1944, neither the generals nor the Allied governments had paid much attention to the Italian resistance which was organizing itself behind enemy lines. Their lack of knowledge of the Italian situation led the Anglo-Americans to believe that an underground anti-Fascist movement could not gain much support in a country that had appeared to be so united behind Mussolini's regime. Only the Allied intelligence representatives operating in Switzerland were prepared to listen seriously to what the partisan spokesmen had to say. Allen Dulles of the OSS and John McCaffery of the British SOE met two partisan leaders, Leo Valiani and Ferruccio Parri, in Switzerland during November, 1943. The partisans wanted financial assistance and air drops of supplies and military equipment, but Dulles and McCaffery feared that the movement's ambitions were greater than its capabilities. They wanted the partisans to eschew attempts at large-scale combat with the Germans and concentrate on sabotage and intelligence operations.[20]

Nonetheless, through these early contacts the OSS and SOE representatives received significant intelligence information, and they also came to trust some of the resistance leaders, especially Parri, who they saw as a useful mediator between the Communist and non-Communist bands. Still, during the first six months of the war in Italy, the partisan movement only received a handful of aerial drops, and these were tied to intelligence and sabotage operations. The OSS played a marginal role at this stage, while the SOE, which shouldered most of the responsibility, directed its limited support to the more conservative and monarchist patriot bands.[21]

Only in the spring of 1944, when the Allied offensive began to press the German defenses south of Rome, did the Anglo-American military start to take the resistance seriously. For the first time the Allies were approaching zones in which patriot formations of substantial size existed. The successful harassment of the German retreat by these units inclined the Allied military command to rate their combat role more highly. In an effort to force a German withdrawal, the generals decided to increase sharply their aid to the partisans. Air deliveries for northern Italy in the summer months were accelerated so they averaged approximately 350 tons in each of the three months—June, July, and August, 1944.[22]

But the new-found Anglo-American interest in the patriots was political as well as military. When the resistance movement showed that it could play a meaningful role in fighting the Germans, the Western generals began to wonder what the partisans would do if German rule in northern Italy collapsed. To exert more control, the Allies, in the summer of 1944, encouraged the resistance movement to create a supreme partisan command and they also pressured the partisans into appointing as commander a pro-Allied Italian general, Raffaele Cadorna. Parri and Luigi Longo were then named vice-commanders of the partisan forces. Since Longo was a Communist, and Parri represented the Action Party, the two largest political actions in the resistance movement were represented in the command structure.

Much of the Anglo-American concern about the patriots came from their uneasiness regarding the Italian Communist Party and the role of the Soviet Union in Italy. Although the Soviets had been excluded from the Allied administration of the country, they still exerted indirect influence through the Communist Party, which manifested its strength not only in the government of the south, but also as the core of the resistance movement. The Soviets followed a policy of warmly supporting Anglo-American actions in Italy, but the Western powers still feared that the Russians might use their growing strength and influence to attempt a Communist takeover. Italian public opinion was modifying much of its pro-Western sympathy in light of the indiscriminate Allied bombing, the slowness of the advance, and the controls imposed by Allied military government. The rapid Soviet offensives in Eastern Europe contrasted dramatically with the snail-paced destructiveness of the Anglo-American operations. Inevitably, the Soviet Union began to enjoy growing respect and sympathy in the eyes of Italians.[23]

No one in the Allied command was so tormented by Communist hobgoblins that they expected direct Soviet intervention, or a coup by Communist partisan bands, while the war in Italy continued. But there was a general apprehension that a strong resistance movement in the north, especially if it came under Communist or Soviet direction, might be able to exploit the political situation occasioned by a German withdrawal or disintegration. A general insurrectionary movement could then spread to the rest of the country and present the Allies with a "leftist" political challenge that would be difficult to control. The British were especially nervous about what they saw as the radical Communist danger among the partisans. This was one reason why the SOE sought, from the very beginning, to maintain close relations with the resistance movement and to get political control over it. In the early days of Allied support, the SOE tried to take advantage of the relative slowness of the American response to create a special British zone of influence. In late 1943 and early 1944, the British actually managed to reserve two-thirds of the monthly air drops for "their" partisans.[24]

But the predominance of the British was short-lived. In its fear and suspicion, the SOE used many Italian monarchist officers as liaisons with the partisan bands, but these men, loyal to the Badoglio government, were far too conservative for much of the resistance. The majority of the partisans did not recognize Badoglio as the head of a legitimate popular government, and the British political effort failed to make headway among the numerous bands which the SOE labeled as leftist. The SOE's grandiose political dreams were further undercut by the OSS, which by mid-1944 had recovered from its initial lethargy and was putting together a strong partisan support organization in northern Italy. Relying more heavily than the British on missions organized by the CLN in Rome, as well as on Italo-Americans of very diverse political views, the OSS quickly equaled the level of SOE operations. Recognizing the changed situation, and eager to tap the partisan military potential, AFHQ ordered in mid-1944 that henceforth OSS and SOE supported bands should receive equal airdrops. In subsequent months the influence of the OSS steadily increased until its operations absorbed the lion's share of men and material intended for the resistance.[25]

The basic reason for this development was the well-worn principle of military necessity. In the summer of 1944 partisan fighting potential was the most important consideration. The liaison officers played a critical role in determining which bands got supplies, and as it gradually became clear that the OSS was less hampered by political considerations, and better able to work with partisan groups on the basis of their military capability, the victory-minded generals in AFHQ were eager to funnel supplies through American channels. The relative success of the OSS did not mean that it was totally apolitical, only that the Americans were politically more open-minded than the British, and it was easier for them to keep their eye fixed on the overriding principle of military effectiveness.

Still the SOE kept its significance in Allied-partisan relations, in part because it made extensive preparations for dealing with the most critical political point in the campaign—the moment of German withdrawal or disintegration. To stop a massive scorched earth retreat by the German army, the partisans would have to be ready to harass the enemy mercilessly. The Allies put high priority on this "antiscorch" campaign, because, should the Nazis demolish northern Italy, the area would not only be difficult to govern, but the cross-Alpine advance would be further delayed. If, on the other hand, the partisans were strengthened to a point where they could serve as an effective antiscorch force, the door to civil war, or a leftist coup, might be opened before the Allies arrived in force. The British answer to this dilemma was to send out what were referred to as "Rankin B" missions, liaison officers instructed to take control of the partisan bands at the critical moment in order to carry out antiscorch operations, and then freeze the patriots until Anglo-American units arrived. Obviously these officers were in a sensitive, perhaps a critical, position. American authorities decided that the operation was so chancy that they forbade participation by OSS officers, since their men did not possess the "requisite qualifications" to carry it off. But the SOE persevered with its Rankin B plans; such missions were sent out in the summer of 1944 before the Allied offensive bogged down, and henceforth the plans were continually updated in preparation for the day when the SOE thought that Rankin B would decide the fate of northern Italy.[26]

Seen from the partisan point of view, this tugging and pulling between military and political operations did little to engender confidence in the Western cause. The Allied authorities neither understood nor strongly sympathized with the Italian men who daily did battle with the German army and the Gestapo. When AFHQ thought them militarily useful, they were called to action with trumpets blaring, but at the first hint that they might have minds or wishes of their own, the Anglo-Americans and the Royal Italian government took fright and tried to reduce them to impotence.

As the Allied front moved northward, and a zone was occupied by the troops, the partisans were then seen as a menace to security and order. They were disarmed and ordered to disband, with internment frequently used for those who did not immediately comply. Individual partisans might enlist in the Italian army, but the Allies refused to allow partisan units, as such, to join the Royal Italian armed forces. Granted insufficient food and medical support, while treated as political pariahs, these "victorious" partisans became an ever-growing center of resentment and disillusionment. They fought and endured the humiliations which followed their triumphs, because their hatred for the Nazi and Fascist regimes transcended every failure and ineptitude of the Western powers.[27]

By the fall of 1944, however, both the partisans and the Anglo-Americans were caught in a marriage of convenience. The Allied efforts in the summer of 1944 had flooded partisan ranks with new recruits, and drastically increased the scale and intensity of operations. Despite chronic shortages of equipment and supplies, the patriots had carried out mass attacks on German and RSI forces, succeeding here and there even in liberating entire areas (the so called "free zones") where they established democratic—not communistic—governmental systems. But the partisans were spread much too far and much too thinly to function effectively on their own. Without a steady stream of supplies and a continuing Allied advance in the fall of 1944, the German and RSI forces would have little difficulty inflicting heavy punishment on the movement. The Allies needed the partisans to facilitate an advance, but if they decided to cut the supply flow and slow down the offensive, the patriots could be decimated.

Already, the Italians were the orphans among the resistance movements supported by the Allies. In 1943 and the first part of 1944, the French Maquis had received the bulk of available supplies, with Tito's partisans coming a close second. When the battle in France ended in the fall of 1944, aid to the Maquis ended with it, but this did not mean an equivalent increase in assistance to its Italian counterpart. Instead, Tito's forces received the bulk of the airdrops because the London government prized the fighting value of the Yugoslavs and still hoped to develop a British "presence" in the Balkans through cooperation with Tito. A British official in October, 1944, reported that in the preceding four months the Yugoslavs had received twenty tons of Anglo-American supplies for every ton obtained by the Italians.[28] This divergence may have been exaggerated, because the official in question, Lord Shelborne, was a great champion of the Italian patriots. However, in every Allied allocation priority, the Italians did come out last with the least.

The fall and winter of 1944–45 held an even worse fate in store for the Italian resistance movement. The first bad sign came during August. In that month, the resistance fighters of Warsaw rose in an effort to drive the Nazis from the city, and the Western powers rerouted to Poland the heavy aircraft and most of the supplies that had been assigned to the Italians. This desperate and futile effort to sustain the Warsaw rising was occasioned by the failure of the Red Army, poised across the river from the Polish capital, to raise a finger to assist the beleaguered Poles. Both then and now, the reason for Soviet inaction appears to have been a desire to let the Nazis destroy the non-Communist forces of the Polish resistance. But what has not previously been recognized is that the Allied decision to abandon most of its support for the Italian resistance in favor of airdrops to Warsaw put the Italians in almost as precarious a position. The Anglo-American action was surely not intended to give the Nazis a chance to exterminate inconvenient leftist partisans in Italy, but it is true that the Western powers gave little heed to the fate of these people.

This combination of circumstances was serious enough, but winter was approaching and poor flying conditions made it increasingly difficult to carry out large-scale supply drops. The Italian partisans also found themselves the target of massive counteractions by German and RSI forces. Many bands were smashed and some "free zones," including that of Val d'Ossola, were recaptured by Axis forces. At this critical juncture, the Allied military commanders made a series of strategic planning shifts which spelled disaster for the patriots.

In the second half of October, 1944, generals Wilson and Alexander finally recognized that, with or without the aid of the partisans, their battered armies did not have sufficient strength to make a midwinter breakthrough of the Gothic line. But Wilson also saw that German forces in the Balkans were beginning a general retreat which could open up the Eastern shore of the Adriatic to Allied attack. If landings were made on the Adriatic coast, Wilson theorized, then a combined Allied-Yugoslav force might succeed in unhinging the German defensive position, and if such an attack was coordinated with a renewed assault in Italy, Kesselring could be trapped by a gigantic Adriatic pincer movement. Wilson presented this scheme to the Combined Chiefs of Staff in a cable of 24 October, 1944, and though he admitted that it involved risks, he urged that the Supreme Allied Command authorize him to undertake it.

One of the parenthetic weaknesses of the proposal, as Wilson conceded, was the lack of air forces "essential to early and decisive results in the Balkans." The only solution to this problem which Wilson could see was to take aircraft from Italy and "give priority for air supply to the partisans in northern Yugoslavia over those in northern Italy."[29] For six weeks, Wilson did not hear whether his Adriatic pincer plan had been approved, but in the meantime the general gradually shifted the focus of partisan support operations ever more decisively away from Italy and toward Yugoslavia.

In the meantime, a policy battle raged among Allied authorities over whether the Adriatic pincer scheme was feasible and if so, whether the Italian partisans should be abandoned. On the surface one might have supposed that this would be a rerun of the conflict over Churchill's old Balkan proposal, but at this late stage in the war, the British seem not to have taken that possibility seriously. The core of the controversy was whether to sacrifice the Italian partisans to the offensive capabilities of Tito's forces, and on this issue the Italians found supporters in a number of quarters.

From Switzerland, Allen Dulles argued in favor of continuous strong aid to the Italians. In a letter to OSS Chief Donovan, which was relayed to President Roosevelt on 1 November, Dulles contended that this was a critical time for the future of the Italian resistance movement. While granting that the partisans in northern Italy had heretofore been viewed "largely from the angle of their military importance," Dulles claimed that there was "another side of the picture." If the resistance could be kept in the hands of the democratic CLNAI "until a German withdrawal," the OSS man asserted, this could be "a real aid in . . . [the] administration of the country." But Dulles warned that "if, due to lack of Allied support, the resistance organization is dissipated, we will probably find in northern Italy rather chaotic conditions upon liberation, and both administration and rebuilding of a sound political structure will be made much more difficult." [30]

In London, and Caserta too, there were other strong advocates of maintaining the existing aid to the Italian partisans. When word first reached the British capital that the Balkan Air Forces were demanding absolute priority for Yugoslavia and that General Wilson supported this claim, it brought down the wrath of Lord Shelborne, the minister in charge of aid to the Italian resistance. On 24 October—the same day on which Wilson dispatched his Adriatic pincer proposal to the Combined Chiefs—Shelborne sent Churchill a strong memorandum on the "Italian Maquis." According to Shelborne, the Italian partisans had 150,000 men in the field supported by eighteen British missions and fifteen Italian military missions, with an additional fifty missions waiting to be sent in. Shelborne made no mention of OSS support operations, but he did claim that Italian patriot formations had inflicted heavy casualties on the Germans and had tied down tens of thousands of Axis personnel that might otherwise have been turned against the Anglo-American armies. Despite these achievements, the Italian partisans had only been allotted minimal supplies and, of these, but a small portion had actually been dropped. Bad weather conditions were partly to blame, and the airlift to Poland had also hurt, but now even this pittance was threatened by what Shelborne called the "insatiable appetite"[31] of Marshal Tito. If overall reductions in aid to resistance movements was necessary, then Shelborne felt the cuts should be made by reducing the number of sorties to the Balkans. If on the other hand, it was aircraft delivery capacity which was the issue, the minister held that undue reliance should not be placed on American flights to Italy, because, "for political reasons," it was important "to maintain the British effort as well."[32]

Before the prime minister had an opportunity to reply to this message, he received another long paper which Shelborne had penned upon seeing a copy of General Wilson's Adriatic pincer proposal. While granting that Allied operations in the Mediterranean had to "marry in with the advance of the Russian armies," he was obviously outraged by what Wilson's plan had in store for the Italian resistance. "Maquis warfare is not altogether like other warfare," the minister lectured Churchill. "Acting on instructions[,] I called the Italian maquis out and they have done a magnificent job, far better than I ever expected[,] in fact just as good as the French did."[33] But, Shelborne continued, "when you have called a maquis out into open warfare it is not fair to let it drop like a hot potato." Mixing his metaphors with gusto, Shelborne continued: "those men have burned their boats and have no retreat. If we fail them with ammunition, death by torture awaits them. . . ." Summing up all the moral force he could muster, Shelborne concluded his message with the plea "that if more support is to be given to Marshal Tito it should not be at the expense of the Italian partisans."[34]

Shelborne's impassioned memorandum gave a fair estimate of the situation, and it also made a significant impression on the prime minister. On 28 October, Churchill wrote General Ismay, chief of staff to the minister of defense, that at the next meeting of the British Chiefs of Staff, the question of aid to the Italian partisans ought to be considered. While cautiously granting that the opinion of General Alexander should be sought in the matter, Churchill added that "it was of the utmost importance to keep the Italian maquis in the field," and that a means ought to be found "to move these small quantities [of supplies] without abandoning our other plans."[35]

The two meetings of the British Chiefs which occurred on 30 October showed how well the British generals had mastered the game of military necessity. Without even considering whether General Wilson's idea of an Adriatic pincer was feasible or desirable, they turned their attention directly to the relative military merits of the Yugoslav and Italian partisans, concluding that due to weather, terrain, and the position of the German forces in the two areas, "the Yugoslav partisans could, under present circumstances, make a greater contribution to operations against Germany than could those in northern Italy." Once this had been decided, the British Chiefs washed their hands of the affair and referred the question of."priority for air supply to the two areas" directly to General Wilson.[36] In the afternoon session of the same day, Churchill meekly remarked that "an effort should be made to give them [the Italians] something" since the amount of air tonnage in question was small.[37] But once the generals had informed him that Wilson and Alexander had discussed and settled the matter, the prime minister acquiesced and let it drop.

Meanwhile, at Supreme Allied headquarters in Caserta, Alexander and his aides were getting down to the rough business of actually determining what the air tonnages would have to be if Wilson's Adriatic pincer movement was to be implemented. At a conference on 5 November, it was admitted that a minimum of 550 gross tons of supplies was needed in northern Italy each month just for "winter maintenance of [the] partisans at a reduced scale of activity."[38] Nonetheless, the Allied Mediterranean Command demanded that the monthly allotment be reduced to 250 tons, an amount which, in favorable circumstances, would only maintain the Allied missions in partisan territory, and perhaps provide "safe harborage for the partisan members themselves." To make the arrangement more palatable, Alexander's spokesmen described it as "a temporary expedient only." The "Italian resistance has paid[,] and is paying a very valuable dividend," the minutes of the military planning conference at Caserta declared, "and once depleted it can no longer be restored to meet the needs of a spring campaign, or an earlier enemy withdrawal. It is still to our military and political advantage to keep this organization in being."[39]

This statement, balancing bouquets and cold calculation, was merely rhetoric, because the large Italian partisan formations were to be cut to a suicidal allotment of 250 tons of supplies per month. In a second meeting at Caserta, on 7 November, the Allied deputy commander in Italy, the American General McNarney, argued passionately that aid to the partisans should be maintained, and if possible, increased. He contended that the partisans were containing one or two German divisions and that as a result their "military value" required that "the target of 550 tons had to be aimed at from the outset."[40] In addition, McNarney called for more efficient dropping operations, which would actually increase the amount of supplies in partisan hands. General Wilson blandly "approved" McNarney's suggestions, but emphasized that the maximum air support effort would go to the Yugoslav partisans.[41]

In fact, the support of the Italian cause put forward by McNarney, Shelborne, and Churchill accomplished less than nothing. In the first week of November, the prime minister discovered that of the 600 tons of supplies that had been earmarked for delivery to the Italian partisans in October, only 100 had actually reached their targets. Again Churchill turned to General Ismay for an explanation, and once again he came away with little but the principle of military necessity for consolation.[42] The deliveries had not been made because the weather was bad and some transport aircraft had failed to perform up to expectations. Furthermore, Ismay reported, since the November allocations had been made at a time before it was obvious that Alexander's advance was not "going to achieve the degree of success previously hoped," it was not then recognized that partisan activity would be "much reduced." Freed from its military double-talk, this meant that the airdrops for November were going to be cut to the bone. Alexander had set his November requirements at 250 tons, and General Wilson conceded that 320 tons might be dropped. Even if weather conditions were good and the available aircraft operated effectively, Ismay concluded, the 320-ton figure was the maximum that the Italian resistance was going to get.[43]

With that, Churchill was silent. The generals had gone through channels, and had made their decision on what they claimed were military grounds. That was the way the Anglo-American decision-making game was played, and short of a major political crisis, there was little more that anyone, including Churchill, could do but accept it.

Once the support allocations had been cut, someone had to tell the partisans, and since Alexander was the general in charge of the Italian campaign and was also the strongest advocate of reducing the airdrops, it was fitting that he should be the one to do it. On 13 November, the general broadcast a message to the partisans urging them to restrict their actions during the winter, and announced that few Allied supply drops would be made.[44] This message was a terrible shock to the partisans who were locked in a battle of annihilation with German and RSI forces. The Axis antipartisan command had stepped up its campaign to wipe out the bands, and with little place to hide, the partisans were taking heavy punishment. Alexander's message was a serious psychological blunder, and the partisans naturally reacted to it with disillusionment and anger. To make matters worse, the propagandists of the RSI seized the opportunity to chortle that the Anglo-Americans had exploited the partisans and were then throwing them away like "squeezed lemons."[45]

Then and since, many partisans bitterly accused the Allies of abandoning them because they were afraid of the political threat posed by a large and powerful resistance movement. These fears did exist in London and Washington, but the politicians, by and large, had surmounted them sufficiently to favor continued support to the Italian patriots. The generals in AFHQ Mediterranean, especially Alexander and Wilson, were the ones who choked off the flow of supplies to the north. Ostensibly they did it to further

Wilson's Adriatic pincer plan, but the driving force behind their action seems to have been a growing sense of powerlessness in Caserta. The fall offensive had failed, and within a week of Alexander's broadcast, Wilson had to admit that with a slow Yugoslav advance in the Balkans, neither he nor Tito had the strength to clear the Germans from the Adriatic in the immediate future. Bitter pill though it was, Wilson was forced to recognize that the most he could hope to accomplish in the winter of 1944–45 was a limited thrust toward the German-held communications center of Bologna.[46]

Once Wilson had to concede that he could not mount a large-scale offensive—double-talk was in its full glory, and Allied generals described standing still as "passing temporarily to the offensive defensive"—little effort was made to deny that the Italian campaign was only a holding operation.[47] In early December, the Combined Chiefs of Staff ordered Wilson and Alexander to try to take Bologna, but after another month of useless sacrifices in the mud of Emelia, it was obvious that it was all in vain.[48] Wilson was reassigned to the post of British military representative in Washington (replacing the late Field Marshal Sir John Dill), and Alexander was made Allied Supreme Commander in the Mediterranean. Alexander retained his command of the Italian campaign because, with the low priority now allotted to the peninsular war, one general could easily do what had earlier required two.

Among Alexander's first acts as Supreme Commander was an admission to the CCS that Bologna could not be taken before the spring. The general asked for an opportunity to rebuild his tired and battered forces so as to make a spring offensive possible.[49] The Combined Chiefs replied on 2 February, brushing aside most of Alexander's requests and ordering him to hand over to General Eisenhower three Canadian or British divisions, together with related air units. In the view of the Combined Chiefs, there was little possibility that either Alexander or the Germans could mount a "sustained offensive," and the troops would therefore be more effectively used in the west.[50] Alexander was ordered to stay put and through deceptive maneuvers, grandiloquently called "Operation Goldflake," he was to try to pin down the twenty-seven German and six Fascist divisions facing him, by pretending that his forces were still at full strength.[51] If this drama could be performed effectively, a large element of the German army would be tied down in a secondary theater, while Eisenhower and the Russians destroyed the Third Reich north of the Alps.

Therefore throughout the rest of the winter, Alexander was not so much an army commander as he was the director of a magic lantern show, making formations pop up here and there to fool the Germans and to keep them off balance. Behind the lines, the Anglo-Americans scrambled madly to shape their remaining units into a force capable of advancing in April-May, 1945. If Alexander had earlier been nervous about his ability to control the situation in Italy, he had far more legitimate reasons for uneasiness now. By all odds, the Allies would defeat Germany in central Europe, and at war's end, the German forces in Italy would likely either make a suicidal last stand in the Alps, or disintegrate and leave northern Italy an arena for what Allen Dulles called "communism. . . [or] at least a kind of anarchy."[52] When the Germans disappeared—however that was accomplished—fights might well break out between the partisan forces and the dismembered divisions of the RSI which were now mainly engaged in antiguerrilla and police actions. Yugoslav and French forces would perhaps also use the opportunity to seize disputed areas, provoking still more clashes with the partisans. Reports were already coming into Caserta in February, 1945, indicating that the French were moving toward Italy's western border, and that in the east fights were taking place between Communist-controlled partisans who wanted to place themselves under Tito's orders and other resistance units that did not want to give up Italian territory.[53] With a minimum of fresh troops in his command, and without strike forces capable of making lightning advances into contested areas, Alexander had reason to be a bit queasy.

To add to his nervousness, the winter of 1944 had produced a frightening example of what could happen when Allied forces entered a politically explosive area unprepared. The British landed in Greece in October, 1944, just as the Germans began to withdraw; almost immediately clashes occurred between Greek partisan forces (ELAS) and the royal administration of Papandreou, which was supported by the British. In mid-November a full-scale civil war broke out, and by the first week of December, the British had intervened openly on the side of the Papandreou government. For six weeks in December, 1944, and January, 1945, British units fought those of the ELAS, while their common enemy, the army of Nazi Germany, made a leisurely and largely uncontested retreat from the peninsula. The fight with the partisans, and the resulting British embarrassment, did not end until the second week of January, when a compromise was finally arranged whereby Papandreou and the Greek king both stepped aside for the moment, and Archbishop Damaskinos was made regent.

Sober observers might conclude that the Greek debacle was caused by a British imperialist bite which was larger than its belly could hold, especially since the London government had supported a political group more conservative than the local population. But to many Allied generals, the message of Greece seemed to be that one should avoid going into areas without overwhelming force, and even more important, one should not allow independent resistance movements to gain significant strength. Applied to

Italy this meant that since the Anglo-Americans would probably not be going into the north with commanding power, it was all the more important for Alexander and his aides to gain control over the resistance.

Actually, the Italian partisans had never sought a clash with the Anglo-Americans, and they were inclined to be doubly cautious and cooperative in light of the Greek experience. It was now clear that a revolutionary initiative in the moment of victory over Fascism might bring down a crushing repression from the Western powers. Thus the revolutionary danger in northern Italy, which had always lacked substance, became increasingly remote as the war drew to a close. As a bogy in the minds of the Allied generals, however, it became ever larger and more threatening during the winter of 1944–45.

The first step that Caserta took to make the partisans totally pliable and obedient was a three-way agreement between the Allied authorities, the CLNAI, and the Italian government, which was executed at the beginning of December. The CLNAI agreed to carry out the orders of the Allied command in exchange for regular monthly financial assistance and an acknowledgment by the Italian government that the CLNAI was its official representative in northern Italy.[54] This arrangment, which was accepted by all three parties as a lesser evil, did not dispel Allied fears or suspicions. Reports continued to come into Caserta indicating that the CLNAI was Communist controlled, that it would try to set itself up as the real Italian authority in the north after liberation, and that it would oppose Allied military government. The Anglo-American generals, whose insecurity inclined them to suspect the worst, reacted by taking additional measures to pull the mythical fangs of the CLNAI.[55]

An AFHQ directive of 4 February 1945 ordered that "indiscriminate armed expansion" of the resistance movement was to be discouraged, and that supplies should therefore be directed solely to support "organized acts of sabotage, demolitions . . . and antiscorch."[56] Arms and provisions were to be selectively provided in each of three zones in northern Italy. The northwest sector, comprising Piedmont, Lombardy, Liguria, and Tuscany, was the area where the partisan movement was strongest. It was to receive a maximum of nonwarlike supplies (food, clothing, medicine) but "an absolute minimum of arms," and these only when the Allies were certain that the weapons would be used "solely for action against the enemy."[57] The area of north-central Italy, comprising Eilia, Venezia Tridentina, and Veneto, was the heartland of the communication system for the German army. Consequently, the partisans in this region would be provided with some warlike stores, but the drops were to be made selectively and only when "considered essential for missions" against the enemy.[58] The third zone, the northeastern region of

Venezia Giulia, was considered the most inflammable. "The overriding consideration in this area," stated the directive, was to control special operations so that "Italo-Jugoslav frontier problems[,] which already exist[,] will not be aggravated, even if this involves forfeiting a military advantage."[59] The directive asserted that "self-organized bands" in Venezia Giulia "were already getting out of hand" and were not complying with the instructions of the Italian government and the CLNAI. Consequently, the Anglo-American command ordered that "no warlike or nonwarlike stores" would be issued to Italian partisans in Venezia Giulia who operated under Tito's authority.[60]

Throughout February, Allied military planners in Caserta looked for new ways to limit or restrain the resistance movement. A system of exchange missions between AFHQ and the CLNAI, which had been developed in the first week of 1945, was quashed because, in the words of the Joint Planning Staff (Caserta), "our policy is now to play down the patriots" and therefore exchanging missions did "not appear desirable."[61] Instead the Anglo-American planners concentrated on ways to make the partisans lay down their arms once northern Italy was occupied. Details were worked out for the creation of holding facilities which were to be given the Orwellian name of "patriot centers."[62] Within these camps, partisans who gave up their guns would be provided with food, clothing, money, and an opportunity for local employment or enlistment in the Royal Italian Army.

But as the generals in Caserta saw it, only the military capability for effecting a "speedy occupation of vital areas" would give them complete soul-satisfying security against a repetition of "what happened in Greece."[63] That, of course, was exactly what they did not have. By March, 1945, they were worriedly piling one controlling measure after another on top of the partisans and at the same time attempting to put together an offensive force for a late spring advance. But these were disheartening times for Alexander and his aides. Every other Allied commander from Eisenhower to Tito was likely to end the war in a blaze of military glory. Only Alexander stood to finish as an also-ran.[64] Unless a surrender of the German army in Italy dropped from the blue, there was little prospect of much to show for the Italian campaign—only a stalemate on VE Day, and the unsavory postwar task of trying to play policeman in northern Italy.

CHAPTER 3

The Senders

T HE FIRST WEEKS of 1945 found Nazi Germany a grim and battered land. The euphoria which had accompanied the start of the German offensive in the Bulge had vanished as the Anglo-Americans first contained, then hurled back, the German attack. Once again the Allied armies were advancing from west and east, and the decisive battle for the German homeland, its cities already blackened and reduced to rubble, was clearly at hand. Nonetheless, the government of the Third Reich clung stubbornly to its policy of resistance, as if oblivious to the enormous losses and the doom so obviously impending. Adolf Hitler, ensconced in his Berlin bunker, continued to toy with the details of military operations, moving paper units hither and yon, while the Allies smashed relentlessly forward. The failure of Hitler and his entourage to face the political facts was so colossal that one might reasonably have expected others to seize the initiative in order to lessen the impact of the disaster. A government which had failed as patently as Hitler's, especially when it showed no sign of trying to change course, would seem to offer a ready target for a coup or a popular rising. But the Third Reich was no ordinary regime, and it showed itself nearly as adept at dealing with potential opposition in its days of defeat as it had in the days of Blitzkrieg victory. The myths and propaganda gimmicks of nazism effectively tied the population, and most of the country's leaders, to Hitler's course of resigned self-destruction. Ever since 1934, the German military had been bound to Hitler's fate by a personal oath pledging to follow wherever he led. The regime made officers and men reluctant to break this oath by branding such action treason and a disastrous breach of the Prussian-German tradition of loyalty and obedience.[1] However contrived and unreal the German military's devotion to this code of honor may appear in retrospect, most officers clearly took it seriously, and Nazi propagandists showed great skill in playing on their sense of duty and tradition.

The German officers' corp had also made itself vulnerable to one especially paralyzing theme of Nazi ideology and propaganda. Following the armistice in 1918, the German High Command had fostered the myth that the army had not been defeated on the field of battle, but had been "stabbed in the back" by the desertion and ultimate revolution of the civilian population. The Nazi Party had subsequently refined this rationalization by heaping the blame for the revolution exclusively on "Jewish Marxists" who had allegedly led gullible Germans astray. A central tenet of nazism soon became the pledge that no matter what else might happen after Hitler seized power, there would not be another "November 1918." This was, in effect, a promise to the army that in any military showdown, the government of the Third Reich would ruthlessly crush any opposition which threatened the military's ability to carry on the fight. The army leadership rejoiced in this Hitlerian commitment and, in fact, frequently rationalized much Nazi repression and brutality within Germany as necessary to produce a disciplined and reliable Volk.[2] After twelve years of parroting this line, it became extremely difficult for anyone with military authority to move against the government in 1945. Such individuals were paralyzed less by fear than by a conditioned belief that this would be the ultimate act of disloyalty and hypocrisy. Many of them also realized that such a move was likely to trigger a German collapse and thereby create the basis for a new legend. For if the surrender of one front, or one army, set off a general disintegration, the officers who initiated the surrender would subsequently be blamed for the German defeat. After the war, General Roettiger, the last deputy commander of the German forces in Italy, stressed that the selection of the right moment for capitulation had been critical. The leading officers on the Italian front had been determined to avoid a postwar charge that they were the reason that "the war had not ended more favorably for Germany."[3] The man who commanded the German forces in Italy during April–May, 1945, was at least as candid as Roettiger. In April, General von Vietinghoff refused to make a surrender proposal to the Allies because he feared that it would "clear the Reich's leadership of responsibility for the collapse" and create a "new stab-in-the-back legend."[4] The generals had no interest in producing a myth in which Hitler was the martyr and the army was the assassin.

The oath of loyalty to Hitler and the determination to avoid another November 1918 were probably the two most important Nazi themes which helped keep the military moving like lemmings along the path toward defeat. But other standard Nazi leitmotifs helped to hold much of the civilian population as well as the military on the same course. The constant

Nazi drumming on the theme that authority had to be monopolized at the top, the *Führerprinzip,* reinforced the traditional German respect toward those in power, and made defeatist or revolutionary action even more difficult in the face of disaster. Though he sank himself into the Chancellery bunker, Hitler's personal magic did not disappear, and until the end, many Germans looked to the Führer with childlike hope and affection.

For example, as late as March, 1945, a number of Germans on the Italian front showed that Hitler's charisma could be as strong as ever. Though admitting that the war was not winable, Field Marshal Kesselring (commander of the Axis forces in Italy until the second week of March) repeatedly dismissed as unfeasible any secret deal with the Allies, simply because Hitler was still allive.[5] Kesselring's successor, General Vietinghoff, was prepared to go a bit farther and consider a separate surrender, but he concluded that the troops would disobey any command that they capitulate against Hitler's orders. Vietinghoff noted that even in the last month of the war, "the mass of our soldiers were still under the influence of the Führer's proclamation declaring that the Battle of Berlin would turn the course of the war in Germany's favor."[6] This explained why the general was unwilling to initiate any surrender effort until "the collapse of the Reich had become obvious to the people themselves."[7] In the opinion of Vietinghoff, and most of the other generals, the public would not see that all was lost until Adolf Hitler was dead.

Nazi propagandists also played a part in holding the German people in line by portraying the advancing Allies as monsters. Goebbels had always presented the methods and designs of Bolshevik Russia and the Western plutocratic democracies in the darkest tones. With the outbreak of the war, the propagandists outdid themselves with dire predictions of the fate that would await any German who survived a Nazi defeat.[8] Not only were the Soviets certain to bring death and brutal repression in their wake, but, according to Berlin, the Western powers, with all their smooth-tongued trickery and greed, would contrive to find some means of breaking Germany and subjecting the population to slavery. The ruthless advance of the Soviet armies in East Prussia seemed to bear out Goebbels's frightful predictions, and the horrors heaped on German civilians by the attacks of the RAF and the United States Army Air Force indicated that little besides suffering would result from a Western triumph. Many of the Nazi prophecies, such as those alleging that the Anglo-Americans planned to exterminate, enslave, or sterilize the German people were somewhat discounted by many civilians and members of the armed forces, who showed a rising willingness to surrender to the Western powers in the spring of 1945. But the Anglo-American proposals for the deindustrialization of Germany (the Morgenthau plan), and the refusal of the Allies to discuss peace terms, that is, the rigid adherence to the principle of unconditional surrender, heightened German fears and suspicions. Furthermore, even though only a small number of Germans clearly grasped the scope of the atrocities and exterminations which had been committed by the Third Reich, there was nonetheless a vague general sense that the regime's endless threats to annihilate or exterminate its enemies had resulted in terrible things being done, especially in the East. Even a flicker of awareness about the *Einsatzgruppen* killing squads, or the gas chambers, was enough to give credence to Goebbels's claim that if the enemy was victorious, no mercy would be shown, and the cost of vengeful Allied justice would be high.

Goebbels provided Germans with a partial antidote to this fear in the endless promises of wonder weapons about to turn the tide. The V-1 flying bomb attacks, and then the V-2 rocket assaults on England rendered a certain credit to such claims, and the appearance of jet aircraft and improved U-boats kept a flicker of hope alive into the spring of 1945. SS Obergruppenführer Karl Wolff, for example, did not abandon his faith in wonder weapons until the Luftwaffe failed during the battle of the Bulge, and Field Marshal Kesselring still hoped that the Führer could come up with a military miracle in March and April.[9]

But none of the wonder-weapon messages or propaganda tricks would have availed much if there had been significant institutional centers of opposition within Germany. From the start of his career, Hitler had sensed that to establish a system capable of eliminating internal opposition, organizational alternatives to nazism had to be eliminated. Not only had other political parties and such quasipolitical institutions as free trade unions been suppressed quickly, but the Third Reich had also striven to infiltrate, and at least partially nazify (via *Gleichschaltung*) schools, social clubs, churches, and every other organization within reach. This process of repression and nazification was carried quite far in the years of 1933 through 1936. Then the political successes of 1936 through 1938, and the astonishing military triumphs of 1939 through 1942, temporarily obviated the need to further tighten the reins. However, in 1943, Hitler responded to the downturn in Germany's fortunes by appointing Heinrich Himmler minister of the interior, and a new phase of tighter control and stronger punishment followed. Apparently it was the success of these repressive measures, and the fear of imminent arrest, which finally goaded one opposition group into direct action in the summer of 1944. The attempt to assassinate Hitler on 20 July was surely heroic in intent, but its effects were disastrous for any non-Nazi peace initiative in the last stage of the war. The failure of the attempt gave the fanatical Nazis occasion not only to root out every trace of organized opposition, it also unleashed an intensified reign of terror which further cowed the general population. Institutions which had managed to escape full nazification, especially the army, were hounded by the minions of Himmler and Bormann, who pushed Nazi control into every corner of German society. The aftermath of 20 July so intensified the nazification of German institutions that, ironic as it may seem, at the moment of defeat the Party was in more complete organizational control of Germany than at any time in its twelve-year history. If there was to be an effective German peace initiative in the spring of 1945, it would therefore probably not come from opponents of nazism, but out of the ranks of the NSDAP itself.[10]

Twelve years in power had sapped much of the enthusiasm and youthful energy which had characterized the early years of the Nazi Party. Of the prominent leaders, only Goebbels and Himmler had managed to hold on to significant positions close to Hitler. Bormann and Speer had captured powerful posts in the course of the war, but many figures, such as Goering and Ribbentrop, had become mere shadows, as war and defeat took their toll. The elite formations of the Party, such as the Hitler Youth and the SS, had either been cannibalized for service in the Wehrmacht or decimated on the field of battle. By 1945, the Waffen SS units were composed of draftees, foreigners, a few volunteers, and a handful of fortunate veterans who had survived six years of savage combat. Even the SS leadership bore little resemblance to that of the prewar period. Aside from Himmler, who remained RFSS, both the deputy SS chief, Reinhardt Heydrich, and the creator of the concentration camp system, Theodor Eicke, had been killed in the course of the war.

The Party, which posed as an all-powerful elite, while possessing more power than elitism, was a vast tableau of squabbling factions and internal conflicts. The dominant tendency among the leaders was, of course, to try to ignore the huge signs of defeat while clinging firmly to a simple-minded faith in Führer, Volk, and ultimate victory. No one in the isolated atmosphere of the Party was immune from this attitude; as Albert Speer has noted, "There were differences of degree in the flight from reality . . . but these differences shrink to nothing when we consider how remote all of us, the illusionists as well as the so-called realists, were from what was really going on."[11] Only here and there did some leaders, including individual officials in the Western Gaue and Speer himself, give at least partial recognition to a higher obligation to the civilian population by trying to save as much as possible for the German people. If this motive seldom led to the initiation of even local surrenders, it did, on occasion, produce orders to put up only token resistance and frequently prevented excessive loss of life and property.

OPERATION SUNRISE

A handful of realistic party and state officials who had kept their hands fairly clean also eased the way for a rapid advance and occupation by the Western powers.[12] In part such individuals were surely motivated by a desire to curry favor with the Anglo-Americans and to protect themselves against possible war crimes prosecution. In addition, most of them were so caught by the force of their own ideology and prejudice that they actually believed that defeat would turn the population into a howling mob racing toward Bolshevism. The Nazi message that only iron control barred the door to anarchy and communism now rebounded on the Nazi leaders, making some of them believe that the most prudent course would be to arrange a smooth transfer of authority from the Third Reich to the Western Allies. Virtually every German official who tried to contact the Anglo-Americans in 1945 asserted that he was motivated by the desire to maintain order and domestic peace inside Germany. *"Ordnung muss sein,"* goes the old German phrase, but in 1945 this idea contained not only some Nazi fanaticism and a fear of the masses, it also embodied a dread of Soviet Russia and of the rapid advance of the Red Army.

The fright engendered by the Russian advance also, paradoxically, ran close to one of the few points of optimism left in Germany. A nearly universal conviction prevailed among Germans that the alliance between the Soviet Union and the West was so artificial that it was on the verge of collapse. Hitler never tired of stressing that the East-West coalition contained impossible contradictions and could not long endure. That the East-West union had been formed by wartime necessity and was showing increasing stress and strain as hostilities drew to a close was surely true, but Nazi extremism and Hitler's very existence were the best guarantees that it would hold together until Allied victory was achieved.

Yet Hitler categorically rejected any thought of surrender and he also refused to initiate negotiation approaches aimed at hastening an East-West split. He was firmly convinced that deliverance could only come if he showed superhuman determination and endurance. On another level, how-ever, he understood that his program and the atrocities perpetrated by the Nazis made a deal with any of the Allies impossible. Perhaps he also realized that a military triumph was unattainable and only dreamed of some kind of stalemate out of which a bargain might evolve. But as Marshal Kesselring noted, the Führer "was downright possessed by the idea of some kind of salvation, an idea to which he clung, like a drowning man clings to a straw."[13] Held fast in a posture of fanatical resistance, Hitler's answer to approaching defeat was to continue fighting and to prophesy that the East-West alliance would break up soon. Now and then he gave an indulgent nod to subordinates who hinted that parleying might produce a break, but for himself, Hitler was not prepared openly to try anything. Better a fiery end, if he could not elude defeat or humiliation.

The hope of splitting the East-West alliance nonetheless played a significant part in the thinking of all those who actually made negotiation overtures in 1944–45. Most would have rejoiced if their activities had produced a rupture which allowed Nazi Germany to survive. Yet the majority of these individuals also had some sense that defeat was at hand and that the time had come to cut losses and get the best terms available. Between these two poles hovered the other factors cited (p. 54) such as the desire to gain favor with the victors and the fear of communism in Germany. Obviously this spectrum of motives was highly inconsistent, but it appears to have been held in toto by a significant number of people in positions of power. In fact, just this mental and motivational muddle seems to have made it possible for individuals to elude the full debilitating force of Hitler's personality and to try for some alternative to collapse and destruction.

Rather than emphasize the internal conflict in these motives it is therefore more fruitful to stress that far more peace feelers came from Nazi leaders in 1944–1945 than has heretofore been realized. The OSS records show that the well-known overture which Himmler made in April, 1945, actually came near the end of a series of approaches, most of which were only slightly less bizarre than that of the RFSS. After a few cautious probes by individual Nazis in 1943,[14] and similar attempts by anti-Nazi German diplomats at the Vatican following the failure of the 20 July plot,[15] more serious Nazi and Italian Fascist initiatives began in September, 1944. In that month an agent claiming to speak for the German Foreign Ministry's representative in the Balkans approached the OSS with a proposed deal whereby German forces would withdraw to the Danube, allowing the Western powers to occupy the Balkans while Germany used her troops "to fight the Soviets."[16] Faced with a cool response from the OSS, the German agent warned that if the Western powers did not accept the German proposal, "America would have the responsibility for plunging Germany and the entire continent into communism."[17] Nonetheless, the OSS categorically refused to negotiate on any basis which would endanger Allied unity. The Combined Chiefs of Staff and the Soviet government were then informed of the content of the German approach, as well as the OSS response, and with that, the episode ended.[18]

Almost simultaneously with this German feeler came a second approach made in Switzerland by a representative of General Glaise Horstenau, an Austrian officer who had entered German service after the *Anschluss* in 1938. Glaise Horstenau suggested to the OSS that he might encourage his fellow ex-Austrian officers to open the front to the Western powers so that Austria would be occupied by the Anglo-Americans rather than fall to the

Red Army. Once again, the OSS shied away from an approach which threatened to produce trouble between the Allies, especially at a time when Western forces were far away from the old Austrian border.[19] The Glaise Horstenau proposal, like the Balkan surrender overture, was therefore not followed up by the Western powers.

However, during this same period—the early fall of 1944—the OSS launched its own campaign to use captured enemy officers as links to the German army commanders on the Western front in hopes of arranging local surrenders. The terror-laden atmosphere following 20 July was hardly conducive to such efforts and the German field commanders showed themselves very wary of any association which might compromise them or draw suspicion from the SS or the Gestapo. In addition, the Joint Chiefs in Washington were cool toward anything that resembled a deal with the enemy. Consequently the effort of the OSS to prime the negotiating pump through German military channels failed.[20] Indirectly, however, via rumor and innuendo, it may have contributed to the impression held in some German circles that the Western powers might yet be interested in separate peace negotiations. Furthermore, the OSS initiative seems to have reawakened negotiation interest among non-Nazi or anti-Nazi German diplomats in Italy. During October-November, 1944, an official of the German Embassy at the Vatican, Albrecht von Kessel, contacted the British with a suggestion that he be allowed to try to persuade the German army commanders in the West to open the front to the Anglo-Americans. Kessel claimed that he could count on the protective silence of his chief, the ambassador to the Vatican, Baron von Weiszäcker, presumably because the object of the proposal was to prevent "the complete ruin of Germany," the avoidance of which would benefit not only Germany and Britain, but all of "Western Civilization."[21] However, due to Kessel's inability to develop effective contacts with the German generals in the West, this thinly disguised anti-Soviet, pro-Western proposal was also aborted.

In the same period, the British received another approach from Axis authorities in Italy, this one initiated by a faction of the SS. Franco Marinotti, the president of a large rayon combine and a man with close ties to the Germans, had been happily ensconced in a Swiss refuge until he was called home in October, 1944, to meet with SS Gruppenführer Wilhelm Harster, commander of the security police in Italy.[22] The meeting, which took place on 25 October, was attended not only by Harster and Marinotti, but by a number of other SS men and German diplomats, including two men destined to play roles in subsequent surrender overtures: the head of the SD's Amt VI (Intelligence) for the Italian area, SS Sturmbannführer Dr. Klaus Huegel, and the consul in Lugano, Alexander Constantin von Neurath, son of the

56

former German foreign minister. Harster told the group that he had been authorized by Himmler to try to contact the Allies. Although firm evidence is lacking, this assertion may have had some basis in fact. Harster apparently had not informed the top SS official in Italy, Obergruppenführer Karl Wolff, of his negotiation efforts, but he was in close touch with Walter Schellenberg, the chief of the SS intelligence service. In any event, Harster directed Marinotti to inform the Anglo-Americans that Germany was ready to give up its plans to totally destroy the industries of northern Italy, if they would allow the German army to withdraw from the peninsula and then throw its full force against the Russians.

Marinotti seems to have been genuinely worried by the threat that if the German proposal was rejected, the SS and the Wehrmacht would transform northern Italy into a "burnt land." But when he journeyed to Switzerland, Marinotti's fearful pleas did not impress the British intelligence men with whom he spoke. They categorically refused to deal with the Germans on this basis, and when Marinotti approached the OSS, his luck was no better. Allen Dulles reported to Washington that he had been contacted by Marinotti, but neither he nor any other United States official chose to follow up the approach. The incident alerted Anglo-American intelligence men to the possibility that SS authorities in Italy might be interested in negotiation, but beyond that the Harster-Marinotti contacts came to nothing.[23]

No sooner had this attempt failed than another one came to the surface. The Vatican was also interested in smoothing the way for a German evacuation of Italy and used Cardinal Ildebrando Schuster, Archbishop of Milan—a man who had actively supported the Fascist regime—to author its mediation effort. After the Italian surrender in 1943, Cardinal Schuster had tried to use his influence with the Neo-Fascists and the Germans to ameliorate the harsh living conditions of the Italian population. Then on 14 October 1944, through one of his secretaries, Don Giuseppe Bicchierai, he sent a note to SS Standartenführer Eugen Dollmann,° offering to help work out an agreement between Field Marshal Albert Kesselring, the German army commander in Italy, and the leadership committee of the Italian partisans, the CLNAI. In this scheme, the Germans were to abstain from destroying Italian industry not directly connected with the war, while the partisans would cease sabotage and other acts hostile to the German armed forces. The declared aim of the proposal was to stop destruction which could be "the basis for the success of Bolshevism in Italy."[24]

The Germans seemed well disposed toward the Schuster-Bicchierai project because they had nothing to lose. The partisans, on the other hand, had nothing to gain from it. In exchange for a vague promise which could easily

° See p. 72.

be broken at the last moment, the Italian resistance would throw away months of preparation and condemn itself to inactivity and disintegration. It is therefore understandable that although a few liberal and Christian Democratic resistance members gave it sympathetic consideration, the CLNAI categorically rejected the proposal.

However, the partisans' negative reaction did not discourage Don Bicchierai, and in late November he went to Switzerland to give Allied secret services a five-page outline of the plan. In this paper, which Allen Dulles later characterized as "a rather unusual document,"[25] Bicchierai reported the favorable comments of some German authorities and the unfavorable views of the CLNAI. But he also contended that General Cadorna, commander of the resistance forces, was "not opposed in principle to the plan" because the partisans' military position was weak at the moment. Bicchierai further claimed that the Germans knew about partisan plans to harass their retreat, so that the advantage seemingly given to the Axis "would be more apparent than real." In conclusion, the cardinal's secretary admitted that the proposal could only succeed if "strong pressure"[26] was brought to bear on the northern Italian Communists by Anglo-American or Soviet authorities. He therefore appealed to the Allies to recognize their self-interest by acting to prevent a partisan rising that could bring Communist domination to Italy.

Once again, it was the British who took the lead in flatly rejecting the proposal. A War Office report of 1 December ticked off the reasons why Bicchierai's plan should be rejected.[27] It would place the partisan groups in an impossible position, exposing their leaders to German reprisal while nullifying all the preparations which had been made to press the Germans and prevent Nazi scorched earth actions. Politically, the plan offered nothing but trouble. To the British, it was "definitely undesirable" for the Western powers to ask Moscow to intervene in trying to "control the Communists." Yet if Bicchierai's scheme was accepted by the Allies, many of the partisans, including the Communists, would surely refuse to go along. If the CLNAI broke apart and there was "no Allied military government at hand," chaos, not order, was likely to follow. Furthermore, all these risks and liabilities were to be incurred to implement a scheme which the British felt smelled "strongly" of a "back door endeavor" to dissolve the CLNAI with the aim of strengthening the "Church and [the] Demo[cratic]-Christians at [the] expense of [the] Communists." This was no bargain in British eyes, and they resolutely closed the door on Don Bicchierai.

The initial reaction of OSS officials in Switzerland was not so categorically negative. Dulles's first dispatch to Washington merely reported that a meeting with Bicchierai had taken place and summarized the main points in the Churchman's proposal. Only then did Dulles discover how determined was the partisan opposition to the scheme. A few days later the OSS man informed Washington that the CLNAI had forbidden members of the resistance movement to negotiate with German authorities. Furthermore, CLNAI representatives, who were at that moment meeting with officials of the Italian government in Rome, flatly declared that if the Germans withdrew, the CLNAI could maintain order and that the Church's fears about communism were greatly exaggerated. The prominent partisan leader, Ferruccio Parri, also characterized Bicchierai as "untrustworthy" and dismissed the whole proposal as preposterous.[28] Faced with a solid front of partisan opposition, Dulles notified Washington on 8 December that "the plan would appear difficult of realization and possibly undesirable from the viewpoint of the Allied military situation."[29]

With that, the Bicchierai scheme was dead. But it is noteworthy that Dulles gave the proposal any consideration at all. Not only was it hopelessly complicated and loaded with political hazards, it also seems to have been completely out of touch with the realities existing inside the Axis camp. At that time there were no plans for an immediate German withdrawal from Italy, and in any event, neither Marshal Kesselring, nor the SS commander in Italy, Obergruppenführer Wolff, seem to have been consulted before Bicchierai traipsed off to Switzerland. Furthermore, no one had discussed the idea with Mussolini or any other top Fascist official; even Bicchierai admitted to the Americans that the Fascists probably would not go along. Yet Dulles had been willing to listen and had only slammed the door on Bicchierai when the partisan pressure forced him to do so. Little wonder that Axis officials wishing to negotiate kept coming to the door of Allen Dulles.

No sooner had Bicchierai been ushered out than a German diplomat came knocking. The consul in Lugano, Switzerland, Alexander Constantin von Neurath (the man who had been present at the Harster-Marinotti meeting in October) informed the OSS that he was willing to try arranging a surrender of German forces in the west. Neurath's idea was to play on the supposed defeatist attitudes of Field Marshal Kesselring, Obergruppenführer Wolff, and Rudolf Rahn (the German ambassador to Mussolini's Fascist Republic).[30] Neurath hoped not only to nudge these three toward capitulation, but to use Kesselring's influence as a bridge to Field Marshal von Runstedt (commander and chief on the Western front), who might bring down the whole German position facing the Anglo-Americans. The OSS gave this suggestion a green light, but Neurath only established effective contact with Rahn, Kesselring, and Wolff in late January-early February, and even then, the field marshal showed himself to be very cautious. The only interesting feature of the discussion was the cryptic remark attributed to Kesselring, that if Field Marshal Paulus, then in Soviet custody and an officer who had made numerous pro-Soviet statements, would "agree to form a government," then "this might have substantial effect upon the Wehrmacht." [31] To have asserted that the actions of an imprisoned pro-Soviet field marshal would have had any significant influence on the commanders fighting in the west, not to speak of the Western powers, merely indicates how out of touch with reality was Field Marshal Kesselring.

Neurath was merely the first of a series of individuals interested in arranging surrenders who was disappointed by the sympathetic but ultimately uncooperative response of Kesselring. It was obvious to all that the field marshal held many of the cards necessary for a smooth surrender. He had been commander in Italy since 1943, and unlike many German field marshals, he enjoyed the confidence of both his troops and Adolf Hitler. Furthermore, Kesselring was the only high-ranking Reichswehr officer who had transferred to the Luftwaffe in the early 1930s and then successfully come back to command both ground and air forces. By early 1945, the field marshal realized that there was little chance for a German military victory, but he also believed that total defeat was not inevitable. He had boundless faith in Hitler and thought that the Führer might yet turn the tide militarily, or, failing that, produce a political agreement which would save Germany from complete defeat. Kesselring was somewhat sympathetic to the idea of making approaches to the Allies which might help nudge Hitler toward negotiation, and he seems to have thought it possible to lure the Western powers into combining with Nazi Germany against the Russians.[32] Kesselring may also have believed that if Field Marshal Paulus proclaimed a pro-Soviet German government that this might encourage the Western powers to come to some agreement with the Nazis. In any event, if Hitler could be shown that the Western powers was willing to deal, Kesselring expected the Führer to make a political move. Since the German military command in Italy controlled twenty divisions in a formidable defense position, Kesselring toyed with the hope that he had strong bargaining counters which might move the Anglo-Americans to open the door to a Hitlerian initative.

Kesselring's political ideas were transcendent in their naïveté and innocence, but the confused and tense atmosphere of late Nazi Germany helped conceal their full foolishness. Germany was cut off from the outside world, and it was difficult to see things in perspective. One of the emissaries advocating surrender who visited Kesselring in April told him that it "would be a good idea" if the field marshal "spent three days in Switzerland sometime" just to find out what was really going on in the world.[33] But as long as higher officers were afraid of betrayal and constantly badgered by the Party and police, clarity was virtually impossible. Discussions were carried on in hushed whispers by hint and innuendo, so misunderstandings were inevitable. Neurath and many others who talked to Kesselring thought that he was interested in some kind of surrender, when in fact the field marshal was determined never to break his oath to Hitler or jeopardize other German forces by surrendering on one front. Perhaps as one of those favoring surrender remarked later, what the field marshal desired above all was to finish the war with a "clear record" free of the taint of treason.[34]

Despite this confusion, the efforts of Neurath and Kesselring did not end merely with an exchange of verbal winks and nods. In the second week of February, while visiting with his father, the former foreign minister, young Neurath received a message from Kesselring arranging for him to meet secretly with the commander of Army Group H, General Johannes Blaskowitz, and the chief of staff to Field Marshal von Runstedt, General Siegfried Westphal. When the meeting occurred, the two generals were cool to young Neurath's suggestion that they work together to open the front. They noted that it was difficult to deal with the SS troops in their commands and that those soldiers whose homes were in East Prussia, or other areas already occupied by the Red Army, felt that they had nothing more to lose and were ready to fight to the end. Westphal and Blaskowitz also indicated that there was little reason for them to assume the risks of attempting a local surrender "if they were merely to be considered war criminals."[35] Despite these doubts and reservations, neither Westphal nor Blaskowitz categorically rejected Neurath's suggestion, and the diplomat reported to the OSS that even though they were not ready to make "definite suggestions,"[36] the two generals might be approaching the point where they would carry through a capitulation.

The possible surrender contacts with the Western front generals were left hanging for the time being, but the OSS continued to receive misleading indications that Kesselring was inclining toward capitulation. From Swiss sources, the American intelligence agency was informed that a German diplomat in northern Italy had recently reported that Kesselring was ready to quit.[37] Such rumors were so rife in the fourth week of February that a British reporter picked them up in Switzerland and soon they were spread over the pages of the *London Daily Dispatch*.[38]

In the meantime, Allied intelligence authorities were receiving a number of feelers emanating from the German SD (*Sicherheitsdienst*), a branch of the SS which dealt both with intelligence and the vilest police actions, including "liquidation" of political enemies. In mid-January, an SD agent attempted to contact British authorities in France with a proposal for peace negotiations.[39] In the fourth week of January, an SD official in Verona tried to get in touch with the Vatican, urging the Papacy to serve as an intermediary for Germany. Although this approach was not acted upon by

Church authorities or the OSS, it too had vague anti-Soviet overtones because the SD official implied that the Church owed the German government special consideration because it alone was carrying on the fight against Soviet Russia.[40] Then in early February, an agent representing Walter Schellenberg, the SS intelligence chief, hinted that the SD leadership wanted to establish a line of communication with the Western Allies. The gist of Schellenberg's message was that if the Anglo-Americans refused to modify their demand for unconditional surrender, the Germans would open the Eastern front and allow the Red Army to seize all of central Europe.[41] Two weeks after the arrival of Schellenberg's threat came another SS-SD approach. This one was passed along by an Austrian industrialist who allegedly represented a top SD agent, Wilhelm Hoettl, who in turn claimed to speak for the deputy head of the SS, and chief of the SD, Ernst Kaltenbrunner.[42] The contact stated that Himmler and Kaltenbrunner were ready to restrain the extreme "war mongers"—presumably Bormann and Goebbels—and for this purpose they wanted to establish contact with the Western powers. Although the first overture was vague, and was treated very gingerly by the OSS, subsequent messages trickled in from this source in the course of March. These indicated that in hope of escaping designation as a war criminal, Kaltenbrunner was toying with the idea of championing a special "Austrian" peace overture, because he had been an Austrian Nazi prior to the *Anschluss* of 1938. Although listened to, these approaches were not pursued aggressively by the OSS.[43] Still they did indicate to the Anglo-Americans that the straight hard line of the Nazi leaders was wavering and that surrender initiatives from the SS were not out of the question.

Yet even this series of rather peculiar peace feelers did not encompass the full variety of German approaches to the Western powers. In the course of March, General Ritter von Epp, an old freecorp commander from the early 1920s, and the first Nazi chief of Bavaria in 1933, cautiously suggested that he might be able to persuade the field commanders to lay down their arms on the southern wing of the front if this would help to prevent Bavaria from becoming a battleground. Again the OSS ignored the proposal; it was far too little and too late in the spring of 1945.[44]

A more interesting and symptomatic offer was one made in February by a group of German army officers in Venice.[45] Claiming, falsely, to be part of an extensive resistance network spread throughout Germany, these men informed Italian partisans that they were prepared to turn Venice over to the Western powers and would try to arrange a general surrender of the German forces in Italy. Although there is no evidence indicating that Kesselring knew of their madcap plan, they proposed that the field marshal cooperate with the imprisoned pro-Soviet Marshal Paulus, and with General von Arnim (the last commander of the Afrika Korps), who was in Anglo-American custody. In order to make their plans operable, the conspirators not only wanted Allied landings at select points on the Adriatic coast and parachute drops to shield Kesselring's headquarters from German reprisal, they also asked for political concessions. Kesselring and "a few others" should not be declared war criminals, and Arnim, Paulus, and Kesselring should also be granted "an appearance of authority" for a period after the surrender.[46] The latter request was presumably intended to save face and to obviate the omnipresent German belief that anarchy was just around the corner. But the clearest indication of the paranoia and confused state of mind which existed among officials of the Third Reich in its dying days was the request by the Venetian officers for a guarantee that the German people would "not be exterminated or sterilized."[47]

If the prospects for the Axis appeared so dark by February, 1945, that Germans as possessed by the demons of fear and suspicion as these officers could contemplate capitulation, then it was a foregone conclusion that the members of Hitler's satellite armies would be searching for an escape route. The men of different nationalities whom the Germans had recruited in Russia, Yugoslavia, Czechoslovakia, and elsewhere, as well as the Italian divisions of the Neo-Fascist army, were the first to realize the hopelessness of the struggle. As the end approached, they were also among the first to try to negotiate their way out. The four divisions of the Fascist Republican army included some draftees who had enrolled out of fear of reprisal to themselves or their families. Most of the men in these units, however, were soldiers in the Italian army who, after capture by the Germans in 1943, had been taken to the Reich as laborers. They received military training in Germany and were then sent back to Italy where they were used at the front, but also as a police force and in operations against the partisans. A wave of desertions started as soon as these units crossed the frontier and increased in following months despite a hastily imposed death penalty for deserters.

In February, 1945, an offer to surrender came from officers within one of these divisions. The surrender spokesman claimed to speak for "substantial elements" of a 6,000-man contingent of the Monte Rosa division which was spread out from the Ligurian coast to the Garfagnana. After having established contact with an OSS officer, the spokesman proposed that instead of retreating with other units, the men of Monte Rosa would remain in their position in order to maintain order and "to prevent [the] plundering" which had been planned by the Germans.[48]

Due to the practical problems involved, the Allies refused to consider surrender of troops behind enemy lines. The OSS suggested therefore that the Italian troops try to pass through the lines, if necessary firing on any

Germans who attempted to stop them. Initially the men of Monte Rosa were told that if they reached Allied lines they would receive "full Geneva Convention treatment with possible special status." Almost immediately, however, the Allied fear of privileged surrender terms asserted itself and in conformity with an order from higher OSS authorities "not [to] commit [the] Allies except to unconditional surrender," the offer of "possible special status" was withdrawn.[49] In the aftermath, there was no formal surrender of Monte Rosa and no large breakout effort. Like the rest of the Neo-Fascist divisions, Monte Rosa splintered during the collapse of April-May 1945; some of its men ended up in the hands of the partisans, while the rest fell into those of the Anglo-Americans.[50]

February, 1945, also saw a similar overture from an SS unit, composed of Czechs, which was stationed in an area north of the Po river. Fearing that the Germans would move them to another front, the Czechs decided to change sides and join the Allies. They offered to kill their German officers and, with white handkerchiefs on their helmets, to fight their way to the Allies' line. The OSS handled this proposal very cautiously. Discouraging a mass surrender, they recommended that the Czechs desert in small groups which would have a better chance of reaching the Allied positions unharmed. Once again the OSS hinted at the possibility of preferential treatment, but in fact was reluctant to move far from unconditional surrender. The Czechs, like the men of Monte Rosa, were left to take their chances by fighting their way out in small groups or going over to the partisans.[51]

The surrender approaches by the German officers in Venice, the men of Monte Rosa, and the Czech SS troops show that Axis dreams of a German victory had largely faded by February, 1945. Taken together with the host of probes and contacts made by high-level German and Italian-Fascist officials between September, 1944, and February, 1945, they also indicated to Allied authorities in the Mediterranean that the German monolith finally seemed to be breaking up.

Yet none of these probes or surrender efforts played a direct role in actually ending the fighting. Only one approach that emerged from this cauldron of defeat and fear significantly influenced the final stages of World War II—the contact made by SS Obergruppenführer Karl Wolff, dubbed by the Allies, "Operation Sunrise."*[52] At the time of his negotiation effort Wolff was Higher SS and Police Leader in Italy, and among his other duties was responsible for the struggle against the Italian partisans. An army volunteer in the last stages of World War I, and a businessman in the early

---

* It should be noted that "Sunrise" was an OSS code word; the British and the military authorities often used the code word "Crossword."

1920s, Wolff had drifted into the Nazi Party in 1930 and had joined the SS the same year. After making an impressive record at SS officers school in 1932, Wolff was appointed Himmler's adjutant in 1933 and became head of the Reichsführer's personal staff in 1935. While retaining his position as adjutant, Wolff also served as liaison officer at Hitler's headquarters from 1939 to 1943. In March of the latter year he had a falling out with Himmler because the Reichsführer objected to Wolff's divorce. Himmler had rather strict attitudes about the public conduct of married SS men, even though his own marriage was far from smooth and one of his secretaries was also his mistress. As a result of the rift between Wolff and Himmler occasioned by the divorce, the Obergruppenführer lost his positions at Hitler's and Himmler's headquarters, and, in September, 1943, was sent to Italy as SS and police commander.[53]

Despite the rebuffs involved in his transfer, Wolff's position in Italy was far from impotent disgrace. For over a decade he had known, and had close relations with, all the top SS officials and many high figures in the Party and army. Although he was no longer the special one whom Himmler had earlier called "Wolffchen," the Reichsführer still treated him with respect and some measure of affection. Above all, Wolff's position was unusually powerful because he had been close to Hitler for a long time and remained one of the Führer's favorites.

On the job in Italy, Wolff revealed himself to be a tough and resourceful SS and police commander. The Italian theater was relatively calm and almost humane, compared with other areas such as Poland, where the SS carried out its butcheries. Wolff's SS units nonetheless tortured hostages, slaughtered whole villages, such as Marzabatto, and carried out the Fosse Ardentine massacre. Wolff later dismissed these as "a few little lapses," maintaining that his actions were "humane, and decent and soldierly and above all just."[54] Judged by the standards of military and police conduct which prevailed in prewar Western Europe, this was nonsense, but compared with what was done at Auschwitz or by the *Einsatzgruppen* in Russia, Wolff's characterization had a measure of validity. As an SS chief in Berlin, he had known about, and participated in, some first-rate atrocities—he was sentenced to fifteen years imprisonment by a West German court in 1964, primarily because of his administrative role in 1942 in transporting Jews to extermination centers. In his own eyes, and compared with his colleagues in the rogues' gallery of higher SS leaders, Karl Wolff's actions in Italy might therefore have appeared relatively moderate.

After ten years at the seat of SS power, Wolff was also something of a politician, and a man willing to make contacts which might be useful if the future became cloudy. In May, 1944, for example, he sought and obtained an audience with Pope Pius XII. Although Wolff knew that rivals within the Nazi heirarchy would look on him with suspicion because of his dealings with the pontiff, he was prepared to take the risk. Convinced that the Vatican was the most important power left in Italy, Wolff told the pope that he was ready to do everything in his power to end the war as soon as possible. Even though the meeting did not bring an immediate direct benefit to Germany or himself, Wolff still thought, to use his own words, that he had done "good business."[55] As he explained to another SS man after the war, a "contact was very nicely established," and in Wolff's view this connection might be important if it became necessary to have "dealings with these people again."[56] As it turned out, when the time came for a negotiation approach, Wolff chose not to go through the Vatican, which was then in enemy territory, believing it too slow and unreliable. Yet the incident shows that Wolff was far more subtle, and much more of a politique, than the average SS officer.

Still, with all his political sensitivity, it took Karl Wolff a long time to recognize that Germany could not militarily win World War II. Until January, 1945—if we can believe his statements—Wolff continued to accept Hitler's and Goebbels's fables that waves of new planes would turn the conflict in Germany's favor. Only when he talked to the disillusioned SS men who had been in the Bulge and been battered by Allied airpower did Wolff grasp that the wonder weapons were all a dream and that unless a political initiative turned the trick, all was lost.[57]

Soon after being disabused of his faith in military victory, Wolff was contacted by Neurath, who, at that time—January, 1945—was trying to arrange a contact between the OSS and German generals on the Western front. Wolff, quite understandably, concluded that the Western powers were interested in making a deal with Germans, an impression that was strengthened by what he learned of the apparent dickering which was going on between the partisans and Cardinal Schuster in Milan.[58] The anxious SS general thought he saw an opportunity to help split the Allied coalition and perhaps consummate a deal between the Western powers and the Nazis. Armed with the idea that the Anglo-Americans wanted to contact him, Wolff set off for a showdown meeting at Himmler's headquarters on 4 February. When the Reichsführer SS was unable to reassure him sufficiently with more tales of wonder weapons, Wolff turned directly to Hitler on the sixth. According to his own account, the SS general told the Führer that he knew of "an increasing number of feelers" from the Allies, and he also claimed to have evidence from interrogations that there were "differences among those unnatural Allies."[59] Yet he did not believe that the alliance would break up of itself "without our own active intervention."[60] Hitler reportedly listened calmly to this explanation and only remarked that he was afraid of adverse effects on troop morale if reports of dickering with the enemy reached their ears. Both Wolff and Foreign Minister Joachim von Ribbentrop, who was present at the meeting, concluded that Hitler had tacitly consented to contacts being made in an effort to split the alliance. In Wolff's convoluted explanation: "I inferred from the fact that he appeared to agree in general with what I had said that he was authorizing that something should be attempted, though without giving any specific directives." [61]

Wolff was accustomed to working in a setting where the Führer allowed his aides to try their luck. Hitler had used this approach frequently in the past, as in the Austrian crisis of 1938, and then had followed up whatever lead best fitted his mood and the circumstances. Wolff therefore returned to Italy believing that he had Hitler's indulgence, if not his support. Still, he had to proceed warily, because any move toward the Allies would make him vulnerable. A misstep would give a Bormann or a Kaltenbrunner an opportunity to poison Hitler's mind with stories that Wolff was trying to sell out the Third Reich to save his own skin. Only a man who believed fanatically in Germany's destiny, the Nazi cause, and his "star" would accept such risks; only a man long schooled in the deadly game of Nazi politics could hope to make the risks pay off. [62]

Soon after his arrival back in Italy, Wolff was strengthened in his resolve by what seemed to be an additional indication that the Western Allies wanted to deal. A British agent, together with two members of the Italian resistance, had been captured by the Italian Fascists. The chief captive, a British Special Operations (SOE) officer, who passed under at least four cover names in Allied documents (Tucker, Drucker, Wallaby, and Mallaby), [63] had told the Neo-Fascist minister of defense, Marshal Graziani, that he was in northern Italy to try to limit loss of property in the last stage of the war. Graziani apparently concluded that Tucker-Wallaby had been sent by the Allies to make contacts with Fascist and Nazi authorities. After hearing him out, Grazinai turned him over to the Germans. Wolff also listened to his story and apparently he too thought that Tucker-Wallaby was there to establish a line of communication between the Allies and the German command in Italy. Like most Nazis in that theater of operations, Wolff believed that the Western capitalists dreaded an end to the war if it occasioned heavy destruction of productive capital by the retreating Axis forces. In this view, Anglo-American companies coveted such prizes as the industrial plants of Milan and Turin, while the London and Washington governments believed that installations like the electric generating plants were essential to the postwar life of Italy. If the Western powers put a sufficiently high value on such property, they might be willing to pay a political price for it. Furthermore, Wolff and other German officials were certain that the Western powers had little interest in seeing "Red" partisans seize power in the wake of a German retreat.[64] Here again, the Allies might be willing to make concessions if the Nazis were prepared to bypass the partisans and hand authority in northern Italy directly to the Allies.

Of course while such arrangements were being made, it might reasonably be expected that the Germans could go on to bigger things, such as splitting the alliance and making a deal with the West. In any event, all such arrangements would first depend on establishing a communication line between the Germans and the Allies. In the confusion of February, 1945, Wolff—who wanted to see hopeful signs—surmised that Tucker-Wallaby's mission was an attempt to make just such a communications contact. So while holding the two Italian resistance men as hostages, Wolff released the Englishman on parole and sent him back to the Allies via Switzerland, to report that a connection had been made with the top Nazi authorities in Italy.[65]

For thirty years this incident has confused accounts of Operation Sunrise. Even in the postwar period the British general in charge of intelligence at Allied Mediterannean headquarters, General T. S. Airey, stated that the British, as well as the Americans, had made contact with Wolff in the spring of 1945. According to Airey, Alexander decided that the Allies "could only deal with one" channel, so the British contact had ultimately been abandoned.[66] In fact there never had been a firm British contact, because, as the contemporary documents show, Tucker-Wallaby had simply lied when he told Graziani that he was in northern Italy on "an antiscorch deal."[67] He was there to give assistance to the partisans and, when captured by the Fascists, had invented the story of preventing destruction as a cover which might save his life. This "clever ruse," as Dulles labeled it when he learned the whole story in mid-March,[68] not only misled future historians of Sunrise, it also strengthened Wolff's belief that the Allies would be willing to receive negotiation overtures.

When he made his move, however, Wolff chose not to use an Allied officer like Tucker-Wallaby, or a pro-Allied German like Neurath. Instead he decided to employ agents over whom he believed he could exercise more immediate control. An Italian businessman named Baron Luigi Parrilli, who had purportedly worked for an American firm (Kelvinator) before the war—and for the Fascists during it[69]—made the initial contact with the Allies in Switzerland. Parrilli had connections to a number of SS officials in Italy. He was especially close to SS Hauptsturmführer Guido Zimmer, an SD officer in Milan, but he also had contact with Zimmer's superior, SS Sturmbannführer

Dr. Klaus Huegel, the SD AMT VI official who had been involved in the Marinotti affair,° as well as with Standartenführer Eugen Dollmann, Himmler's special liaison officer to the Italian Fascist Republic. All three of these Nazi officers had, at one time or another, considered using Parrilli as a contact man with the Allies. In January, at Zimmer's suggestion, Huegel had discussed with his boss, the ubiquitous Walter Schellenberg, the idea of sending Parrilli to Switzerland to sound out the Allies on peace terms. The Italian may not have been informed of the details of the plan, and in any event, Schellenberg failed to give Huegel an immediate go-ahead. But the baron, who had extensive manufacturing interests in northern Italy, was himself eager to undertake a mission that would produce a smooth transition from the authority of the Fascists and Germans to that of the Allies.[70]

In late February, Huegel decided to wait no longer for Schellenberg, and through Zimmer he told Parrilli to go to Switzerland to see if he could make contact with the OSS. Although it is not clear whether Wolff was behind the decision to send Parrilli, he certainly knew the whole story immediately upon the baron's return.[71] In Switzerland, Parrilli had used his acquaintanceship with Professor Max Husmann, who operated a private school near Lucerne, to get in touch with a Swiss intelligence officer, Major Max Waibel. In turn, Waibel arranged for Husmann and Parrilli to talk with Gero von Schulze Gaevernitz, a German-American OSS man who served as Dulles's closest collaborator in Switzerland. To Gaevernitz, Parrilli and Husmann described the miserable fate which awaited northern Italy if the Germans carried through their plans to fight to the finish. In addition, both men offered their services to the cause of peace and to help bring about an orderly end to Fascist-German authority. Gaevernitz responded with platitudes about Allied devotion to peace and order, but he was skeptical about the whole affair. Parrilli had reported that he was working with Zimmer and he had made a passing reference to Dollmann, but he did not state that he was speaking for any top German officials. Believing that February, 1945, was too late for such seemingly low-level and indirect approaches, Gaevernitz told Parrilli that nothing less than a talk with Dollmann, Wolff, or Kesselring would be "worthwhile," and then sent him on his way.[72] With that, both Gaevernitz and Dulles believed the incident finished. They only sent a routine summary of it to Washington, and apparently filed no report with the OSS office in Caserta.[73]

However, when Parrilli returned to northern Italy and reported to Zimmer, the SS man was very enthusiastic. Every intermediary in Sunrise seems to have had a rare talent for making one side look good to the other, and Parrilli probably exaggerated the warmth of the welcome he had

°See p. 56.

received from Gaevernitz. But the OSS man had implied that he was ready to talk with SS men, so Zimmer had some legitimate grounds for optimism. The report of the incident which he made to his superiors was glowing, apparently so glowing that he may have contributed to the impression held by Wolff that the Anglo-Americans were desirous of initiating talks with the Nazis.[74] The Obergruppenführer's mind was already inclined toward the myth that the Western Allies wanted to negotiate and that they looked on him sympathetically because of his supposed reasonableness and moderation. Now Parilli's report, relayed and perhaps amplified by Zimmer, indicated that the OSS was willing to talk with him or with Dollmann.[75]

Wolff therefore prepared Zimmer and Dollmann for a special mission to Switzerland to open discussions with Dulles or one of his representatives. Before their departure he sent Dollmann to get the political advice of the German ambassador to the Fascist Republic, Rudolf Rahn. The ambassador had quietly advocated negotiation with the Western powers for a long time, and had, on various occasions, cautiously taken soundings with Wolff about this possibility. In February, Rahn gave his blessing to Wolff's efforts and supported them to the end, despite some resentment because his negotiation dreams were being pursued by members of the SS, the very organization which had earlier opposed them. The ambassador apparently used the occasion of his talk with Dollmann to caution that it would be best to avoid trying to disrupt the alliance by playing blatantly on the anti-Soviet fears of the Anglo-Americans.[76] Perhaps inclined to be more realistic because of Rahn's advice, Dollmann and Zimmer set off for Switzerland on 2 March.

If Wolff had been preparing to arrange the secret surrender of the German forces of northern Italy, as Dulles and most subsequent writers have assumed, his dispatch of Zimmer and Dollmann to Switzerland on 2 March would have been a step so foolhardy as to border on madness. Sending two SS officers on such a mission—especially a man so well known in diplomatic and intelligence circles as Dollmann—would have invited denunciation by a host of fanatical Nazis ready to gain credit with Hitler and Himmler by denouncing Wolff. But from all indications, Wolff had not the slightest thought of unconditionally, or secretly, surrendering anything. He remained a devoted Nazi and still adhered to Hitler and the SS mission. Both before and after his dealings with the OSS, he upheld the "ideals" of the SS and never went beyond the most tepid apologies for "mistakes" such as "the concentration camps and gas chambers and incinerators."[77] Even after the capitulation in May, 1945, it was the creation of a racial ruling elite "first for Germany and then for the whole of Europe" which he prized, and when speaking with Allied officers he still used phrases like "Slavonic mongol" to refer to groups such as the Poles.[78]

In March, 1945, Wolff was prepared to limit senseless destruction, and he was eager to impress Western authorities with his own virtues and those of the "idealistic" members of the SS. Perhaps he was looking ahead to protect himself against war criminal charges, but more central to his thinking was the conviction that the Nazis would have to come to terms with the Western powers. At the time Dollmann and Zimmer were sent to Switzerland, Wolff knew that the war could not be won militarily, but he also believed that he had a tacit blessing from Hitler to find out what could be salvaged by negotiations. A deal had to be made with the West—Wolff was sure of that. He hoped that it could be done in such a way that the alliance would disintegrate and the Western powers would join forces with Nazi Germany to fight the Soviet Union. In all likelihood his mind had not yet touched seriously on the question of what should be done if the East-West alliance held firm. In any event, treason to Nazism or a simple surrender were not in his mind or his idiom. Rather than a Götterdämmerung, or a capitulation, Wolff chose to deal with the West, and for this reason alone, Zimmer and Dollmann were sent over the border.

CHAPTER 4

Parleying in Bern

MANY GERMANS talked about negotiating with the Western Allies during World War II, but Standartenführer Eugen Dollmann was the first important SS officer who actually tried it. Long resident in Rome, where he had worked as a translator and writer before the Nazis came to power, Dollmann had the gentility and suave manners of a professional diplomat. He had translated for Hitler and Mussolini and then had found Himmler's special favor. The Reichsführer-SS realized the value of Dollmann's connections with Italian clerics and aristocrats, and the historian/translator soon emerged with the rank of SS colonel (*Standartenführer*) and a reputation as the top SS expert on Italy. Dollmann managed to stand as far as possible from the dark and murderous side of the SS, and along with a handful of other officers such as Gunter d'Alquen and Walter Darré, he helped to give the SS some veneer of culture and respectability.[1] But no one in Himmler's kingdom could totally distance himself from the SD, the Gestapo, and the death squads. As an OSS summary on Dollmann put it in March, 1945, he had allegedly saved individuals in Rome from "destruction," but, reportedly, he had done it "for a price."[2] Whether completely true or not, the story suggests that Eugen Dollmann's sophistication did not raise his vision above Nazi standards and Nazi methods. He was Himmler's special agent in Italy, and even among Germans he had a reputation for harshness and unscrupulousness.[3]

Soon after his arrival in Switzerland, Dollmann began to get some glimmers of how myopic the Nazi view of the world had become by the spring of 1945. Dollmann, Parrilli, and Zimmer were met at the border by Professor Husmann and a Swiss intelligence officer, Lieutenant Friedrich Rothpletz, who was assigned to them by Major Waibel. Rothpletz took the four men to Lugano, where, on the afternoon of 3 March, they waited in a private restaurant dining room for the arrival of an OSS agent. As tends to happen in real-life spy stories, the OSS agent was late, and as the hours dragged by, Professor Husmann seized the opportunity to lecture Parrilli and the SS men on the hopeless situation facing the Axis.[4] The Swiss professor told them that there was no possibility that the East-West coalition would break up before the Allies' overwhelming military preponderance crushed Hitler's forces. Only the mad will of the dictator was prolonging the struggle, claimed the agitated Husmann, and Hitler's suicidal resolve was also drawing Europe to a finale of useless death and destruction. There was no way out but unconditional surrender, and Husmann called upon the SS men to help avert meaningless chaos by arranging their own capitulation in Italy, if the Hitler government continued down its fatal road. In the course of what had become an impassioned moral lecture, Husmann indicated that those on the German side who rose to meet the challenge would be "an elite" who could play a part in the rebuilding of the destroyed European continent.

Dollmann's initial reaction to the agitated arguments of Husmann was hot anger. He had not come to Switzerland to commit treason by unconditionally surrendering the Italian front, but was there to arrange contacts for German negotiation with the Allies. The Axis still had an intact army in Italy, and according to Dollmann, there was no need for him to come cringing to the Allies like a beggar. The SS man's flash deflated Husmann, and in the aftermath, tempers cooled and calm chitchat again took possession of the Lugano dining room. But Husmann's lecture may have left a mark on Dollmann. He probably discounted some part of what the professor said, assuming—wrongly—that Husmann had been briefed by the OSS and was following Allied instructions. But Dollmann surely did realize, along with everyone else involved in Sunrise, that the Swiss were vitally interested in seeing a smooth end to hostilities in northern Italy.[5] This was an area with which the Swiss had close economic ties, and mass destruction there would produce serious economic losses. Furthermore, if the Allied armies were compelled to smash the Axis forces, and no formal surrender occurred, masses of disorganized and fleeing soldiers would be driven up against the Swiss borders. No one in Bern relished the prospect of the border becoming a war zone, bringing with it the dangers which inevitably accompany groups of desperate men trying to find a safe haven.

But even if Dollmann allowed for all this, the fact remained that here, in the middle of delicate contacts, a neutral Swiss was baldly declaring that the alliance between Russia and the West could not be broken quickly, and that the Germans had no choice but unconditional surrender. Coming on the heels of Ambassador Rahn's warning to avoid trying to split the East-West alliance, Dollmann must have begun to realize that much of the whispered mumbling about negotiating a separate peace with the Western Allies that had recently occurred in northern Italy was far removed from reality. The only possible bit of light which had shone from Husmann's diatribe had been the remark that those Germans who arranged a surrender would be an "elite" with a future. For an SS man like Dollmann, long familiar with ruling elites, it was a reference to be kept in mind.

After the five men had spent three to four hours in the Lugano dining room, arguing, chatting, and pondering, the OSS agent finally arrived around 4:00 P.M. Since Gaevernitz was away on another assignment, this time the OSS was represented by Paul Blum, an officer who happened to be in Lugano to interrogate a captured Italian agent. Blum had been instructed to probe for indications about who was behind Dollmann and Zimmer, as well as what they were after. All he was able to obtain by direct questioning were hints that Dollmann was associated with Wolff; the Standartenführer flatly refused to state on whose behalf he was in Switzerland. He also declined to provide hints as to German objectives or conditions, merely stating that if contact was satisfactorily established, he would return to Switzerland on 8 March "with credentials and definite proposals."[6] Blum subsequently learned that Dollmann had told Husmann and Rothpletz that he was there as a spokesman for Wolff, Rahn, and Kesselring, and the OSS man therefore concluded that the point at issue "would bear upon the future disposition of the German forces in northern Italy."[7]

If Blum was not very successful in penetrating Dollmann's mask, the SS man made little dent in the Allied demand for unconditional surrender. Dollmann skirted the touchy issue of East-West relations, but he did ask cautiously whether the Allies would deal with Himmler if the Reichsführer-SS championed a separate peace in northern Italy. The OSS man, representing the antiracist cause, fittingly replied that such an approach would not stand "a Chinaman's chance."[8]

With that, Dollmann quit probing, but Blum gave him additional indications about where the Allies, or at least the OSS, stood. On instructions from Dulles, Blum handed Dollmann the names of Ferruccio Parri and Antonio Usmiani. Parri was an Italian partisan leader while Usmiani was apparently a member of the Royal Italian Secret Service (SMI). Both men had been captured by the Germans. Although denying that their freedom was a precondition for discussion, Blum indicated that the OSS would see the release of Parri and Usmiani as a sign of sincerity. Since Parri and Usmiani were probably the two most important pro-Western Italian prisoners in German hands, their release might be considered a stiff test of serious intent. But the formidability of the challenge was more apparent than real, for if the SS was ready to parley, the lives of a couple of Italian patriot leaders meant nothing to them. Furthermore, Blum gave Dollmann two indications that the OSS would try to remain open-minded. At the start of the discussion he deliberately shook hands, not only with Parrilli, but with both Dollmann and Zimmer. This simple gesture implied that the OSS would not let the rigid demands of unconditional surrender or the beastly reputation of the SS stand in the way of gentlemanly treatment and a fair deal. Blum, who realized that the unconditional surrender policy, and Goebbels's threats that the Allies intended to exterminate Germany made discussion extremely difficult, tried to reassure Dollmann that the Western powers would not be vengeful. Citing the enormous "material and moral destruction" in Europe, Blum stressed that the Allies would need the help of "every available man of goodwill." To the SS men in front of him, Blum added specifically that anyone who helped shorten the war would give the Allies "proof" of this "goodwill."[9]

Strange as it may seem, the whole exchange between Blum and the SS men lasted only twenty minutes. Dollmann, Zimmer, and Parrilli then left immediately for northern Italy to report that contact had been made, and to obtain further instructions from Wolff. Understandably, Dollmann and Zimmer were somewhat uncertain about the meaning of what had transpired. On the one hand, Husmann and Blum had barred the door to any direct effort to split the alliance or deviate from unconditional surrender. But by handing over the names of Usmiani and Parri, the OSS had shown a willingness to talk, if certain assurances were provided. Blum's decision to shake hands with the SS men further suggested that they would not be treated as pariahs. But the most encouraging sign for the Germans was Husmann's reference to the creation of a postwar elite and Blum's remark that men "of goodwill," such as those who helped arrange a surrender, would be important in the reconstruction of Europe. To SS members whose minds were filled with elitist dreams, yet pinched by the censorship and propaganda of Nazi Germany, this seemed like a veiled offer of preferential treatment. Men like Dollmann and Wolff simply could not accept the idea that all was lost and that the Third Reich would be destroyed root and branch. To their muddled minds, Blum and Husmann seemed to be saying that the OSS would play along with the unconditional surrender formula, but if the SS men played ball, the good and idealistic elements among the Nazis would find a respectable place in the new Europe. This not only meant that the handful of individuals directly involved with the negotiations would gain Allied favor; Dollmann and his colleagues concluded that somehow the men in the organizations to which they belonged would be looked upon with respect and treated honestly and decently.

So strongly did those Germans who took part in Sunrise come to believe this that they clung to it even after the war. Zimmer, for example, maintained long after hostilities ended that Blum had told them that the Allies "desired German participation in the task of postwar reconstruction." The story had grown to such proportions for Zimmer that he claimed that Blum as well as Husmann had seen surrender as the first step leading to the creation of "a postwar elite."[10]

Nor was Zimmer the only one for whom the dream of special surrender terms assumed a transcendent reality. When the formal capitulation ceremony actually occurred, seven weeks after the meeting at Lugano, the German representatives were frozen speechless when actually confronted with the terms of unconditional surrender.[11] All the weeks of haggling and discussion had not eradicated the impression which flowered at Lugano that if the Germans played along with the OSS, some softening of the surrender terms would occur. Sitting in his cell after the capitulation, the wily Wolff still held to this faith. He told a fellow prisoner that "certain promises were made and certain hopes aroused during the talks which took place before the actual surrender," but he cautiously concluded that "at the moment it is wiser not to mention these things or to make too much of them."[12]

When Dollmann met with Wolff and Ambassador Rahn on 4 March, the day after his return from Lugano, the Standartenführer was able to provide them with some information pointing toward guarded optimism.[13] The OSS was willing to talk, and the Germans had reason to believe that Dulles and his associates might be flexible, indeed, even pliable. Wolff quickly agreed to the release of Parri and Usmiani, and after talks with Zimmer and Parrilli, he decided to go to Switzerland himself on 8 March, in order to deal directly with Dulles. It is possible that Parrilli played a significant role in persuading Wolff to go by insinuating that he had good connections with the Allies, and that if Wolff could convince the Anglo-Americans of the "Russian danger" there would be a "just basis" for discussion.[14]

In any event, once Wolff made the decision to contact the OSS himself, he immediately received the backing of Ambassador Rahn. Although the top Germans involved in the enterprise do not seem to have formally agreed on what they would ask for in Bern, Rahn did provide Wolff with a handwritten scheme for ending the war in Italy. Rahn's proposal was remarkable for its complexity and lack of contact with reality. First off, the ambassador wanted the Allies to abandon their offensive in Italy in exchange for an Axis pledge not to carry out attacks or destruction of property. The cease-fire would be kept secret—"in order to avoid any basis for a stab-in-the-back legend"—until Kesselring agreed to end hostilities formally.[15] This was to occur no later than "the day after the fall of Berlin." Furthermore, both Rahn and Dollmann seem to have hoped that after the capitulation, the German forces would continue to exist as military units, though disarmed except for officers' sidearms. In Rahn's plan these units would be sent home after capitulating in order to prevent "unrest or plundering by foreign workers who had been brought to Germany."[16] The German soldiers would then only be interned for a short period and, following that, they would be free to go to any part of Germany they chose, that is, they would not be forced into the Soviet zone.

Although Rahn tried to make his proposal attractive to the Allies by noting that it would free them from the danger of a redoubt, the scheme offered the Anglo-Americans very little, and was hopelessly impractical. Kesselring had not even been consulted, and the Allies were thus being asked to take a theoretical pig in a real poke. To have kept secret a de facto cease-fire for six, eight, or ten weeks was obviously impossible, especially as the Western powers were being asked to go behind the back of their Russian ally while dealing with the enemy. Finally, the only thing that the Allies were to get for this was a pledge of an orderly withdrawal and a host of commitments to the German leaders involved.

Whether Rahn's plan was approved by Wolff, or whether the Obergruppenführer intended to present it to Dulles is not clear. But elements of the scheme, such as the need to preserve order, avoidance of a stab-in-the-back legend and the honorable withdrawal of the German forces, paralleled points in a number of other surrender or negotiation approaches. In their subsequent attempts to explain what they had done, Axis participants in Sunrise repeatedly made reference to points in the Rahn proposal.[17] Therefore it seems likely that Wolff was hoping to obtain Allied approval for something of this kind when he left for Switzerland on 8 March.

Obviously, once Wolff decided to cross the border himself, the period in which Dulles could shield himself behind secondary agents had come to an end. Dulles had managed to keep in the background up to this point by using the Swiss and OSS men like Gaevernitz and Blum. He had thereby unwittingly created the basis for future trouble because of Husmann's and Blum's statements implying that the Allies might give special favor to those who surrendered. But Dulles's own actions were the direct cause of Wolff's decision to go to Switzerland. It was Dulles who had decided to tell the Germans that the OSS was willing to talk, and it was Dulles who made the release of Parri and Usmiani a precondition, or at least a necessary indicator, of serious intent.

The OSS representative in Bern was not a man reluctant to make important decisions or an individual racked by doubt regarding his own judgment. Long experienced in international relations, the future director of the CIA came from a line of distinguished American diplomats. His maternal grandfather, John W. Foster, was secretary of state under President Harrison, and one of his uncles was Robert Lansing, Wilson's second secretary of state. After education at Princeton, Dulles entered the diplomatic corps, serving as a member of the American delegation to the Paris Peace Conference in 1918 and then in various European capitals. In 1926, he resigned from the diplomatic service to join the well-established law firm of Sullivan and Cromwell, in which his older brother, Foster, was a partner. Among its clients the firm included American corporations with cartel interests in Europe as well as a number of German firms. In the 1930s, Dulles acted as legal adviser to American delegations to various international conferences and participated in the neutrality law controversy which followed the Italo-Ethiopian war. On this issue he published (in cooperation with Hamilton Fish Armstrong) an important volume, titled *Can We Be Neutral?*, sponsored by the Council on Foreign Relations in 1936. The book strongly attacked mandatory embargo of United States exports, which to Dulles's mind seemed a needless hindrance to American trade. He pleaded that United States action should be directed solely toward America's "best interest" and should not be influenced by "any fetish of neutrality, impartiality, or even consistency."[18]

When the time came to establish an intelligence organization, Dulles's knowledge of international, especially German, finance, and his long experience as a diplomat in Europe were considered of great value. Dulles was also drawn into the planning of the OSS because he was a friend of the director, William Donovan, and of David Bruce. The latter, another lawyer and corporation executive (a son-in-law of Andrew Mellon), was assigned to London and became the chief OSS official in Europe.

In November, 1942, Dulles asked for and received an assignment to Switzerland, where he could have an active role rather than remaining an administrator in London. Dulles wanted to play spy, and when given even a small opportunity, he played it with gusto. Though it was soon common knowledge in Bern that he was a top American intelligence official, Dulles insisted on regularly performing such low-level spy routines as leaving restaurants through different doors than the ones he had used when entering.[19]

On a more significant level Dulles was strongly committed to the idea that an organization dedicated to intelligence-gathering and covert operations could make possible a quick end to the war. His post in Bern soon became the most important juncture for continental intelligence activities and for the exchange of information between the Allies, the neutrals, and the Axis. In addition to collecting data on the economic, political, and military condition of occupied Europe, the OSS office in Bern maintained contact and support for various resistance movements. The chief effort was aimed at assisting the

French Maquis until France was liberated by Allied armies in the fall of 1944. Dulles also collaborated closely with some anti-Nazi and dissident groups inside Germany, but these activities were nullified by the failure of the assassination attempt of 20 July. By early 1945, the most ambitious covert OSS operation remaining on the continent was support for the Italian partisans.

From his sensitive vantage point in Bern, Dulles anxiously watched the growing prestige and influence of the Soviet Union as the Red Army succeeded in reversing the tide of the German advance.[20] To counteract Soviet prestige in Italy, Dulles strongly advocated massive aid for the Italian partisans. He thereby hoped to strengthen the anti-Communist groups and to convince Italians that they were not being neglected by the Western powers.[21] In Germany, after the failure of his effort to assist the resistance, Dulles thought that the post-July 20 repression might drive any remaining anti-Nazi sentiment into a pro-Soviet position. By creating the Free Germany Committee, the Soviets had shown a willingness to restore a German state after the war, while the Western powers aimed at a division of the country as the only means to prevent a resurgence of German power. Dulles believed that in order to counter Soviet influence, German authorities should be given some hope for the future.[22] Only so would an opposition inside the Party and the government be able to produce an early capitulation.

Due to the military value of the Italian partisans, the Combined Chiefs of Staff may have been given a measure of credence to Dulles's advice. The Italian resistance did receive aid, though never as much as it, or Dulles, thought appropriate. Regarding Germany, however, Dulles's proposals ran head on against the policies of military necessity and unconditional surrender. On these basic points, the Allied command was not prepared to give an inch—especially in the last days of hostilities—and Dulles was not authorized to offer any concessions to top Nazi or Fascist officials.[23]

Unable to obtain maneuvering room at the top levels of the Nazi system, Dulles also failed to bring off important local capitulations. The plan to use German generals in Allied hands to get access to the enemy commanders on the Western front had collapsed by February, 1945.[24] Thwarted at both the highest and lowest levels, Dulles was forced to stand back, watching the Germans, while waiting for someone to make a move. Even so, it does not appear that he tried to anticipate developments, nor did he have a clear grasp of what was going on inside Germany. Much OSS data on the Third Reich was hopelessly out of date by February-March 1945, and Dulles's special point of view added to the confusion. While the Anglo-American military authorities looked upon the SS with extreme suspicion because they thought its fanaticism and deviousness would most likely lead to last-minute atrocities or attempts to drive wedges between the Russians and the Western powers, Dulles saw the SS in a more positive light. The crushing of the July 20 conspiracy by the Blackcoats, their responsibility for the repression of the resistance movements, and the pervasive fear of the SS led Dulles to conclude that no opposition to the war could organize without SS support.[25] This view easily slipped over into the belief that only the SS had the power to carry out a capitulation. Such an impression was a gross oversimplification, however, for many crosswinds blew in Germany. Not only were party and state riddled with apathy and disaffection, but the SS itself had long been torn by bitter personal conflict and Byzantine intrigue. Most important, as events in Italy and later at Rheims clearly demonstrated, the SS could lend its support to a capitulation, but only the German army had the power and means to carry one out.

Generally, one may conclude that Allen Dulles was not in a very strong psychological position to cope with a direct approach from Obergruppenführer Wolff. Along with putting too much value on an SS initiative, Dulles was hobbled by his tendency to overestimate the strength, and underestimate the weakness, of every real or imagined opponent. The SS official could only see Soviet power and prestige in the spring of 1945; he could not see Russian sensitivities, or the soft spots left by four years of slaughter and decades of fencing with capitalists. Similarly, despite numerous indications that Hitler and Germany were near their end, Dulles was one of the last to really believe it. Throughout the spring of 1945 he continued to act as if victory was a mile down the road, rather than just around the corner. Most of all, the OSS man seriously underestimated the political risks involved in dickering with the representatives of the SS or any secondary Nazi leaders. Inherent in such attempts was the danger that the Axis officials could wriggle their way into the confidence of individual Allied officials, thereby laying the basis for a softening of the peace terms either before, or after, capitulation. Even more dangerous was the likelihood that since the Soviets would not be parties to OSS talks with the Germans, they would have reason to believe that a villainous Nazi-Western deal was being hatched behind their backs. Nothing would be better suited to produce the East-West rupture which was every Nazi's fondest dream.

But Dulles gave little thought to the basic political hazards. For him, the central problems in peacemaking were technical ones; how to get emissaries over borders, how to protect potential capitulators from publicity, and how to keep the lines of communication open once contact had been made. In his subsequent explanations of the role he played in Sunrise, the technical and practical considerations were the ones which received the stress.[26] From the beginning, Dulles had this same concern. When the first reports of Parrilli's and Dollmann's journey to Switzerland reached Allied Mediterranean head-quarters, authorities there were less than enthusiastic, and Dulles was told "that if Kesselring wished to dispatch an emissary with an official message he could always find ways of doing it."[27] But Dulles immediately cited an obstacle that would stand in the way of Kesselring "or those around him" following such a course. The "greatest secrecy" would be necessary so that the advocates of surrender would not be "betrayed by fanatic Nazis in Kesselring's entourage." Therefore, Dulles advised, rather than send emissaries through the lines, it would be more practical to arrange contacts in Switzerland, since the OSS had experience in slipping "high officials" into the country "without arousing suspicion."[28]

This message not only reveals Dulles's narrowly practical focus, it also shows the degree to which the OSS man's muddled view of the situation came to serve his own interest. Heretofore, the OSS had maintained that secrecy was necessary in dealing with German army officers because of the dangers of betrayal to the Gestapo and the SS. This time Dulles claimed that clandestine methods were needed regarding SS officers because of the risks of disclosure by unspecified fanatics in the army. The only point of consistency was the assertion that whatever happened, the OSS's practical expertise placed it in the best position to facilitate a capitulation.

The war was coming to an end, yet the OSS had achieved relatively little in Europe. Although Dulles had obtained valuable information from Fritz Kolbe and other informants, his intelligence successes were modest when compared with the coups which the British had achieved through code-cracking ventures like Ultra. The OSS's liaison and supply work with the resistance movements had also been overshadowed by the operations of the British SOE. Dulles's dabblings with the German opposition had produced little and he had therefore not become a conduit for significant German capitulation approaches. After 3½ years of talk about the importance of political warfare, nothing notable had been accomplished. By March, Dulles and the OSS in Europe could not help but feel the need to produce a stunning coup which would make all the effort worthwhile.

Then on 8 March came the word that Parri and Usmiani had been released and that Parrilli, Dollmann, and Wolff himself had crossed the border. Dulles made a heroic effort to control his elation, but the prospect of finally achieving a notable success against the Nazis, especially against the SS, proved too strong. To his mind, the events of 8 March marked a Sunrise, not only for the Allied cause, but for his mission, and that of the OSS, as well.

Dulles immediately decided that he and Gaevernitz should travel to Zurich to arrange a contact with Wolff.[29] The Obergruppenführer was traveling with a rather large party: Dollmann, Zimmer, Parrilli, and Wolff's adjutant, Sturmbannführer Eugen Wenner. At the border, they had been met by Major Rothpletz, and the omnipresent Husmann, who accompanied them to Zurich. En route, Husmann lectured the Obergruppenführer, as he had previously done Dollmann, stressing that the East-West coalition could not be broken by the Nazis. He also managed to extract a guarded statement from Wolff that he had not come as a representative of Hitler and Himmler—an assertion that was almost correct, because the Reichsführer SS had not specifically been informed of Wolff's mission, and Hitler had only listened passively while the Obergruppenführer urged that contact be made with the Allies.[30] Once in Zurich, the SS men waited in Husmann's residence to see what Dulles and the OSS would do. Dulles realized that he was in a tricky situation because if the press learned that he was dickering with an SS commander, there would be a mighty outcry. Deciding to play it somewhat cautiously, Dulles chose first to meet with Parri and Usmiani to ascertain whether they were well and had been freed unconditionally. Once this was accomplished, he told Husmann that he and Gaevernitz would meet Wolff alone in an apartment which the OSS maintained in Zurich.

In the discussion which occurred on the night of 8 March and in a subsequent meeting with Gaevernitz and Dollmann the following day, Wolff made an impression on Dulles and Gaevernitz so favorable that it sustained him throughout all subsequent developments. Dulles immediately concluded that he was a "distinctive" and "dynamic" personality.[31] The OSS officials were somewhat nervous about Wolff's possible manipulation by Himmler, but they were pleased that the Obergruppenführer revealed himself to be "a man of power." They had not expected him to be "a Sunday School teacher," and as they reported later, they were "more interested in his power than in his morals."[32]

Wolff also said most of the right things, or avoided saying the wrong ones. He did not ask for immunity from war-criminal prosecution and in fact made "no request concerning his personal safety."[33] He did not deny that the war was lost for Germany, and he raised no objection when Dulles declared that all discussion would have to be based on the principle of unconditional surrender. Wolff asserted that the time had come for "some German with power" to "lead Germany out of the war in order to end useless human and material destruction."[34] To provide further guarantees of his sincerity, Wolff offered to take a number of steps beneficial to the Allies. He assured the safety of 350 Anglo-American POWs and the release of the last handful of Jews held in northern Italy. In addition to promising that he would try to release another Italian resistance fighter, Edgardo Sogno, Wolff pledged that the forces under his command would cease "active warfare against [the] Italian partisans, merely keeping up whatever pretense is necessary."[35] The concern which Wolff and Dulles shared about the maintenance of order in the postwar period was reflected in an assurance from the SS man that he would facilitate "the return to northern Italy of Italian officers presently held in Germany, who might be useful in the post-hostilities period." [36]

What Wolff proposed actually to do to end the war in Italy emerged less clearly. Realizing that there was no hope for fantasies like the Rahn plan, Wolff prudently wrapped his ideas in many folds of vagueness. He dismissed the execution of a "simple military surrender" as "difficult" to arrange, and suggested instead that he try to persuade Kesselring to participate in a general declaration by the German leaders in northern Italy that further resistance was useless. [37] While granting that of these leaders, only Rahn fully supported him, and that it would be difficult to persuade Kesselring to break his oath to Hitler, Wolff still maintained that the idea was feasible. He proposed going to Kesselring immediately after his return from Switzerland. His close "personal relations" with the field marshal would allow Wolff to convince Kesselring that "the senselessness of the struggle" required him "to admit that his duty to the German people is higher than that to the Führer." [38] Once Kesselring was won over, Wolff, Rahn, Kesselring, "and others" would draft a radio message to the German people "setting forward the uselessness of the struggle" and while urging "Germans in general to disassociate themselves from Himmler-Hitler control," also announce that the German authorities in northern Italy were terminating hostilities. [39]

Despite the complexities and uncertainties involved, Dulles was enthusiastic about Wolff's proposal. The release of Parri and Usmiani impressed him mightily, as did Wolff's promises to end the war against the partisans. The question marks hovering around Kesselring made the OSS man somewhat nervous, and he still harbored doubts about whether Himmler had his finger in the affair, but grasping the larger hope, Dulles exulted on 10 March that if "the Wolff-Kesselring talks are favorable, this plan may present a unique opportunity to shorten the war, permit occupation of northern Italy, possibly penetrate Austria under most favorable conditions, and possibly wreck German plans for establishment of a maquis." [40] One may fairly conclude that Dulles was far too optimistic, and that during the talks with Wolff, he and Gaevernitz were not sufficiently cautious or skeptical. But compared with the serious errors made in the preparation and transmission of the OSS reports relating to the events of 8 and 9 March, Dulles's conduct in the actual meetings seems exemplary.

The first cable in which Dulles notified London, Washington, and Caserta that Wolff had crossed the border contained a very serious error. The OSS man stated that the reports he had received—from Waibel—indicated that Wolff's party included not only three SS men, but also an "OKW representative"—a German army officer—"presumably from Kesselring['s] staff."[41] In fact, there was no army (OKW) officer in Wolff's group; either Waibel or Dulles had mistaken Wolff's adjutant, Eugen Wenner, for an army officer. This mix-up inevitably led the Allied military authorities to conclude that the German army was expressing an interest in surrender, when the Axis army leadership in Italy had not even been informed of Wolff's mission. On the following day, 9 March, Dulles caught his error and in the next two telegrams stated correctly that all the Germans in the group were SS men, but he did not go back and specifically indicate that the first report had been mistaken. Dulles does not seem to have grasped that to Field Marshal Alexander and the Combined Chiefs of Staff, a deal with the SS was of secondary importance; they wanted the capitulation of the German army in Italy and thus were hypersensitive about any indication that Kesselring might surrender. Because Dulles failed to read the Allied military attitude correctly and did not clear up the confusion, it is likely that the army authorities never recognized that their initial elation about Wolff's mission had arisen from a reporting blunder. Consequently they may have—consciously or subconsciously—considered the whole Sunrise affair to be more important to them than it actually was, simply because of that first electrifying message indicating that an "OKW representative" was in Switzerland.

The tendency to overprize Sunrise was increased by two alterations made by the OSS Director, William Donovan, in this same telegram of 8 March. It was customary for the OSS Washington office to paraphrase field reports before they were circulated, partly to remove incidental information, and partly to thwart enemy code-cracking efforts. But in this case Donovan also made changes affecting the content of Dulles's dispatch. The OSS representative in Bern had stated that Wolff and his party were "allegedly prepared to talk definitely," but in Donovan's rewording, the sentence came out much stronger: "They are allegedly prepared to make definite commitments in regard to terminating German resistance in northern Italy."[42] Furthermore, Dulles had ended his cable with a doubting sentence which read, "[The] question is[,] how much does Himmler know about this[?]" Donovan omitted this sentence entirely.[43] If one adds Donovan's alterations to the initial mistake over the OKW representative, the message that emerges gives a far more positive picture of Wolff's mission than the facts warranted. Yet this was the picture which the OSS presented to the secretary of state, the Combined Chiefs of Staff, and President Roosevelt himself. After 8 March, Dulles's messages were more accurate, and Donovan's paraphrases much closer to the originals, but the damage had probably been done. Henceforth Dulles and the rest of the OSS embraced Sunrise as their cause, and the highest authorities in the American government were not able to shake off the impression that an operation was underway which would end the war in Italy.

Field Marshal Alexander was especially susceptible to the Sunrise fever because he was vividly aware that the Germans still had a powerful force in northern Italy. Reportedly "very enthusiastic" about the news of Wolff's arrival, Alexander made his plans on the assumption that Dulles's assertion that an OKW representative had come to Switzerland was correct.[44] Although troubled by the fact that the leading personalities in the venture were SS men, Alexander was less concerned about the uncertain attitude of Kesselring. In his telegrams to London and the Combined Chiefs of Staff, the field marshal proposed to follow Dulles's advice and send military representatives to Switzerland so that they could verify the Germans' readiness to surrender before passing them on to Caserta for a formal capitulation. While adding the qualification that this should only be done if the German approach "appear[ed] genuine," Alexander's planned course of action was predicated on the assumption that Kesselring would authorize a surrender agreement.[45] The first message dispatched by Alexander was sent to the British Chiefs in London on 10 March; they in turn registered their suspicions of the fact that SS men were involved, but recommended that Alexander's plan to send military representatives be approved with the proviso that the Soviets "be informed" of the situation. At the bottom of the memorandum summarizing the recommendations Churchill jotted the words, "I agree." On the following day the prime minister reacted more cautiously, instructing Alexander not to send representatives until authorized by the Combined Chiefs of Staff to do so, because "the Russians must be informed before any meeting takes place."[46]

When Alexander's message reached Washington, American government officials immediately realized that it was a matter "of great importance."[47] The Joint Chiefs of Staff agreed with the British Chiefs that the Soviet Union should be notified to prevent "any future criticism."[48] But the Americans were anxious to avoid "asking their concurrence" for fear that it might "delay or jeopardize a possible success."[49] When Secretary of War Stimson learned that the British Chiefs had received Churchill's approval for their action, the secretary journeyed over to the White House on the afternoon of 11 March to see the president. Roosevelt knew of Sunrise from the information provided by the chairman of the Joint Chiefs, Admiral Leahy, as well as from the OSS, but he did not know that Churchill had specifically approved the decision to inform the Soviets before proceeding. "Very glad" to receive Stimson's message, Roosevelt also okayed the idea of notifying the Russians.[50]

On 11 March, both the British Foreign Office and the State Department made preparations to cable paraphrases of Alexander's telegram to their respective ambassadors in Moscow. But before the British message was dispatched, Churchill and Eden added a cover note asking for an expression of Soviet opinion and assuring the Russians that no contact would be made until a "Soviet reply is received by the British government."[51]

Churchill, thereby, on his own initiative, altered the policy of the Combined Chiefs of Staff; the British message not only notified the Soviets of the surrender overtures, it requested an expression of Soviet opinion with the concomitant implication that Soviet views would be given consideration by the Western powers. This was not the first occasion on which the British prime minister had independently, perhaps arbitrarily, modified Anglo-American policy to suit his own views. Naturally energetic and impetuous, Churchill chafed at bureaucratic routine and had limitless confidence in his own insight and judgment. His action in this case was especially high-handed because the surrender discussions in Bern were primarily an American, not a British, enterprise.

Yet Churchill's underlying concern was surely correct; he understood that the Soviets would be suspicious of anything that resembled a separate peace discussion. The alliance of the Big Three was based on mutual need in wartime, and as the Allied armies advanced, the basis of this unity would dissolve. Realizing that Britain's strength was waning and that she would face a postwar Europe basically altered by the rise of Soviet power, Churchill was anxious to avoid unnecesary friction with Russia. But in his eagerness to reassure the Soviets by asking for their opinion, he had provided an opportunity for them to impose conditions which might jeopardize the Bern negotiations and thereby provide a new basis for inter-Allied disagreement and irritation.

The British Staff Mission in Washington learned of Churchill's action late in the evening of 11 March, and the next morning proposed to the Americans that they accept the situation as a fait accompli. The Americans acquiesced and the Combined Chiefs directed Alexander to send his representatives to Bern, but ordered him not to allow them to speak to the Germans until authorized to do so.[52] This procedure was intended to provide time for the receipt of an answer to Churchill's message to Moscow, but it was not necessary to wait long, for on the same day, 12 March, Molotov replied to both Washington and London.

The Soviet foreign minister stated that the Russian government did "not object to the proposed conversations," in fact it considered them so important that it designated three Soviet officers to participate in the Bern talks.[53] Assuming that Soviet participation would be acceptable to the Anglo-Americans, Molotov merely asked for United States assistance in getting the

Russian officers to Bern since the Soviet Union did not have diplomatic relations with Switzerland. The British Joint Staff Mission in Washington accepted Molotov's statements without demur and asked the Combined Chiefs to direct Alexander to get the Soviet officers to Bern. Once they were there, the British urged, Alexander should immediately begin discussions with the Germans.[54]

The American government had not sought a Soviet opinion in the first place, however, and it was not willing to follow the resulting British recommendation. The Combined Chiefs had been preempted by Churchill, and the Americans had gone along with that, but they had not been happy. In his diary entry of 12 March, Secretary of War Stimson remarked that Churchill had "moved into the matter" and Stimson thought his interference "a grave mistake." "It adds delay to a movement which must be conducted rapidly," the secretary wrote, and noted further that "Churchill had no business to do it without our assent." As a result "two discordant notes have gone to the Russians" and Stimson obviously felt that the whole affair was now likely to produce trouble.[55]

He was right, in part because American officials were virtually unanimously opposed to Soviet participation in the talks in Bern. The United States ambassador in Moscow, Averell Harriman, cabled the State Department that he felt there was "no justification" for the participation of Soviet officers. The Bern talks were solely concerned with an Anglo-American front, and, in Harriman's view, the Soviets had no legitimate military interest in the question. Furthermore, if Soviet officers were present they might make "embarrassing demands" and thereby jeopardize the discussions. Harriman's objections went far beyond practical military considerations, for he believed that this incident involved a question "of policy in our relations with the Soviet government." The ambassador asserted that in a comparable case on the Eastern front, the Soviets would not concede participation to the Anglo-Americans; if the Western powers accepted Molotov's plan, it would not improve relations with the Russian government; "rather it would lead to even more intolerable demands from them in the future."[56]

On the heels of this chilly percursor of the cold war came a second telegram from the American Embassy in Moscow, this one from the head of the American Military Mission, General John R. Deane, to General Marshall. Deane also "strongly recommend[ed] that the Soviet request [sic] for participation in the proposed negotiations be disapproved," and cited the possible adverse effects which the presence of Soviet officers might have on the German negotiators. But Deane's basic argument was that Bern was simply an Anglo-American military problem comparable to the surrender of twenty-eight to thirty German divisions on the Eastern front. Therefore, he concluded, "from a military point of view it would appear to be neither [sic] necessary, desirable, nor proper to approve the Soviet request [sic].[57] Since the American government's wartime decision-making system gave transcendent priority to military necessity, the form and content of these two telegrams was bound to have a strong impact in Washington. Harriman's telegram used military considerations to reach political conclusions—not surprising for an ambassador. But even though Deane's telegram put still greater stress on military facts and speculation, he too came to political conclusions, especially in his penultimate sentence which read: "Approving the Soviet request will be an act of appeasement which will react against us in future negotiations."[58]

Harriman's and Deane's arguments were accepted as valid by the State Department, but there was concern about the possible consequences of too intransigent a stand. Charles Bohlen pointed out that "a flat refusal" would have adverse effects on the alliance and would "open up the possibility of a 'surrender race' in regard to Germany." To avoid the danger of having the Soviets raise further "impossible conditions," Bohlen suggested that the Russians be told it was not possible to delay the discussions in Bern until Soviet "observers" arrived, but that such observers "would be welcome" at subsequent negotiations at the Allied Mediterranean headquarters. Bohlen felt that the Soviets also had to be made aware that the final "responsibility of decision" lay solely with Alexander.[59] These arguments were discussed at length within the State and War departments, and FDR also considered the problem. The president's major concern was apparently one that had been raised by both Deane and Harriman, namely that the mere presence of Soviet officers might have an adverse effect on "the willingness of the Germans to surrender."[60]

Consequently the Joint Chiefs of Staff proposed to instruct Alexander to start discussions with the Germans at once in Bern; at the same time, the Soviets were to be informed that they could not be present there, but would be "welcome" at any subsequent discussions at Alexander's headquarters. The reasons that had been advanced by Harriman, Deane, and Bohlen were cited to support this decision and in addition the Joint Chiefs made the practical observation that if even two Soviet generals went to Bern they would have equal representation with the Anglo-Americans.[61] Secretary of War Stimson was nervous about this controversy and still angered by what he considered "Churchill's erraticness." The secretary of war emphasized to FDR that the American action was aimed at establishing negotiations on a "strictly military level without going into political affairs at all and not therefore handled by politicians." With the issue thus cast in the familiar

nduct of separate negotiations by one or two of the Allied powers with
rman representatives without the participation of the third Allied power
ruled out."[67]

The Soviet worry and anger over the Western handling of the Bern affair
uld only have been increased by a message which Field Marshal Alexander
nt to General Deane and the British military representative in Moscow,
eneral Archer, for relay to the Soviet general staff on 17 March. Alexander
ad, by all indications, not been told that the Soviets had demanded the end
the Bern talks. He also seems to have been unaware that the Western
overnments were trying to justify their refusal of Soviet participation on the
ender grounds that these were only preparatory talks and not negotiations.
lexander's message stated that he wanted Soviet representatives to come to
is headquarters for final talks "if the negotiations being conducted in Bern
were successful."[68] Thus one Allied message reached Moscow stating that
here were no negotiations going on, while another message frankly admitted
hat there were. Generals Deane and Archer, faced with Alexander's message
and knowing of the Allied contention that there had been no negotiations, as
well as Molotov's demand that the talks be ended, made the amazing
decision to transmit Alexander's message to the Russians "as though we had
heard nothing of Molotov's letter to our ambassadors."[69] Under these
circumstances, the Soviet reply to Alexander, which was given to Deane and
Archer on 18 March, was surprisingly restrained. After summarizing the
reasons why Molotov had demanded that the talks be broken off, General
Antonov merely observed that Alexander's message had "been based upon a
misunderstanding."[70] Deane and Archer then made another important and
surprising decision: they sent Antonov's reply to Washington but they did not
send it to Alexander, "since to our knowledge Field Marshal Alexander has
not been informed of Soviet insistence that the Bern negotiations be broken
off."[71]

This incident, and the decisions made by Deane and Archer, throw into
bold relief how clumsily the Western powers handled the exchanges and how
generous they were in supplying the Soviets with information that would
give grounds for concern and suspicion. Most important, the telegrams
clearly show how unrealistic and contrived was the Western claim that there
were no negotiations going on in Bern. The Anglo-American military and
political leaders themselves repeatedly described them as negotiations in
their own messages.

In Washington, the responsibility for trying to develop a solution to the
problem, and an answer to Molotov's cable of 16 March, fell to the military
authorities. Since General Marshall was out of town, Secretary of War
Stimson personally drafted the American reply to what he called Molotov's

language of military necessity, Roosevelt backed up
the final message prepared by the Joint Chiefs.[62]

On 14 March, the British Chiefs received the Unite
tions; but since their original proposal—that the Sovie
Bern—had been rejected by the Americans, they had
prime minister for guidance. This time Churchill's resp
of his earlier regard for Soviet suspicions and sen:
demonstrate anew his remarkable capacity for makin;
course. The American proposals taking a firm line w
logical and also extremely important." His only objec
passage which stated that Soviet representatives would b
negotiations occurring at Alexander's headquarters: "We
wrote at the bottom of his note to General Hastings Ism;
the minister of defense), "they have nothing to do with
surrender of the German army in Italy."[63] With this stat
basic attitude was set for the rest of the negotiation contro
toward the Soviets had overcome his caution, and this ten
grow stronger as the Bern dispute became more serious.

The British Chiefs and the Foreign Office readily adap
Churchill's new course and the Foreign Office revise
proposal to meet the problem of ambiguity cited by the
Eden was anxious to avoid using the word "observer" bec:
offensive to the Soviets; the resulting British revision, wh
Washington for final approval, merely stated that Alexander
arrangements "for the presence of Soviet representatives" a
headquarters, but added that Alexander alone would be '
conducting negotiations and reaching decisions."[64] British
avoiding the word "observer," produced a message even h;
American original. As soon as the British revision reached Was
quickly accepted by the Combined Chiefs of Staff and
Moscow. Only then did Churchill see a complete summary
original telegram. In a two-sentence note to Eden he showed
desire to draw a sharp line with the Soviets: "These are
arguments," he wrote. "I feel we were too complaisant—I esp

It was only natural that the Soviets would react strongly to t
Anglo-American stand. On 16 March Molotov sent a reply c
Western refusal to admit Soviet representatives to Bern, an acti
found "utterly unexpected and incomprehensible from the poir
Allied relations."[66] Molotov considered it impossible to give his cc
talks and insisted "that the negotiations already begun in Berr
off." Further, Molotov demanded that "from now on all possit

"very quarrelsome letter."[72] The secretary attempted to smooth over the trouble by using the same word as had General Antonov; for Stimson, the whole crisis was only a "misunderstanding."[73] The memorandum by Stimson stressed again the American contention that the question was not political, but simply a matter of military expediency. "No negotiations whatever are to take place at Bern," Stimson wrote, and he went on to claim that General Lemnitzer (one of the military representatives sent from Caserta to Switzerland) was in Bern merely as a staff officer for Field Marshal Alexander and had received "no instructions whatever from the United States government."[74] But the secretary was not prepared to make any concessions on the substantive points raised by the Russians: The Americans were determined "to stand fast"[75] and go ahead in Bern without the Soviets. Stimson's memorandum was approved by the secretaries of navy and state, as well as the Joint Chiefs of Staff. After Admiral Leahy added a comment stressing the need for cooperation with the British, it was also initialed by FDR.[76]

The American policy was being shaped by the military authorities rather than the State Department, but this did not mean that it was thereby made more harshly anti-Soviet. While Stimson was preparing a message conciliatory in tone, if unyielding on the disputed issues—"firm but not insulting" he called it—Ambassador Harriman was sending Washington another, less compromising appraisal of the situation. After claiming that Molotov's message of 16 March confirmed his belief, and that of General Deane, that since the Yalta conference "the Soviet leaders have come to believe that they can force their will on us on any issue,"[77] Harriman asserted that Molotov had been "arbitrarily" distorting facts in order to place his own interpretation on a series of issues from Poland to Bern. In the ambassador's view, Molotov had originally only "expressed the wish that the Soviet government might be represented" at Bern, and had subsequently made this participation a condition for Russian assent to the talks. In fact, Molotov's telegram of 12 March, as transmitted by Harriman, had agreed to talks and named Soviet representatives simultaneously, as if it was self-evident that the Western request for an expression of Soviet opinion was tantamount to an invitation to participate. But Harriman only saw what he construed to be "the arrogant language of Molotov's letter" and concluded that this had brought into the open "a domineering attitude toward the United States which we have before only suspected." Believing that this would ultimately create an "intolerable" situation for Americans, Harriman decided that the time had come to "face the issue by adhering to the reasonable and generous position that we have taken and by advising the Soviet government in firm, but friendly terms to that effect."[78]

Thus although there were differences of opinion on how sharply the line should be drawn, Stimson's memorandum expressed the consensus within the American government on the crucial point that the Soviets should not be allowed to participate in the Bern talks. On this occasion it was the British who showed more confusion and less determined leadership. The British ambassador in Moscow, Sir A. Clark Kerr, was not as upset by Molotov's message as his American colleague, and there were no characterizations of the Soviet position as "distorted" or provocative, in his dispatch to London. Still, his more generous view did not lead the British ambassador to suggest that Anglo-American policy should be altered. The military advantages which might accrue from a German surrender in Italy were sufficient, in Clark Kerr's view, to justify continuing the talks in Bern, while assuring the Soviets that they would be "associat[ed]" with any resulting negotiations at AFHQ.[79]

The British foreign secretary, Anthony Eden, did not bring an equally calm and steady approach to the problem, however. The rapid shifts of position which had been made by Churchill and the sharpness of Moscow's most recent response seem to have thrown him off balance. In a rambling and rather petulant message to Washington on 14 March, Eden claimed that the British government had "always been ready to agree" that the Soviets should be present at Bern[80] (hardly an accurate description of some of the views of the prime minister). But no sooner had Eden made this assertion than he backed away again and admitted that it was by then "probably too late to bring the Russians to Bern."[81] The only positive suggestion that the foreign secretary made was that Churchill and Roosevelt should try to mollify the Soviets through personal messages to Stalin. But Eden also gave this proposal an anticlimactic twist by suggesting that the prime minister and the president should only send Stalin a rewording of the Stimson message. The British were rightly worried because the Soviets had become angry at the Anglo-American handling of the Bern affair, but Eden's cable completely failed to drive home the point with the Americans.

On 19 March, Admiral Leahy, speaking for the Joint Chiefs, made short work of the Eden message. He amended the text to remove a passage which he felt gave too much initiative to the Soviets, and he also rejected the suggestion of top-level messages to Stalin, presumably because this would have created a more overtly political tone than the American military desired. Eden's message accomplished nothing except to produce a few inconsequential rewordings in the Stimson telegram. On 20 March, this polished message was approved by FDR and dispatched to Harriman in Moscow.[82]

In the course of the eight days which had passed from 11 March to 19 March, the tone of the diplomatic volleys between the Western capitals and

Moscow had become sharper. In part this was the natural consequence of Churchill's action in asking the Soviets for their opinion and the American decision not to permit the Russians in Bern. But it also arose from a gradually increasing awareness that a large-scale German surrender in Italy would have many, and significant, consequences. With the German forces in the west already crumbling, the loss of an additional twenty to twenty-five divisions in the south might lead to a total collapse of resistance to the Anglo-Americans. In any event, such a surrender would enable the Western powers to dash forward rapidly both to the north and east, as well as dissipating much of the danger of a last-ditch Nazi stand in an Alpine redoubt. With the Soviets slowed by continued stiff German resistance on their front, the Western powers would be able to sweep over the sensitive areas of the north shore of the Adriatic and on into Central Europe. The war would thus end with a dynamic Anglo-American offensive which would give them possession of many of the territories whose fate had not been settled by the Allies, as well as a large portion of the zones of Germany and Austria intended for Soviet occupation.

These possibilities were not the result of a concrete Anglo-American plan to gain a march on the Soviets; there is no extant documentary evidence to support a contention that the British and Americans plotted at Bern to help themselves to Central Europe. As the end of Nazi Germany approached, the political differences and rivalries which the Big Three had played down during the earlier stages of the war were bound to come more into the open in any case. Serious clashes had already occurred on issues as big as the future of Poland and as small as the treatment of United States POWs liberated by the Russians.[83] But the Bern affair was a perfect funnel to point, and perhaps to accelerate, this process. Yet even as the diplomatic exchanges passed back and forth between Moscow, Washington, and London, it gradually became clear that the Western leaders had made Wolff's approach seem more promising than it really was. To read the summit telegrams, one would think that a surrender in Italy was virtually assured, but with each passing day, Sunrise had become ever more complicated, and a simple unconditional surrender ever more remote.

The first indication that the ground was shifting under the feet of Wolff and Dulles reached Washington on 13 March, four days after the first Dulles-Wolff meeting had taken place in Zurich. Dulles learned from Wolff, via the Italian intermediary, Baron Parrilli, that Kesselring had left Italy for Berlin in accordance with a direct order from Hitler. Wolff was unclear about what caused Hitler to summon Kesselring, and he was even less certain about when the field marshal might return, noting ominously that "he might never come back."[84] To add to the trouble, a report of Wolff's trip to

Switzerland had reached the deputy chief of the SS, Ernst Kaltenbrunner. Apparently the pressure of serving two masters—Wolff and Kaltenbrunner—had been too much for the SS and police chief in Italy, Gruppenführer Wilhelm Harster, and to protect himself he had notified Kaltenbrunner that Wolff had gone to Switzerland. Kaltenbrunner sternly warned Wolff to break off his contacts, explaining that he himself was involved in high-level efforts to deal with the Allies which might be jeopardized by Wolff's activities.[85] In fact, a tournament of negotiation attempts had begun among the SS leaders, with Hoettl, Schellenberg, Wolff, Kaltenbrunner, and Himmler himself among the participants. For the moment Kaltenbrunner might appear to be ahead because he was simultaneously trying to initiate a contact through the Vatican and also attempting to negotiate as the leader of a fictional group of Austrian opponents of nazism.[86] Thus in addition to the usual dangers of intrigue within the SS hierarchy, there now existed a jealous competition to see who could make the best contact with the Allies. None of the people involved were very clear about what their negotiation efforts were supposed to accomplish, but all of them were deadly aware that it was best not to be left behind while another SS chief made a deal with the West.

Faced with Parrilli's report of Kesselring's trip to Berlin and Kaltenbrunner's warning to Wolff, Dulles was thrown into something of a quandary. In an effort to get a clearer picture of the situation, he had Parrilli relay a series of questions to Wolff about what he intended to do now. Wolff replied via Parrilli on 15 March that if Kesselring did not come back he was prepared to work out a "plan" either on his own or with Kesselring's successor. The Obergruppenführer was not very encouraging about what he could do on his own authority aside from "the possibility of facilitating a coastal landing or the seizure of airfields," but at least he did declare flatly that if he was summoned to Berlin, he would stall, and if necessary would "refuse, stating that it was impossible to leave the situation in northern Italy without a chief."[87]

While Dulles carried on his long-distance exchanges with Wolff, a vital decision regarding the future of Sunrise was being made by Alexander in Caserta. On 12 March, the Combined Chiefs told Alexander that he could send military representatives to Bern but that these men were not to contact the Germans until "further instructions" were received.[88] Alexander had selected as his representatives his British chief intelligence officer, General Terence Airey, and his American deputy chief of staff, General Lyman Lemnitzer (the latter subsequently served as Commander of NATO forces and Chairman of the Joint Chiefs of Staff). While Lemnitzer and Airey were preparing to depart for Switzerland, Dulles's messages arrived indicating that Kesselring had been called to Berlin and that Kaltenbrunner was on

Wolff's track.[89] Alexander decided nonetheless to send Lemnitzer and Airey to Bern because the preparations were "so far laid" that he did not want to scrap them.[90] Even with the scanty information that Alexander then had, this was a longshot. Apparently he was so apprehensive because of the strong Axis forces opposite his front that he was prepared to seek out a military capitulation against long odds.

On 13 March, Lemnitzer and Airey left Caserta; on 15 March, they were met by Dulles at Annemasse, the French border town opposite Geneva. The OSS man explained that Wolff's overture had been based on what he called "team play" between Kesselring and Wolff[91]—in realiy Kesselring seems to have had little or no idea of what was going on. In any event, Dulles admitted that all this was finished, at least for the time being, and that it would therefore be necessary "to build anew."[92] Dulles was still not discouraged and predicted that a meeting between Wolff and the Allied representatives, if held "soon," would lead to "a full surrender, or confusion behind German lines, or the destruction of German development of a Maquis."[93] Reflecting Dulles's optimism, Lemnitzer and Airey decided that "having come so far, they did not wish to turn back," and would proceed to Bern.[94] They told Dulles to send Parrilli to Wolff's headquarters with a message that it was "desirable" for the SS man to come to Switzerland for another "conversation."[95] Through this step-by-step, almost frivolous, process, the Western powers moved closer to a meeting between Wolff and Allied military representatives. The Obergruppenführer's messages showed that the surrender prospect was now merely a shadow, but still the Allies pressed on, and this time the responsibility lay clearly with them. On 15 March, it was the Allies, not Wolff, who asked for a meeting in Switzerland.

Once in Bern, Lemnitzer and Airey surveyed the OSS's plans for a meeting. Rather than have Wolff run the risk of traversing Switzerland by train, Dulles was preparing to meet him at Ascona near the Italian border. Even though the Combined Chiefs' ban on their talking to Wolff was still in force, Lemnitzer and Airey reported to Caserta that they intended to be in the neighborhood of Ascona when the Obergruppenführer was there, so that they could give advice to Dulles "if it was necessary."[96] On 16 March, this contrived arrangement was overtaken by events. Caserta received a message from the Combined Chiefs stating that Russian officers would not be coming to Switzerland (though they were invited to any subsequent proceeding in Caserta); at the same time the ban was lifted on Lemnitzer and Airey talking with the Germans.[97]

Dulles, Alexander, Lemnitzer, and Airey had all argued against bringing a Soviet officer into Switzerland, because the diplomatic and security risks were monumental. AFHQ Mediterranean was also afraid that if a Russian came, he might destroy all hope for a capitulation, or try to deal with Wolff on his own.[98] The Combined Chiefs, in their tough mood of 15–16 March, put all these fears to rest by barring Soviet participation in Swiss talks. Alexander then gave Lemnitzer and Airey authority to meet with Wolff if they thought it advisable.[99] Already inclined toward such a meeting, Lemnitzer and Airey were pushed further in that direction by the message Parrilli brought back from Wolff on 17 March. Not only did the SS man indicate that he was willing to come to Switzerland, he also provided more information on the fate of Kesselring. The field marshal had been made commander of the German forces in the west, a position even more significant and potentially more useful than his post in Italy. His new chief of staff was General Westphal, one of the officers whom Neurath had contacted in February when trying to arrange local German surrenders for the OSS. Wolff further whetted the Allied appetite by noting that his "close relationship" with Kesselring might now "open up possibilities on [the] Western front."[100] This point seems to have been decisive in overriding any doubt which the Allied military representatives still harbored, and they decided to meet with Wolff on 19 March. Their purpose, in Lemnitzer's optimistic words, was "to insure that events moved from [the] preliminary conspiratorial phase to [a] definite discussion of [a] plan for military surrender."[101]

In this context of vague but extensive possibilities, meetings occurred between Wolff, Dulles, Gaevernitz, Lemnitzer, and Airey at a villa near Ascona on 19 March. Wolff met with Dulles and Gaevernitz in the morning, then these three were joined by Lemnitzer and Airey in the afternoon. So many guards were stationed around the villa that their mere presence threatened the secrecy of the meeting. Dulles realized the dangers, as well as the comic elements of the situation, and removed the excess guards.[102] But he was less successful in his effort to maintain secrecy within the villa by withholding from Wolff the identity of Lemnitzer and Airey. Since Dulles reportedly presented the two officers as his "military advisors" while Lemnitzer and Airey told Wolff that they were "high-ranking officers,"[103] the German could have had little question that he was facing representatives of the Anglo-American High Command.

As in their previous meeting, Dulles and Gaevernitz looked on Wolff very favorably and were eager to give him the benefit of every doubt. Lemnitzer and, especially, Airey, were somewhat more critical. The Englishman was not enamored by Wolff's "three chins and fat fingers with diamond rings," and even while granting that the SS man was a "strong personality, active and intelligent," Airey thought he had "a crafty appearance" and was "clearly nervous."[104] In the course of the talks, Wolff, once again, went a fair way to allay Allied doubts by providing the Western officials with what they wanted. He made "no attempt to bargain" regarding his own fate and assured Dulles that he was committed to the "enterprise" and would "stand or fall" with it.[105] He also flatly declared his opposition to the creation of an Alpine redoubt, which to his mind was "madness."[106] Wolff further disabused the Allies of their dreams that army generals on the western front, such as Blaskowitz, might produce a surrender on their own initiative. Such people "would not take risks," Wolff rightly concluded, unless they were "90 percent sure of success."[107]

Wolff's tastiest intelligence tidbits, however, related to the situation in Italy. He provided the Allies with a detailed breakdown of the forces under his command and also handed over a "useful map giving [the] German idea of [the] partisan order of battle and [their] dispositions." In an earlier message Wolff had offered to present the Allies with "several truckloads" of Italian corporate securities;[108] this time he gave them his characterization of the Duce. In Wolff's view, Mussolini "was pulled this way and that by the women around him (the Petacci sisters), who really controlled his movements and decisions."[109] In any event, Wolff concluded, Mussolini was not "of any substantive importance"[110] to the question at hand, and with that, Wolff and the Allies gave little more thought to Italian fascism.

On the central question of how to arrange a surrender, however, Wolff still did not provide a direct answer. If the Allies wanted an immediate capitulation of his own command, Wolff could arrange that himself, but his "widely scattered" forces were "not very dependable" and could be crushed by the large German army formations to the north and south of them.[111] An immediate appeal to Kesselring's replacement in Italy, General von Vietinghoff, held few prospects in Wolff's opinion, because he was a simple "nonpolitical soldier" whose participation would have to be prepared carefully, preferably with the assistance of Kesselring.[112] The best course, if he had "five days to a week,"[113] would be for he himself to go to the West and urge Kesselring to participate in the plan. Wolff contended that Kesselring's support would help to tip Vietinghoff in favor of surrender and might also open up the possibility of a capitulation on the whole Western front. Noting that Kesselring's chief of staff was General Westphal—characterized by Wolff "as a man of broad political outlook who was likely to react favorable [sic] in connection with Kesselring"[114]—the SS man hinted that if his mission to the West was successful, he would bring back with him officers prepared to surrender both Vietinghoff's and Kesselring's forces.

By unrolling detailed prospects for a surrender in the West, Wolff was once again playing on a special sensitivity of the Anglo-Americans. He had nodded toward this plum in his message of 17 March, and his detailed presentation of the idea in Bern clearly made a strong impression on the Allied representatives. Not only Dulles, but Lemnitzer and Airey were captivated by hope that Wolff would come up with a general plan for a German capitulation in the south and west. They accepted at face value the SS man's claim that he had prepared a common plan with Kesselring and believed that "he had gone further with Kesselring than he had previously admitted."[115] They were also impressed by his "confidence in gaining support" and thought that he "represented the feelings of certain [army] generals."[116] In summarizing their conclusions for Alexander, Lemnitzer reported that there was "a chance" that Wolff and the generals would "use the opportunity to arrange [a] surrender."[117]

Wolff was also successful in his effort to use the meeting of 19 March to create the impression that he had joined with the Western Allies in a common effort to produce peace. He eagerly agreed to Dulles's suggestion that when he returned from his mission to Kesselring an OSS radio operator should be assigned to his headquarters to improve communication with Bern.[118] He also raised no objections to the surrender procedure set down by the Allies. At the moment of capitulation, German army officers would come to the Swiss border and after their credentials had been checked, they would proceed to Caserta for the actual surrender.[119] In his turn, Dulles showed a willingness to help Wolff with his problem of arranging a cover story for his trips to Switzerland and his release of Parri. The OSS man agreed to try to arrange a prisoner exchange to throw Wolff's suspicious colleagues, such as Kaltenbrunner, off the track.[120]

On only two points did Wolff fail to get his way. He was obviously fishing for a specific Allied acceptance of his plan to get to Kesselring, and he also sounded like he was trying to ferret out the date of the pending Allied offensive in Italy. Repeatedly the SS man asked if he would be granted enough time to make his trip to the West, but the Allied representatives refused to give him an official stamp of approval. They left "to him" the question of what he should do, and gave no hint as to the date of the Allied offensive, except to say that "time was exceedingly short."[121]

Even though the balance of the meeting tipped clearly in the SS man's favor, one must be cautious about portraying Wolff as a man totally in control of the situation, or himself. Despite his ability to manipulate the Allies, the Obergruppenführer was almost as confused as they were. At this point he was nearly obsessed by the conviction that a deal had to be made with the West, but he seems to have had no clear idea of what the deal should consist, or what German authority should actually make it. Apparently discouraged about the prospect of enticing Hitler into negotiations, he still hoped for a split in the East-West alliance.[122] He probably realized that a journey to Kesselring was an extremely long shot, but he was ready to try anything because his main objective was to delay the Allied offensive in Italy until he had time to work his way fully into the confidence of the Western powers. By cooperating in arranging an end to the fighting, and by preventing destruction, he hoped more than ever to convince the Anglo-Americans that he and his "decent" Nazi and SS comrades should be allowed to work their passage in the postwar world. Given enough time, he expected to convince some authority of the Third Reich—Hitler, Himmler, Kesselring, or whoever—that this had to be done to help the Nazi faith, and especially the Nazi faithful, survive an Allied victory.[123]

Wolff had put himself in an exposed position, but so had the Anglo-Americans. The Allied representatives had been insufficiently alert to Wolff's ingratiating efforts, and, on balance, they were satisfied with the results of the 19 March meeting. Erroneously believing that they had put the SS man on the spot, Lemnitzer reported to Alexander that Wolff would have to "come to [the] next meeting either with definite proposals and plans[,] or admit his inability to act."[124] Captivated by the hope that the SS man would develop a general plan for a German capitulation in the south and west, Dulles, Lemnitzer, and Airey sent encouraging reports to their superiors. In their turn, Donovan and Alexander dispatched optimistic summaries to the military and governmental chiefs in London and Washington. Though the reports by Donovan and Alexander exhibited bits of caution, the dominant tone of both suggested that Wolff was making serious surrender preparations. Again, it was the enticing possibility of a capitulation in the West which they stressed. There were references to Westphal's important position as Kesselring's chief of staff, to Wolff's close relations with the field marshal, and to the Obergruppenführer's "considerable confidence" that he could pull off a surrender both on the Italian front and in the West. The reports made by Donovan and Alexander left the impression that Wolff would probably meet again with the Allied representatives in Bern in the near future and that he might well bring with him German army representatives from Vietinghoff's and Kesselring's headquarters.

The accounts of the 19 March meeting prepared by Donovan and Alexander moved rapidly up through the chain of command. Donovan's went to the secretary of state, the Joint Chiefs of Staff, and FDR; Alexander's to the British Chiefs of Staff, the Combined Chiefs of Staff, Roosevelt, and Churchill. By 21 March, Wolff's optimism and his suggestive gambit about a Western capitulation had reached the top of the Anglo-American command system. The combination of this development and the high-level exchanges which had passed between Moscow and the Western capitals thereby committed the British and Americans at two critical points. On the one hand, they were clinging to the tail of a whispy surrender possibility. It promised to drag them through a labyrinth of intrigue within the German armed forces, but they hoped that it might result in a complete surrender of the German southern and western armies. On the other hand, they had drawn a sharp line with the Soviet Union, asserting that Russian officers could not be present at the Bern talks because these only concerned a military situation on the Anglo-American front.

Even while Lemnitzer and Airey were talking with Wolff, the Anglo-Americans still contended that negotiations were not going on in Bern. So pronounced was this dichotomy by 21 March, that only the most benign and tortured logic could make it seem consistent.[125] The Anglo-Americans had thereby made themselves vulnerable to a degree that fairly cried for Soviet Russia to zero in on the differences between Western words and Western deeds.

Karl Wolff, commander in chief of the German SS in
Italy, with Benito Mussolini during the last days of
the German-occupied Salo "Republic." It was Wolff
who was responsible for initiating conversations with
the OSS that ultimately led to Operation Sunrise.
(Reprinted by permission of the Istituto Luce, S. p. A.
Rome.)

Eugen Dollmann, of the German SS, one of the main
actors in Operation Sunrise. (Reprinted by permission
of the Istituto Luce, S. p. A. Rome.)

General Albert Kesselring, commander in chief of the
German army in Italy, shown here between Alessan-
dro Pavolini *(on the left)*, secretary of the Fascist
Party, and the Italian defense minister, Rodolfo Graziani. Kesselring emerged as the major obstacle to
surrender on the German side. (Reprinted by permission of the Istituto Luce, S. p. A. Rome.)

Wolff is shown here *(to the right)* with one of his backers in Operation Sunrise, the German ambassador to Italy, Rudolph Rahn *(center)*, along with the Secretary of the Interior of the Italian Fascist government, Guido Buffarini Guidi. (Reprinted by permission of the Istituto Luce, S. p. A. Rome.)

Allen Dulles, chief of the OSS office in Bern, the key
negotiator for Operation Sunrise, and its enthusiastic
advocate in Allied counsels. He is shown here with
Gera von Gaevernitz, his key aide. (Princeton University Library. Reprinted with permission.)

Henry L. Stimson, U.S. Secretary of War. With President Roosevelt gravely ill, Stimson was primarily responsible for defining U.S. policy and drafting instructions to the U.S. negotiating team in Operation Sunrise. (The Bettmann Archive, Inc.)

The three wartime Allies *(from left to right)*, Stalin, Roosevelt, and Churchill, at the Teheran Conference in 1943. Two years later, Soviet outrage at Operation Sunrise helped usher in the cold war. (The Bettmann Archive, Inc.)

Mission accomplished: on 29 April 1945, General Morgan signed the document of the surrender of all the German forces in Italy at the Allied headquarters in Caserta. Shown standing behind him is General Lemnitzer, and at the latter's side is the Soviet representative, General Kislenko. (From *The Secret Surrender* by Allen Dulles. © 1966 by Harper & Row, Publishers, Inc. Reprinted by permission of the publisher.)

CHAPTER 5

Sunrise on a Chilly, Cold War Morning

IN THE SPRING OF 1945, the perspective of the Soviet leaders, as well as conditions inside Russia, differed sharply from those which prevailed in the Western world. The Soviet Union had suffered war losses on a scale that people in the West found scarcely believable. The country had been ravaged by great German offensives in 1941 and 1942, as well as by Nazi extermination policies and the scorched earth tactics employed by the Soviet defenders. When the Germans and Russians reversed roles in 1943 and 1944, the war impact was still nearly as devastating. As the conflict approached its close, the toll of Soviet military dead topped ten million, and total Russian fatalities, including civilians, may have been double that figure. The four-year struggle had wiped out most of the fruits of the rebuilding and planned expansion which the 1920s and 1930s had produced at such great cost. With another era of costly rebuilding looming on the horizon, the only bright spots that lay immediately ahead for the Russian people were the return of peace and the satisfaction of having decisively defeated Nazi Germany.

Beyond these general conditions, whatever options were open to Russia in the last stages of the war depended chiefly on decisions made by Joseph Stalin.[1] The Soviet premier was notoriously suspicious of the outside world. Despite some expansionist tendencies, his prewar policy had mainly been aimed at blocking "capitalist encirclement" and preventing real or imagined attacks on the USSR. He had rearmed, promoted collective security, and in the end even made an alliance with Hitler, but the Nazis had nonetheless invaded Russia. Forced to cope with the brutal reality of Operation Barbarossa, Stalin reversed alliances, dealing first tentatively with the Anglo-Americans in the summer of 1941, and then more concretely after American entry into the war in December of the same year. These agreements, however, were the product of circumstances, not the result of any basic change in Stalin's views or outlook. Soviet Russia was mortally wounded and needed Western arms and supplies. Stalin took the aid with the same degree of enlightened self-interest as those who gave it. Transactions such as Lend-Lease could not possibly eliminate many of the suspicions he harbored about the capitalist powers, however, and the personal relationships which he established with Anglo-American leaders were likewise unable to wipe the slate completely clean. The Soviet premier seems to have genuinely liked FDR and trusted him, but the long anti-Communist record of men such as Churchill was hardly reassuring in Moscow.

Considering the way they had handled prewar relations with Adolf Hitler, neither East nor West had grounds to be completely optimistic about the strength of the wartime alliance. With the Nazi-Soviet pact of 1939 before their eyes, the Western powers knew that Stalin was capable of making a deal with Hitler. For his part, the Soviet leader had only to look back to the Munich agreement of 1938 to reach similar conclusions about the Western powers.[2]

In light of these and other grounds for distrust, it was of paramount importance to Stalin that he quickly obtain Western agreement to a postwar territorial alignment which would protect Soviet security. Notwithstanding Russia's precarious military situation and the imminent danger of total defeat, the Russian premier wanted to made a deal even in the earliest days of the East-West alliance. When Anthony Eden visited Moscow in December, 1941, Stalin called upon the West to match Hitler's generosity by conceding to Russia the territory she had been granted by the Nazi-Soviet pact as well as a kind of protectorate over Rumania and Finland. Eden dodged this question and the Western leaders kept deftly tiptoeing around it for the next 3½ years. Consequently, the important territorial problems were never completely clarified, much less resolved, in the course of the war. Significant meetings took place at Teheran, Yalta, and elsewhere, but the Americans, in particular, were wary of specific political commitments. Understandings concluded on such issues as the future of Poland, or the zoning of Germany, were couched in language so vague and conditional that postwar cooperation between the three powers would have been essential for their smooth fulfillment. Despite four years of such understandings, clear-cut postwar agreements had not been made, so the alliance continued to be held together more by a common fear of Nazi Germany than by mutual trust between East and West.

As the end of the European war approached, Stalin obviously realized that the Soviet Union would enjoy a tremendous increase in power and prestige due to the crushing victory over Germany. Within his complex and calculating mind, some consideration was surely given to the possibility of exploiting this development to expand Soviet-controlled territory. But judging from his behavior, the dominant feature in Stalin's thinking was not expansive confidence, but a desire to use this new position to protect and rebuild the Soviet Union. He tended, almost obsessively, to underestimate Soviet strength and to overestimate the power of opponents. Like Allen Dulles in Bern, Stalin continued to fear Nazi power even when it was obvious that the Third Reich was crumbling. By March-April, when the top Anglo-American leaders were convinced that Hitler's system was near its end, Stalin—and Dulles—continued to speak of Germany as if it had changed little from the days of boundless Blitzkrieg.

The Soviet leader's constant fear that the West might make a separate peace gained its sharpest edge from this overestimate of German power. Similarly—in this case like the Western governments—Stalin gave too much credence to the idea that Nazi-Fascist ideas and institutions would retain significant strength following defeat. The example of German revival in the 1930s was ever before the eyes of the Allies, and they concluded that only the most thorough cleansing of Germany and her satellites would produce a basis for future peace.[3] Thus when the Anglo-American forces entered Western Germany, they instituted denazification, and when the occupation forces of the Soviet Union ruthlessly "communized" the territories which they occupied, it was not only to destroy capitalist enemies and settle old scores, but was directed at the Nazi-Fascist groups in Hungary, Slovakia, and East Germany, which Stalin saw as possible nuclei for another attack on Russia.

In surveying the postwar power constellation, Stalin judged correctly that the United States would be a military-industrial colossus. But the Soviet premier's estimate of the Western Allies was also colored by his tendency to exaggerate the power of potential opponents. Like the Americans, he overestimated the strength of England, and much of his suspicion of the West was rooted in a fear (shared by FDR) that Britain might once again set off a round of colonial expansion.

The more Stalin's mind was occupied by the dangers and threats which he saw surrounding Russia, the more necessary it was for him to stress Soviet power, importance, and equality with the Western Allies. Despite his suspicions of the Anglo-Americans, Stalin definitely wanted the East-West alliance to continue into the postwar world; with Western support, Germany could be controlled and Soviet Russia would gain the time necessary to recover from the wartime slaughter and destruction. Thus, even as he feared the Anglo-Americans, Stalin sought to get along with them on a basis of mutual respect for each other's power and importance. Symbols of prestige were of critical importance to him, because if the Western powers did not consider Russia an equal, Western contempt might again lead to Soviet isolation and the return of "capitalist encirclement."

The Soviet authorities were especially anxious that people and governments in the West recognize the overwhelming importance played by the Russian army in the defeat of Hitler's Germany. Stalin wanted honors and glory for the Red Army in order to provide the Russian people with recognition for their great wartime sacrifices. But even more importantly, he needed the war to end in a way that would drive the lesson home to the Anglo-Americans that it was primarily Soviet power which had crushed the German army. Yet in March-April, 1945, after having driven the Germans westward for 2½ years, the Red Army found its advance slowed before Berlin. Rather than the Russians, it was the British and Americans, lightly bloodied and only recently arrived on the continent in force, who dashed forward at the last moment to grab the symbols of victory over Germany. What an unjust and frustrating turn of events this must have seemed in Moscow!

When the Western powers then went on to negotiate with the Germans in Bern (under the most suspicious circumstances), the Russians saw themselves threatened by mortal injury as well as dangerous insult. Given these conditions, there was no possibility that the Soviet Union could fail to respond sharply to the convoluted Western justifications of Sunrise. On 23 March, Molotov dispatched a reply to the Anglo-American cable of 20 March which fairly bristled with suspicion and angry accusation. What had happened at Bern, according to the Soviet government, was not a "misunderstanding," but "something worse," far worse.[4] For two weeks, Molotov charged, the Western powers had been negotiating with the Germans "behind the back" of the Soviet Union, while Russia carried "the main burden of the war against Germany."[5] Insisting that this was "absolutely inadmissable," the Soviet foreign minister flatly demanded that the Bern talks be broken off.

The hostile tone of Molotov's letter coincided with a number of other indications that the fruitful cooperation which was supposed to flow from the Yalta agreement was, in fact, rapidly dissolving. Stalin had imposed a puppet government in Rumania and was rigidly excluding the West from participation in the affairs of Poland. The Lublin Committee barred the London Poles from the new government, and Soviet authorities even rejected American plans to airlift relief supplies to Western prisoners who had recently been freed from German camps in Poland by the Red Army. On 23 March, the same day Molotov dispatched his sharp criticism of Allied actions in Bern, the Soviet Embassy in Washington also informed the State Department that the Russian foreign minister had decided not to lead the Soviet delegation to the United Nations Conference, which was due to open shortly in San Francisco. This belated withdrawal seemed to be a deliberate snub, intended to nullify the conference and imperil the new era of cooperation which was supposed to be born there.[6]

Although troubled by what they saw as a rising Soviet negativism, and taken aback by the bitter accusations in Molotov's message on Sunrise, the Western leaders showed little desire to leap into an angry East-West confrontation on the latter issue. In mid-March, 1945, the spirit of wartime comradeship was stronger than the tendency toward icy suspicion and hatred of the Soviet Union which would soon dominate Anglo-American councils. Furthermore, the course that Operation Sunrise had followed made it a singularly inappropriate basis for a self-righteous Western ultimatum. Serious mistakes had been made in Bern, Caserta, and the Western capitals. In addition, a veritable surrender fever was moving through Western officialdom following Wolff's meeting with the Allied representatives on 19 March. The possibility of a German capitulation expanding from Italy to the German forces in the West proved to be too much for Anglo-American caution. Wolff's vague hints about contacts with Kesselring were enough to cause Allied officers at SHAEF to discuss the need for selection of a site for surrender talks which could be "readily accessible" to Eisenhower's staff as well as Alexander's.[7] At the highest level, too, the prospect of a German surrender in the West tended to pass from pious wish to possible fact. By 25 March Winston Churchill was speculating seriously on the significant and beneficial consequences which would follow if Wolff's capitulation initiative extended from "a secondary front like Italy" to the German high Command in the West. Until this possibility was clarified, the prime minister implied, it was better not to beard the Russian bear in his den, especially not on issues where the West was weak, such as Poland or the history of Operation Sunrise.[8]

All levels of the British government, from Clark Kerr in Moscow to the prime minister himself, therefore decided to meet Molotov's angry message of March 23 by stalling and employing conciliatory silence. Ten days previously, the Americans had rejected Eden's suggestion that the first Soviet suspicions over Sunrise should be answered by a direct message to Stalin from the Western leaders. With a summmit approach presumably still blocked, there seemed nothing for Churchill to do after 23 March except to try to control his temper while keeping a hopeful eye cocked on Bern.

OPERATION SUNRISE

Perhaps in the near future more favorable circumstances would allow him to persuade the president that a joint message should be sent to Stalin covering all the sore points from Bern to Rumania. In the meantime, the prime minister was satisfied to stand back and let the Foreign Office and the British chiefs of staff take the lead in attempting quiet conciliation.

The initial British effort focused on developing a policy to deal with any future approaches from the Germans, so that the problems which had arisen at Bern would not be repeated.[9] This was a long and complex undertaking, because the military wanted to allow broad discretion to local commanders while the Foreign Office was anxious to develop a procedure that would pacify the Russians. Endless revision finally divided the problem into two categories of surrender, one local and the other general, but then argument erupted over how to distinguish between the two, and when to apply one or the other. Complexity triumphed over the desire for a quick smoothing of East-West relations, and British officials continued to wrangle over these questions until the end of April.

In the meantime, a more fruitful small suggestion for easing the troubles over Sunrise was advanced by Clark Kerr, the British ambassador in Moscow. Kerr, who consistently sounded both cautious and reasonable, indicated in a telegram of 25 March that the first step to take in dispelling the "genuine suspicion" of the Russians was for the Allies to "scrupulous[ly]" fulfill their obligation "to keep the Soviet government fully informed of developments."[10] This meant above all that the Russians needed to be provided with complete information on what had transpired during the 19 March meeting between Wolff and the Allied representatives in Bern. Kerr's suggestion dovetailed with recommendations by other Foreign Office officials, especially A. W. Harrison, who contended that the best way to calm the Russians was to pull Lemnitzer and Airey out of Switzerland.[11] In this view, once the military representatives had left, Sunrise could be turned over to OSS men who would be able to act as intermediaries, pure and simple. Should a military surrender actually materialize, all Dulles and his colleagues had to do was arrange "for fully accredited German representatives to proceed to Allied Headquarters to discuss [the] details [and] to carry out unconditional surrender."[12] If, on the other hand, the OSS received "detailed proposals for 'opening' either the Italian or the Western fronts"—the prospect Wolff had dangled before Allied eyes on 19 March—it could forward them "to the competent military authorities."[13]

The central contradiction in the Anglo-American handling of Sunrise was neatly embodied in this recommendation by Harrison. The Foreign Office man was seriously concerned about East-West relations and he was surely right that the presence of Lemnitzer and Airey in Switzerland was provocative to the Russians. But at the same time Harrison was perplexed by what he called the "sinister and as yet undisclosed motive"[14] behind Soviet hostility. It seems never to have dawned on him that his own speculations on how to smooth the way for a possible German and Anglo-American deal to open the Western front was a clear instance of the basic trouble. It was precisely this Western adoption of an elastic and self-serving definition of unconditional surrender which lay at the core of Soviet fear and hostility regarding Bern.

Blind to the true nature of the malady, British officials continued scurrying about, trying to remove its ugliest symptoms. On 27 March, the Foreign Office recommendations to recall Lemnitzer and Airey, while informing the Russians of what had happened on 19 March, were laid before the British Chiefs of Staff. The British Chiefs grasped even less of the problem than did their civilian counterparts. Still captivated by the possibility of a general surrender engineered through Sunrise contacts, they flatly rejected the suggestion that Alexander be ordered to withdraw his officers from Switzerland. Instead they contended that since the field marshal was acting within the limits of discretion allowed to a theater commander by the principle of military necessity, he should be permitted "to play out his hand as he sees best." The most that the British military authorities would concede was a recommendation to the Combined Chiefs of Staff that Alexander should be "reminded of his obligations" to keep the Russians informed.[15]

Following this lead, the Combined Chiefs simply informed Alexander on 31 March that he should report to the Soviets the results of any Sunrise contacts. Without providing the field marshal with any information on Molotov's angry accusations, the Combined Chiefs told him that if he had not already done so, he should immediately inform the Russians of what had transpired in Wolff's meeting with Lemnitzer and Airey on 19 March.[16] Considering that twelve days had passed since that event, there was little chance that any information provided by Alexander would have a salutary effect in Moscow. In fact, Alexander's telegram was so muddled and filled with statements that would arouse Soviet suspicions that the Western military representatives in Moscow, generals Deane and Archer, informed the field marshal that they would have to edit it in order to avoid giving "a definite impression to the Soviet authorities that negotiations for a German surrender had been initiated at Bern." Alexander vehemently denied that Lemnitzer and Airey had "enter[ed] into negotiations," but in the end allowed his message to be edited before it was handed to the Russians. The cleansed text, which tried to put the best possible face on Western actions by avoiding words like "negotiation" and "definite discussions," was finally presented to the Soviet military chiefs on 2 April.[17]

In light of these interminable delays and the clumsy efforts to prettify their bungles and sharp practice, it may seem difficult to imagine how the Western position on Sunrise could have been made much worse. But in fact, what Britain had done up to the end of March was only half of a Western response to Russia which, in its blindness and lack of coordination, seems to have been almost suicidal.

The British were wrong when they assumed that the United States government had rejected a summit response to Molotov's letter of 23 March.[18] Actually only the State Department had decided against such a course, while Roosevelt and his top military aides had opted to try mollifying the Russians by means of a direct approach to Stalin. Not only was Britain kept in the dark about this decision, but even the American diplomatic corps appears not to have been informed about it. While the London government's policy of quiet conciliation received encouragement from the State Department, the real power in the United States government made a leap to the summit. Three secret "Roosevelt letters" were sent to Stalin (24 and 31 March and 4 April), and three quick replies returned from Moscow (29 March and 3 and 7 April).

Why this moment was chosen to embark on such a course is not altogether apparent. FDR was generally nervous about the future of East-West relations during the last months of his life, a period in which he also left much of the responsibility for his personal correspondence to Admiral Leahy. Since the American military chiefs had set the main course of United States policy on Sunrise, it is reasonable to conclude that they were as eager as FDR to smooth relations with the Russians by trying to take the sting out of Molotov's accusations against the Bern talks. Although we will probably never know whether a military man, or FDR himself, first advanced the idea of a secret summit approach, it was a proposal which both the president and the top military authorities found readily acceptable. Once the decision had been taken, the chief responsibility for its execution fell to the military. All three "Roosevelt letters" were actually written by Admiral Leahy, with assistance at particular points by Secretary Stimson and General Marshall. President Roosevelt merely added a word here and there, and approved the final drafts before they were dispatched.[19]

The first message to Stalin went over the whole ground once again—called the difficulty with the Soviets "a misunderstanding," denied that there had been negotiations, and claimed that the affair was a military, not a political, question.[20] In Leahy's draft, Roosevelt told Stalin that every possibility, such as Sunrise, had to be exploited if it promised to prevent "additional and avoidable loss of life in the American forces." The president accepted virtually all of Leahy's phrasing, even the admiral's farfetched effort to gain a sympathetic hearing by referring to Stalin's experience as "a military man." Roosevelt added only one additional phrase to the letter. In a shaky hand he tried to minimize the importance of the incident by drawing an analogy between the Bern talks and a local surrender offer by German forces at "Koenigsberg or Danzig on the Eastern front."[21] With that, the letter was put in final form and dispatched to Moscow on 24 March, the day after Molotov's message had been received in Washington.

The propitiatory tone of this Leahy-Roosevelt message failed to make any impression on the Kremlin. Five days later, Stalin fired back a response which reiterated the Soviet contention that the negotiations being conducted by the Western powers would lead to an opening of the Western front with a resulting shift of German forces to the East.[22] The only passage of the American message which Stalin quoted in his reply was the one that the president himself had added, comparing the situation in Italy with that in Danzig or Koenigsberg. Stalin scornfully rejected the parallel, retorting that in the latter case the troops were surrounded; they might surrender, he conceded, but only "in order to avoid annihilation." But the German forces in northern Italy were "not surrounded" and did "not face annihilation" according to Stalin. If they, nonetheless, sought "negotiations in order to surrender and to open the front to Allied troops," it could only mean, the Soviet premier contended, "that they have different, more serious aims relating to the fate of Germany."

Stalin's analysis was close to the mark when he concluded that Wolff had political purposes in mind when he went to Bern, and under these circumstances, the tone of the premier's message to Roosevelt was relatively restrained. Stalin clearly believed that the German move was aimed at isolating the USSR and he also quite openly announced his suspicions that the Western Allies might cooperate with this plan. Once more—this time with reasonable cause—the obsessive fear of a separate peace between Germany and the West had come to the forefront of Stalin's mind.

When the premier's message reached the ailing president at Warm Springs, all he did was pen a note to Leahy stating, "Please let me know if you consider a reply necessary, and if so, prepare and send a draft for my approval."[23] Roosevelt's ill health had virtually eliminated the constitutional supremacy of the chief executive and left most of the responsibility for policy formation to Leahy and Marshall. "Alarmed" by Stalin's message, the two officers met the situation promptly. They immediately prepared a reply to the Soviet cable which was approved by Roosevelt without change and sent to Moscow over his signature on 31 March.[24] The message "categorically" assured Stalin that no negotiations had taken place and that there was no question of allowing the Germans to remove their forces from Italy. Hypothesizing that "the whole episode" might have been a German attempt to "create distrust" between East and West, the Americans called on Stalin to exercise care so that the Nazis would not "succeed in that aim."[25]

This message also failed to pacify Stalin, and his cable to FDR on 3 April was even more bitterly accusative than the first. If the president did not believe that negotiations had taken place at Bern, Stalin charged, then he was not "fully informed."[26] The premier himself had learned from his "military colleagues" that there had been negotiations and that these had "ended in [an] argreement," whereby Marshal Kesselring would "open the front and permit the Anglo-American troops to advance to the East," with the Western powers promising in return "to ease the peace terms for the Germans."

In retrospect we can see that this accusation was obviously a gross exaggeration. If Alexander had been willing to make such an arrangement, the Bern talks would most likely have ended long before. But this kind of suspicious accusation grew easily out of the atmosphere of mistrust existing among the Allies. There had been German overtures to one power or another in recent months, and all of them were aimed at a separate peace. Some of these approaches had originated from efforts of the German SD to split the Allies, or to elicit favorable terms from East or West by threatening that the Germans would open the front to one side or the other.[27] Most likely all, or nearly all, of these German proposals had come to the notice of the secret services of every Allied country. This time, according to recently published Russian accounts, it was a Soviet intelligence agent, or a "foreign friend," who notified Moscow of the talks in Bern.[28] The informer reported that although the German aim of arranging for a separate peace with the Western Allies had been rejected, it was still possible that the Germans would open the way to Berlin for Anglo-American troops. Since in these very days the Western powers were waiting to see whether Wolff would deliver on his pledge that Kesselring could be induced to surrender the whole Western front in addition to Italy, the Soviet intelligence account was substantially accurate.

Not only did Stalin accept it as "close to the truth" in his letter to FDR on 3 April, he went two steps further, assuming that a deal with Kesselring had been made by the West and castigating the president for trying to "conceal this from the Russians."[29] All the premier's resentment and anger came together in the claim that as a consequence of the alleged deal:

> At the present moment the Germans on the Western front in fact have ceased the war against England and the United States. At the same time the Germans continue the war with Russia, the ally of England and the United States.

Leaving no insulting stone unturned, Stalin closed his letter by hurling a final accusation at Britain. Claiming to be mystified by London's silence, he alleged acidly, and incorrectly, "that the initiative in this whole affair . . . in Bern belongs to the British." [30]

When Stalin's missile hit Washington on 3 April, the American authorities found the accusation that they had reached a secret agreement with Kesselring "astounding." [31] Filled with a "very great anxiety," [32] General Marshall sought the opinion of Henry Stimson and Admiral Leahy. The secretary of war advised that they should all move with "the greatest care and the greatest patience and the greatest thoughtfulness," given the "astonishing situation in Stalin's mind and in the minds of his staff." [33] For his part, Leahy once again was inclined to stress the military aspects of the situation and observed to Marshall that:

> This is a new statement of the Soviets' suspicions which might be answered by telling U.J. [Uncle Joe] something about the difficulties that Eisenhower encountered in disorganizing the German armies on the Rhine. [34]

With these slender reeds for support and guidance, Marshall took on the task of drafting a "Roosevelt letter" which would calm Stalin. After registering "indignation" and "deep regret" about the premier's attacks on the president's good faith and integrity, Marshall went on to refute Stalin's allegation that the rapid advance of the Western armies was due to a secret deal with the Germans. [35] That the Anglo-American forces had moved forward so rapidly, Marshall contended, was caused solely by military factors, especially "the terrific impact of our air power." The chief of staff also frankly refuted Stalin's attacks on Great Britain. Admitting that the British had originally wanted Soviet representation at Bern while "we opposed it," Marshall declared flatly that the responsibility for Sunrise "rests on us and not on the British." After defending the Anglo-American conduct at Bern, the American chief of staff then concluded his draft by eloquently urging the Soviets to reconsider their accusations. "It would be one of the great tragedies of history," he wrote, "if at the very moment of victory, now within our grasp, such distrust, such lack of faith, should prejudice the entire undertaking after the colossal losses of life, material, and treasure."

The Marshall draft was sent to Admiral Leahy on 4 April, and the chairman of the Joint Chiefs thereupon prepared his own version for the president's signature. [36] The Leahy message incorporated Marshall's explanation of the military situation on the Western front and his impressive conclusion, but omitted completely the section defending the British. It also tempered some of Marshall's intensely personal references to indignation and integrity. If more muted, the Leahy version still placed the main emphasis on the president's personal "reliability," while defending what had transpired at Bern. Signed by the president almost immediately after it was drafted, the Leahy message went to Moscow on 4 April. [37]

OPERATION SUNRISE

With this done, the American military chiefs could only cross their fingers and wait to see if the third "Roosevelt letter" would do the trick. During the two weeks that had transpired since Wolff's appearance in Ascona on 19 March, both the British and the Americans had put themselves in vulnerable positions while hoping that the Sunrise contacts would hit the surrender jackpot. The Anglo-Americans had followed different routes in dealing with Soviet hostility, but each of them had decided to try to hold on while anticipating that Bern might produce a decisive capitulation, in the south, the west, or both. Layer upon layer of diplomatic scrambling had been piled on this hope, but whatever they did, the Allies could not escape the fact that way down at the bottom of the affair there existed nothing but the activity of SS Obergruppenführer Karl Wolff. His appearance in Switzerland on 8 March had started the whole process, and his meeting with Lemnitzer and Airey on 19 March had fueled all sides of the diplomatic crisis. Like its origin, much of the ultimate form and effect of the crisis would depend on Wolff.

The Obergruppenführer's actions were critical during the two weeks in which the Roosevelt–Stalin exchanges occurred (19 March until the first days of April) because, after he had whetted the Western appetite at Ascona, he was under some pressure to come up with something fast. Yet instead of rushing directly to Kesselring, the SS man took a few days to visit his wife and then traveled west by car. His journey to Kesselring's headquarters at Bad Neuheim, where he arrived on 23 March, failed to net him the support he needed.[38] Wolff was probably loath to be specific in his talks with the field marshal, and, for his part, Kesselring was, as always, *vorsichtig* (cautious) and very coy about making commitments that were dangerous to his reputation or his neck. Kesselring did not categorically reject a possible deal with the West—he made no move to denounce Wolff for activity that might well have been treasonous to the Third Reich—but he also did virtually nothing to advance its prospects. Perhaps inclined to be more cautious than ever because he felt himself "surrounded by strangers,"[39] the commander in chief in the West categorically refused to participate in any project to surrender his command or open the Western front to the Allies. Kesselring may have "authorized," or more likely "advised,"[40] the SS man to speak with Vietinghoff about his plans, but if so, this was still a far cry from the glorious surrender prospects which the SS man had placed before the Allies.

Foiled at Kesselring's headquarters, Wolff then traveled to Berlin to meet with his SS superiors. Contemporary accounts of this episode are so fragmentary and confused that firm statements about his motives in making the trip, as well as what transpired at the meetings, are impossible.[41] Apparently the

SS chiefs were suspicious of his activities and summoned him to headquarters. By going to Berlin and talking with Himmler and Kaltenbrunner, Wolff seems to have hoped that he could cover himself and find some fairly realistic authority in the German capital who would act at the critical moment by opening the western and southern fronts to the Anglo-Americans. Arriving in Berlin on the evening of 23 March, Wolff spent the next four days traveling around Germany—to Bavaria, to Thuringia and back to Berlin—all the time carrying on talks with Kaltenbrunner and also on occasion with Himmler and Schellenberg. Despite all this activity, Wolff finally left the German capital on 27–28 March with his hands nearly as empty as when he had come. He had not been punished for his activities, although both Himmler and Kaltenbrunner were highly suspicious of him. Once again, he was free, but without any significant support. Apparently the nervous Himmler, always so ready to escape reality, claimed that it was still too early for decisive action. He wanted Wolff to spin out indirect talks with the West, but at the same time he seems to have demanded that the Obergruppenführer stay out of Switzerland.

Wolff himself had a muddled view of the situation, but he grasped that the East-West alliance would hold until Germany was dispatched, and that the end was near. Men like Kesselring and Himmler might stand by like paralyzed rabbits, but Wolff was determined to do what he could to enhance the future of Nazis and nazism in the wake of an Anglo-American victory. With his eye on the morrow, and having failed with Kesselring and Himmler, Wolff had no choice but to return to Italy to see if he could at least talk Vietinghoff into surrendering the Italian front at the most profitable moment.

He met with the general at the latter's headquarters on the first of April and informed him of his contacts in Switzerland. As always, Wolff tailored his presentation to the wishes of the listener, and the general was told that the object of the contacts was to secure an "honorable armistice" for Army Group C while preventing the destruction which would be occasioned by "large-scale fighting in northern Italy."[42] Vietinghoff replied that he "entirely approved Wolff's intentions" and that he had already decided to forbid destruction "not immediately required by military necessity."[43] He even conceded that German resistance inside the Reich would collapse shortly. But still he refused to take the responsibility for a surrender initiative. As long as general German resistance continued and Hitler remained in charge, a partial capitulation was impossible. Vietinghoff could not betray his comrades in other German units "who were still fighting stubbornly north of the Alps," and even if he tried to do so, his "own troops would fail to understand such a proceeding and would in part refuse to follow . . . orders."

For Vietinghoff too, it was still much too early. Even though he seems to have gone a bit further in endorsing Wolff's efforts than Himmler or Kesselring, his answer to the crucial question was still negative.

Vietinghoff's sympathetic understanding was small consolation for Wolff, who needed fair words far less than he needed a general who would take the gamble and act. After the war the SS man was full of bitter scorn for army commanders who had lacked courage to put their lives on the line for a higher cause.[44] But Wolff was himself largely responsible for the corner in which he found himself, and Vietinghoff's arguments were not necessarily a mark for cowardice. The army leaders would not be as vulnerable if the Allies won a crushing victory as would the SS men, and Vietinghoff was right when he contended that the German leaders and the troops in the field had not yet faced the imminent reality of defeat. If Vietinghoff had attempted to put through a limited capitulation on 1 April, the likely result would have been insubordination among his troops and his own execution by the SD. Wolff had miscalculated. He had judged the long-term situation correctly, but his pledges to the Allies had outrun the capability of any German leader except Hitler to carry them out at that time.

Wolff was able to elude the full force of his dilemma and keep Sunrise alive because even though he had misassessed the mood in Germany, he had taken an accurate measure of the Allied authorities in Switzerland. He seems to have had no inkling that his trips to Bern and Ascona had produced serious friction between East and West, but he had grasped the hopes dear to the hearts of the Anglo-Americans and possessed a sure touch for providing them with what they wanted to hear. Even as he wended his peripatetic way from Kesselring's headquarters to Berlin and back to Italy, he understood that the Western representatives in Switzerland would be anxious for news, and he timed and molded his messages to coincide with their hopes and changing moods.

For one week he left them without any information, presumably because he guessed—rightly—that the enthusiasm engendered by the Ascona meeting would sustain them that long. In fact, Lemnitzer and Airey scrapped tentative plans for one of them to visit Caserta to report during this period, because they were afraid that the messenger would not return in time for the next meeting with Wolff.[45] While anxiously waiting for the SS man, Dulles and the generals spent considerable time worrying about what to do with Parri. The Italian who Wolff had turned over at the time of his first visit was still in Switzerland and if he had been returned to northern Italy and again fell into German hands, the secrecy covering Sunrise would have evaporated. He could not remain indefinitely in Switzerland either, since rumors about his release, and his own impatience to resume the battle against the

Germans, might expose the whole story of the secret surrender operation. Finally, following a lively exchange with Caserta, it was decided to send Parri, together with General Cadorno, to AFHQ Mediterranean to await the day when he might safely reenter northern Italy as a spokesman for the moderate, pro-Western, resistance forces.[46]

On 26 March, Dulles and the Allied military representatives were pulled back into the mainstream of Sunrise speculation by a message relayed from Wolff. Zimmer had appeared at the Swiss border claiming that he had spoken on the phone with the Obergruppenführer who was, in Zimmer's tale, still at Kesselring's headquarters. The sly Wolff, who had actually met unsuccessfully with Kesselring, Himmler, and Kaltenbrunner by this time, knew how to quiet Anglo-American doubts without making them lose interest. Apologizing for the delay which he attributed to serious but unspecified "difficulties," he begged the "gentlemen"—Lemnitzer and Airey—"not to go away in anger." Wolff claimed that he would soon be coming, not with "half-formulated plans," but with a "complete program." To help strengthen their patience he added suggestively that the affair had taken on "a greater scope than had been initially contemplated."[47]

Showing uncharacteristic caution, Dulles apparently filed no report on this discussion with the OSS headquarters in Washington.[48] But as if following Wolff's script, Lemnitzer and Airey sent two long messages to Caserta on 27 and 28 March, which enveloped Zimmer's report in clouds of confusion and inconsistent evaluation.[49] They covered pages with vacuous speculation about the motives of those who were, or might be, involved in the plot, including Vietinghoff, the Swiss, and even Heinrich Himmler. When they finally descended to the crucial point, it was to declare that there was a "strong possibility" that Wolff intended to return to Switzerland soon, and that he "hopes to bring with him mandates from both Kesselring and Vietinghoff." No sooner had they delivered themselves of this estimate than they added that "we believe there is only a fair chance of success" because Wolff might be eliminated or arrive "empty-handed." Reduced to its basic elements, the generals were saying that Wolff faced great difficulties, but they trusted him and wanted to give him a generous opportunity to try to deliver.[50] If Wolff had written the messages himself, he could hardly have improved on that.

On the receiving end of these dispatches, Alexander decided that little of the speculative muddle should be sent to the Western capitals.[51] Instead, London and Washington received a short cable from Caserta which merely transmitted most of Wolff's optimistic fables without comment.[52] Alexander told the Combined Chiefs the story of Wolff's prolonged journey to Kesselring's headquarters, his desire to return with a "complete plan," and the prediction that he would soon be in Switzerland with "mandates from

Kesselring and Vietinghoff." None of the points of caution made by Lemnitzer and Airey—especially their estimate that there was only "a fair chance of success"—appeared in Alexander's cable to the Chiefs.

Significantly, this message reached Washington just prior to the arrival of Stalin's first angry retort to the "Roosevelt letter" of 24 March. It seems probable that the soothing information contained therein strengthened the determination of Leahy and Marshall to stand up to the Soviet premier in the second "Roosevelt letter" which they sent to Moscow. Of course, the British had not yet been informed of the "Roosevelt letters" to Stalin, so they were allowed a bit more time to slumber with the illusion that time, and Albert Kesselring, might be on their side.

But no one was permitted to remain sublimely ignorant for very long. On 27 March, Zimmer told the OSS that two individuals who had played supporting roles in Sunrise—Ambassador Rahn and SS General Harster—had been summoned to Germany. Although nothing of importance came of this, because Rahn did not go and Harster was apparently only engaged in routine SS business, the message helped to convey the impression to the Allies that Wolff and his friends were risking their lives in a highly dangerous enterprise. With this heroic overture still ringing in his ears, word reached Dulles on 30 March that Wolff had returned to his headquarters at Fasano, and that the OSS should stand by for an important report which would soon follow.[53] On the next day, Zimmer crossed the frontier again, and this time met Dulles near Locarno for the first face-to-face talk in twelve days. Wolff's emissary did the best he could to make his chief sound well intentioned, spinning out long yarns about the Obergruppenführer's trip to Kesselring and the troubles which he had encountered at the field marshal's headquarters. Although he ultimately had to admit that there would be no capitulation in the West via Sunrise, Zimmer struggled manfully to redirect Dulles's attention toward an Italian consolation prize. He reported that Wolff's efforts to contact Vietinghoff and arrange a capitulation for the Italian front had heretofore been foiled only because the army general had been inopportunely absent from his headquarters. But, according to Zimmer, Wolff was scheduled to see Vietinghoff that very day and therefore wanted to assure Dulles that he was preparing to come to a "final conversation" in Switzerland, and that he planned to have "Rahn[,] Dollmann[,] and either Vietinghoff or a staff officer" accompany him.[54]

Zimmer's statements to Dulles actually scotched every trace of reality clinging to the great Anglo-American hope that the Germans might open the Western front to them. Yet when one remembers the clouds of fantasy and expectation which Wolff had released by mentioning this prospect at the 19 March meeting, the Allied representatives in Switzerland seemed to take the news very calmly. In his report to Washington, Dulles only remarked that "any action by Kesselring via Wolff seems excluded," while Alexander was notified by Lemnitzer and Airey that Kesselring was "too much surrounded by untrustworthy personnel to be able to participate."[55] Regarding the possibility of a capitulation on the Italian front too, Dulles merely observed that "despite Wolff's apparent optimism," Vietinghoff's participation was "still [a] matter of conjecture." On this question Lemnitzer and Airey were even more resignedly pessimistic, advising Caserta that although Wolff would "almost certainly" come to Switzerland on 2 or 3 April, they did not "pin much hope on his bringing Vietinghoff." Rather the generals expected Wolff "to make some offer, probably impractical," to surrender the "rear areas under his command[,] in order to reinsure himself personally."[56]

The decisive importance of this Dulles–Zimmer talk seems to have been lost, not only in Switzerland, but also in the labyrinth of multiple authorities and complicated communications systems which characterized the Anglo-American command system. So many messages passed back and forth to so many points, that trivia often took precedence over matters of importance. For example, on the same day as the meeting in Locarno, Alexander's chief of staff, General Morgan, actually made use of the top-secret Sunrise communication system to ask Lemnitzer and Airey if they would purchase a wrist watch for him while they were in Switzerland. Morgan was not even willing to give them a free financial hand and asked for a return message quoting prices![57] In view of this mentality, it is little wonder that the guarded report on Zimmer's trip, which was sent to Caserta, failed to sound the alarm bells there. All Alexander did was dispatch a routine message to the Combined Chiefs of Staff on 2 April, which alluded to some of the relevant information, but did it so indirectly that the hesitant conclusions drawn by Lemnitzer and Airey were softened even further. From the Alexander message one might infer that there was now only a modest chance for a surrender in Italy, and no possibility of a Kesselring capitulation in the West. But it offered these inferences so obliquely that a reader would have had to struggle hard to see this development as anything approaching a turn in the road. Since the field marshal ended his cable by explaining that Wolff would probably come to Switzerland in a day or two, and if a meeting with him failed to produce "concrete" results, Lemnitzer and Airey would be "re-call[ed]," the Anglo-American governments were in fact invited to stand by once more, so that he too could "play out his hand."[58]

Such a tempered message, soliciting further delay, was not sufficient to jolt the British government out of its attempt at quiet conciliation of the USSR. Churchill was becoming increasingly restive, but he still clung to the policy of officially ignoring the "insulting telegrams" which Britain had received from Molotov.[59] If the Anglo-American stances on Sunrise were to be reunited, the initiative would have to come from Washington, and the meeting between Zimmer and Dulles may have nudged the American authorities in that direction. Admiral Leahy, and the other members of the Joint Chiefs of Staff, had not only received Alexander's languid account of the events of 31 March, but they were in possession of the equally tepid, if rather differently worded, version sent by Dulles. These two pieces of soft evidence may have suggested to the American military that the Bern talks held little promise of immediately solving their political and military problems. Then on 3 April, Stalin's second angry reply to a "Roosevelt letter" reached the American capital, indicating that the political problems were more serious than the Joint Chiefs had imagined. Admiral Leahy decided that a bit of prudence was called for, and at this point, in an effort to start lining up with the British again, he sent copies of the first "Roosevelt"-Stalin exchange to London on 3 April.

Yet from all indications, Washington was only slightly more conscious than the British of the negative turn which had overcome Sunrise. In order to drive the lesson home, the Anglo-American governments apparently needed to receive a flat declaration from Alexander that no surrender was in sight. On 2 April a meeting took place in Ascona which was so disappointing to Western hopes that it forced Caserta to dispatch just such a message. Dulles, Lemnitzer, and Airey went to Ascona confident that they would finally see Wolff once more, but instead of the Obergruppenführer, it was Parrilli who showed up. The baron explained that he had been directed to tell the Allies that Wolff was unable to make the trip because Himmler had become extremely suspicious of his activities. Following the directions he had received, Parrilli declared that the Reichsführer-SS had ordered Wolff not to leave Italy and had taken his family into custody with the whimsical threat that he wanted to take "better care" of them.[60]

There may have been an element of truth in this tale. The mood of mutual suspicion and black intrigue which covered Berlin could have prompted Himmler to tighten the reins on Wolff. But certainly the fundamental reason the Obergruppenführer stayed out of Switzerland was that he had nothing to offer the Allies. Contrary to his predictions, neither Vietinghoff nor Kesselring had shown an inclination to act rapidly on any deal with the West, much less on an unconditional surrender. Wolff would have been mad to appear in Ascona announcing that he had failed. It would have been equally disastrous for him to have gone there wrapped in new plans and speculations which would have forced him to run the risk of being unfrocked by close Allied questioning. While caught in this corner, Wolff did the best he could.

118

The SS man pushed an intermediary into the middle, a man who was himself anxious to make Sunrise work through good thoughts and strenuous effort.

Like Zimmer before him, Parrilli did his best to put a good face on a dismal situation. He relayed Wolff's message that in his talks with Vietinghoff the general had agreed that it was "nonsense to go on fighting," and Parrilli implied that Vietinghoff was prepared to arrange a surrender.[61] At one point the Italian hinted, "probably in Wolff's behalf," that the "Germans might like to make some arrangement whereby they would be permitted to withdraw over the Italian frontier after giving up their arms." But when he was told that such a proposal was "entirely out of the question,"[62] Parrilli dropped the matter. He knew that the withdrawal idea was dear to many German hearts in northern Italy, but he was even more keenly aware that his main task was to try to keep the Allies favorably inclined toward Sunrise. Yet even though he tried to put the withdrawal dog back to sleep, and managed to step around most other sensitive issues, Parrilli ultimately had to tell the Allies the bad news: Wolff declared that in order "to hand over northern Italy," he would still need at least "ten more days."[63]

Dulles and the Allied military representatives were politely patient through most of this and seem to have accepted many of the assertions in Parrilli's report at face value. The OSS man even reported to Washington that in his opinion, the threat to Wolff's family might "be real."[64] But all three Anglo-American officials ultimately concluded that Wolff was mainly playing for time. Dulles speculated that the Obergruppenführer and his associates were "probably stalling"[65] until the Allied advance produced such chaos in Germany that their families would be safe, and they would be free to act. Lemnitzer and Airey were closer to the mark when they concluded that Wolff and Vietinghoff were "waiting for the project to be overtaken by events" and that the Obergruppenführer was counting on his contacts with the Allies to make sure that he was personally "reinsured" in any case.[66]

In an effort to shake Wolff into motion, Parrilli was told to remind the Obergruppenführer that he had made pledges to "prevent the destruction of northern Italy" as well as promises to "restrain" action against the Italian partisans. On these matters, as well as on the surrender itself, the Allies relayed the message to Wolff that this was his "last opportunity for action," and that "action alone counts."[67] Lemnitzer and Airey went one step further, directing Parrilli to report to Wolff that if Vietinghoff was really prepared to cooperate, and "they wanted to surrender," all they needed to do was "send parliamentarians to the Allies directly through the lines." At Parrilli's request, they even agreed on a password, "Nuremberg," which would allow such safe passage.[68] Although this was short of an ultimatum, Lemnitzer and

119

Airey believed that they had put the responsibility for surrender squarely on Wolff's shoulders.[69] After reporting what they had done to Alexander, they asked permission to return to Caserta.

The field marshal acceded to their request, and on 4 April notified the Combined Chiefs of Staff of the results of the second Ascona meeting. His cable included a summary of the story that Wolff had not come to Switzerland because of Himmler's threat to his family, and it was overly generous in stating that Vietinghoff, and his chief of staff, General Roettiger, had "agreed" with Wolff's "project." But Alexander, like the Allied officials in Switzerland, concluded that Wolff was playing for time while trying to ingratiate himself with the Western powers. He also informed the Combined Chiefs that at Ascona the SS man had been reminded of his earlier commitments and told that if he and Vietinghoff wished to surrender they could easily pass a plenipotentiary through the lines. The conclusion of Alexander's cable sounded as if he was closing the door on the affair. He stated that he had ordered his "representatives to return to Caserta" and was keeping only the OSS link open to deal with "any future contacts."[70]

When Alexander's cable reached Washington on 4 April, it reinforced the more sober mood about Sunrise and the East-West crisis which had been developing there during the preceding two or three days. The message from Caserta landed in London, however, while British officials were trying to reconcile themselves to the shocking discovery that for a week and a half the Americans and Russians had been locked in a secret summit controversy about the Bern talks. Even while registering his dismay at the news that "though the Americans may have ignored Mr. Molotov's letter, the president has *twice**° sent messages to Marshal Stalin,"[71] A. W. Harrison of the Foreign Office at least took some consolation from the news that Lemnitzer and Airey had finally been removed from Switzerland. "Good," he wrote on 4 April, "I am glad Field Marshal Alexander has withdrawn his representatives . . . we must be careful about allowing any official representatives back into Switzerland."[72]

Churchill's desire to change course also seems to have been strengthened by the news that the Bern surrender initiative was either already dead or barely breathing. On the day before the Caserta report reached London, the prime minister was grumbling about the "insulting messages [from Molotov and Stalin] which we have decided to ignore but not to forget." Even so, he was willing to continue with the policy that Britain should not directly confront Russia over Sunrise.[73] But then Alexander's cable arrived, and close on its heels came copies of Stalin's letter to Roosevelt on 3 April, and the "Roosevelt response" of 4 April. Churchill failed to show any visible

°Underlined in the original.

irritation that the Americans had again jumped to the summit without him,[74] but he was stung by the bitter accusations against Britain that had been made by the Soviet premier. With the dashing of the Sunrise surrender hopes, and with an American summit precedent before him, there was nothing left to deter Churchill from answering the Russians. On 5 April, he quickly abandoned quiet conciliation and prepared his own message for Moscow.

The prime minister's draft repeated the customary contentions that no negotiations had taken place in Bern, and reaffirmed the right of Alexander to arrange a surrender of enemy forces in his theater of operations. Claiming to be "affronted" by Soviet accusations that the West had acted in bad faith, the prime minister rejected the "wounding and unfounded" charges contained in Molotov's original letter.[75] Still Churchill tried to be conciliatory. He was careful not to zero in directly on the assertions and allegations made in Stalin's telegrams and he acknowledged that the rapid Western advance had, in part, been made possible "by the magnificent attacks and weight of the Soviet armies." Yet even while trying to be temperate, the prime minister did not attempt to escape Stalin's wrath against Britain by throwing the blame for the Bern affair on the United States. Instead, Churchill chose to stress Anglo-American unity, and to portray all the Sunrise developments as if they represented the common policy of the two countries.

Not everyone in London was as eager as the prime minister to accept responsibility for the actions of the United States government. Lord Beaverbrook believed that Ambassador Harriman might have exacerbated the confusion over Sunrise because he lacked "experience," and often produced misunderstandings "through a desire to appear . . . fully informed."[76] The English press lord told Churchill that he also had little confidence in the work of General Donovan, who might not have had "a proper understanding of the dangers inherent in his relations with German negotiators." Calling for a "direct inquiry into the OSS's conduct of the affair," Beaverbrook added the surmise that the Germans had probably "given their account of the [Bern] matter to the Russians." Yet all this clever insight was obviated by a final naïve recommendation that the best way to ease the controversy was for Churchill to ask Stalin to tell him everything that Soviet intelligence had learned about the Bern contacts.

More significant criticism, closely attuned to the realm of the possible, was made by the War Cabinet. On 5 April, on the first occasion in which it seriously discussed Sunrise, the Cabinet suggested that the prime minister make a number of small rewordings in his draft message to Stalin, and in addition, tell the Soviets that the British government took responsibility only for its own actions and not for activities which the OSS might have carried out on its own.[77] Churchill incorporated the Cabinet's minor suggestions into the final form of the letter, but he refused to follow the lead of either the Cabinet or Lord Beaverbrook by raising questions or making accusations regarding the OSS. The American intelligence organization was not mentioned in the 6 April telegram to the Kremlin, and Churchill held firmly to his course of not straying from a public appearance of Anglo-American unity.[78]

On the previous day he had sent a letter to President Roosevelt, in which he placed himself squarely alongside the United States. Once more he raised no objection to the independent initiatives taken by the Americans, but spoke instead of possible reasons why the Russians had become so upset over Sunrise. Although granting that "the brutality of the Russian messages" might indicate "some deep change of policy," he was inclined to believe that the core of the trouble was the rapid advance of the Anglo-American armies.[79] Characterizing Russian anger as "their natural expression when vexed or jealous," the British prime minister suggested that the Western powers should push home their advantage by driving "as far to the east as possible, and if circumstances permit, enter Berlin."

Churchill's tough mood seemed to find a responsive echo in Washington. The short answer to the prime minister, written by Leahy, and dispatched over Roosevelt's signature on 6 April, contended that "we must not permit anybody to entertain a false impression that we are afraid," and the message closed with the ominous prediction that "our armies will[,] in a very few days[,] be in a position that will permit us to become 'tougher' than has heretofore appeared advantageous to the war effort."[80]

It is important to remember, however, that these sentiments, bordering on bellicosity, came from the chairman of the Joint Chiefs of Staff and may have had little or nothing to do with the views of the dying president. Roosevelt's hand had slipped nearly free of the helm and the military leaders were assuming ever more responsibility for steering American policy. The generals and admirals were eager to end the European war in a blaze of American military glory, and Leahy's "tough" talk reflected this desire. But even when their military expansiveness reached full flower, they were not ready to take serious risks. They refused to engage in a race for Berlin,[81] and they were pulled up short by any sign that Soviet displeasure might seriously disrupt their operational plans.

On 4 April, the Joint Chiefs had received a message from General Deane in Moscow, which showed that Russian unhappiness could have grave military consequences. Deane had just returned from a trying meeting with representatives of the Soviet general staff. The American had attempted to raise a number of military issues dependent upon Soviet-American cooperation, but to each point the Russians only gave the "terse answer" that "no decision has been reached by the general staff."[82] The United States was particularly anxious concerning the use of Soviet airfields and had its eye on employing Soviet territory for operations against Japan, but the Soviets had become totally uncooperative. Near the end of the meeting, the Russian spokesman raised the question of the Bern talks, and it became immediately clear to Deane "that this was the festering sore." Until Sunrise was resolved, he concluded, "all of our joint projects" could be brought to "a stand-still," and he therefore asked permission to return to Washington for consultation.[83]

On the same day, Harriman had spoken with Molotov about Sunrise and the Soviet commissar was again "extremely suspicious," repeating the charge that the rapid Western advance was connected with some sort of deal made at Bern. Like Deane, Harriman had lost his stomach for lonely confrontations in Moscow, and he too requested a recall to Washington for consultation.[84] But even in the American capital it was apparent that the Russians had become very touchy regarding the whole question of a German surrender. In a paper referring to occupation policy for Germany which the British had recently layed before the European Advisory Commission, the phrase "unconditional surrender" was inadvertently omitted. The Soviet representatives thereupon became highly agitated, and stiff protests were lodged in London and Washington. American authorities tried to reassure the Russians by declaring that this had merely been a trivial oversight and that they would not "modify the agreed unconditional surrender instrument."[85] But obviously, Soviet hostility on surrender problems was no laughing matter.

Consequently, it was with a sigh of relief that Washington received news of an accommodating gesture made by the USSR on 5 April. On that day the Kremlin renounced its neutrality agreement with Japan, clearing the way for Russian entrance into the Pacific war, once Germany was beaten. The Western powers had long desired that the Soviets take this step and the action of 5 April was most welcome, especially in Washington.[86] The Sunrise replies which Stalin penned to FDR and Churchill on 7 April also showed reassuring signs, although the Soviets' angry apprehension was still there. Holding firmly to his position that the Bern affair was not just a military matter, Stalin asked rhetorically why the Germans "surrender without any resistance" in the West, while fighting savagely in the East for "some unknown junction . . . which they need as much as a dead man needs poultices."[87] While inquiring pointedly whether such German behavior was not "strange and incomprehensible," Stalin stopped short of directly accusing the Western leaders of treachery. He assured Roosevelt that he had "never doubted" his honesty, and in his letter to the prime minister—which bore a surprisingly friendlier tone than that to the president—he claimed that he had never intended to "blacken anyone."[88]

Stalin's messages did not wipe away Churchill's pugnacity. "I think the time has come for a showdown," he wrote to Eden on 8 April, "and the British and the United States are completely aligned." Relishing the opportunity, he added, "we may go far and long before finding an equally good occasion."[89] However, in his calmer moments, the prime minister was satisfied to let the Bern controversy fade away and he told FDR that Stalin's letters were "about the best we are going to get out of them" because they came as close as the Soviets "can get to an apology."[90]

Roosevelt and his advisors needed no prompting toward conciliation. It was the last moment of FDR's life, and when Stalin's message arrived he merely penned a note to Admiral Leahy reading: "I think no reply necessary unless you or General Marshall want to make reply."[91] An Admiral Leahy chastened by the serious consequences which had flowed from Soviet anger rejected a staff suggestion that a stiff message be sent to Moscow,[92] and instead he wrote a reassuring response declaring that the Bern incident "now appears to have faded into the past without having accomplished any useful purpose."[93] Emphazing that there must not be mistrust occasioned by "minor misunderstandings," the Leahy message, routinely signed by the president and sent to Stalin on 12 April, looked forward optimistically to the link-up of the Soviet and Western armies and to a final "fully coordinated offensive in which nazism would disintegrate."

Before this message was handed to the Russians, Ambassador Harriman suggested that the word "minor" be struck out, because, in his opinion, the misunderstanding appeared "to be of major character and the use of the word 'minor' might well be misinterpreted here."[94] But the soft line advanced by the American military triumphed over the hard-line objections of the ambassador in Moscow.

In what was the final act of the Leahy-Roosevelt partnership, and the final message of Franklin Roosevelt's life, Harriman was ordered to deliver the letter to Stalin in its original form. "I do not wish to delete the word 'minor,' " the final cable read, "because it is my desire to consider the Bern misunderstanding 'a minor incident.' "[95]

CHAPTER 6

The Long Mile
to Caserta

ONE MIGHT reasonably have expected the Anglo-Americans to stop Operation Sunrise completely in the first half of April, 1945. Wolff had failed to deliver on his surrender promises, causing the consequent withdrawal of Lemnitzer and Airey from Switzerland. Churchill, who had harbored doubts about the enterprise from the beginning, had, after many ups and downs, finally turned overtly hostile. In his final days, Franklin Roosevelt too had become highly pessimistic regarding the undertaking. Once the Anglo-Americans succeeded in smoothing out most of the Sunrise-inspired trouble with the Russians, prudence and good sense seemed to dictate that they at last allow the operation to be laid to rest.

But, in fact, the parleying did not end, and messages between Wolff and Dulles continued to pass back and forth over the Italo-Swiss border. That the SS man would try to curry favor with the Allies by launching one surrender proposal after another is highly understandable. With every passing day, the crushing defeat of Nazi Germany became ever more apparent, and it was clearly in Wolff's interest to pile up all the good credits he could with the victorious Allies. But that Dulles prolonged the Bern affair, after it had lost nearly all positive potential, is both somewhat perplexing and also more serious. It was the OSS man's willingness to let the contacts run on and on which allowed Wolff to achieve his primary aim of wiggling his way into the confidence of the Allies. Dulles seems to have fallen victim to the most basic pitfall of a man engaged in the craft of intelligence; he became so fascinated with the game, so pinched in by his own narrow point of view, and so infatuated with the hope of achieving a dazzling political-intelligence coup, that he failed to see that changing circumstances had undercut his operation.

By early April, the military situation had turned so decisively in favor of the Western powers that local German capitulations were much less important. The Anglo-American armies had smashed their way across the Rhine in force; the Ruhr was encircled on 1 April, and by 12 April—the day Franklin Roosevelt died—the Ninth U.S. Army had reached the Elbe. On 9 April, the long-awaited Allied offensive in Italy finally began, and although initial gains were slow, the Axis armies absorbed heavy punishment from Allied air and artillery power. The Germans were forced to abandon one vital position after another, and by mid-April, their whole position south of the Po had been unhinged.

Even with these crushing military developments, one might still maintain that a German capitulation in Italy could yield advantages to the Western powers. A surrender would spare lives, property, and might allay Allied fears both of a partisan revolution and of a last suicidal stand by Army Group C on the southern edge of an Alpine redoubt. But Lemnitzer and Airey had been right when they contended at Ascona, that if the Germans in northern Italy wanted to capitulate, all they had to do was send an emissary through the lines. Dulles, on the other hand, thought that he could use Wolff to coax the German forces into making a deal to surrender, or at least get them to stop fighting in a nice way. He refused to face the fact that Wolff had not delivered on his surrender promises in time, and the OSS man also did not clearly recognize that the more the Allies advanced, the less importance was left to Sunrise. For Dulles, the Bern affair continued to be the glorious capitulation prospect of 8 March, and it was this illusion which clouded his vision and drew him in ever deeper.

Yet it would be both unjust and inaccurate to lay all the responsibility for the immortality of Sunrise at the door of Allen Dulles. The OSS representative was allowed to keep playing at peace-making because his superiors did not exercise tight enough control over him. The OSS leaders in Washington were ready to run risks and ignore signs of probable failure, apparently because, like Dulles, they hungered for a last-minute political triumph. Donovan and his aides let Dulles go his way, and the Joint Chiefs of Staff, who occupied a spot one link up the chain of command, also failed to exert their authority and stop him. The generals had supported Sunrise on the grounds of military necessity, and had defended it both to the president and to the Soviet Union. But once Wolff failed to produce a capitulation and Soviet protests had finally been stilled, the Joint Chiefs seem simply to have put it out of their minds. Perhaps they decided to let Dulles keep playing with Wolff as a long shot, but it seems more likely that the incident was merely lost among other, presumably more important, problems that called for the Chiefs' attention.

The generals were not brought up short by a strong voice from the White House, due to a number of factors. During the period of Roosevelt's last illness, the Joint Chiefs had become accustomed to operating with little or no direction from the chief executive. Then Roosevelt died just at the critical moment when he seems to have grasped that Sunrise had failed. Although his successor, Harry Truman, received briefing papers indicating that the Polish question and the "negotiations for [the] surrender of the German forces in Italy" were among the most critical foreign policy issues which he faced,[1] the Bern affair nonetheless slipped into the background. Truman tended to let whatever was going smoothly under Roosevelt continue during the early days of his administration unless an issue cried out for action. In mid-April 1945, he apparently concluded that there were more pressing things to worry about than the shadowy dealings of an obscure OSS agent in Bern. So Operation Sunrise was allowed to roll along largely unattended.

Closer to the scene of action, Dulles's dealings encountered more resistance than they did in Washington. Even though the negative reaction at Caserta was neither wholehearted nor decisive, Alexander and his staff seem to have harbored more suspicions about Wolff than did Dulles or the Joint Chiefs of Staff. They also became increasingly cautious as they realized some of the political dangers involved. But it was primarily the rising success of the Allied offensive which made Caserta cooler to Sunrise. When Alexander sensed that he might yet seize the military prize, a chancy surrender deal became less appealing. Still, in mid-April, Vietinghoff was not totally beaten, even on the Po, and it was possible that he might yet rally for a stand in the Alpine foothills. Until the Brenner Pass and the Trieste routes into the "redoubt" were firmly in his hands, Alexander could not breathe easily. So Caserta sounded skeptical and urged Dulles to be cautious, but it did not take decisive action to end the dickering in Bern. Like officials in London and Washington, the generals in Caserta were dragged along by events. They too watched the cables passing back and forth between Wolff, Dulles, and the various political, military, and intelligence authorities in the Western capitals. Like the others, they were left three or four days behind simply because communication was slow and messages had to pass through a myriad of offices and officials. They criticized, and grumbled, and worried more than the others, but in the end they failed to act by seizing the initiative from Allen Dulles and Karl Wolff.

Quite naturally, Wolff, and his companions on the German side, did not clearly comprehend the change in mood which had taken place in Washington and Caserta. Unaware of the summit crisis through which the Allies had passed, and oblivious to the fact that a number of Allied officers were ready to write him off, Wolff plodded on, trying to piece together a surrender coalition. On 6 April he apparently met with his subordinate SS commanders and ordered them to limit action against the partisans and to prevent destruction. The next day, 7 April, he made another try with General Vietinghoff. According to his later account of the conversation, the commander of Army Group C told Wolff that he could not then take responsibility for initiating a surrender until the Italian theater was cut off from Germany or until he received permission from Berlin to make a deal. The threat that his troops would disobey a local capitulation order still paralyzed General Vietinghoff.[2]

Vietinghoff's statements may not have been crystal clear and Wolff, in any event, could not remain inactive forever. Consequently, on 9 April, Parrilli was sent off to confer with Allen Dulles in Bern, taking with him two memorandums. The first, concerning efforts of the Germans to prevent destruction, protect POWs, and limit combat with the partisans, raised no serious problems for the OSS man.[3] The other, which requested Allied concessions to the pride and honor of the surrendering forces, asked that the German army be allowed to carry out a withdrawal (*Abzug*), "with military honor," after the end of hostilities, and that a modest contingent of German forces be held in reserve as a law-and-order force within Germany.[4] When he presented these memorandums, Parrilli also told Dulles that in order to avoid passing back and forth a number of times, Wolff wanted to see an advance copy of the surrender terms.[5] As even Parrilli realized, these various requests, which probably represented a blend of Vietinghoff's minimal demands and Wolff's pious hopes, bore little relation to the disastrous position in which the Axis forces found themselves.[6]

Nonetheless, Dulles and the OSS tried to put the best face they could on a now nearly ludicrous situation. In reports to Caserta and Washington, Dulles chronicled the details of his meeting with Parrilli and then added:

> My view is that they do not expect the somewhat naïve suggestions ... to be accepted but do expect[,] or hope[,] the statement of unconditional surrender will contain some palliative, not perhaps of substance ... but rather as regards the military status of those surrendering."[7]

On this occasion, as on others, the OSS chiefs in Washington outdid even Dulles in putting Parrilli's message in the most favorable light. The official OSS report to the top American leaders emphasized that Wolff and the German army authorities had agreed to prevent destruction, restrict the war against the partisans, and protect POWs. But Edward Buxton, the acting director of the OSS, did not indicate that Wolff's surrender proposal had virtually evaporated, nor did he provide a clear picture of the special requests which the Germans had made. All that the secretary of state, the Joint Chiefs of Staff, and the president learned from the OSS was that Parrilli had indicated a "military honor problem" was involved![8]

However, the army authorities at AFHQ Mediterranean had a cooler and more realistic view of the situation. Although the Caserta generals were being pressured from a number of quarters to take more political chances in the closing days of hostilities, Alexander and his aides were generally restrained and cautious. They had rejected a proposal that the small Anglo-American forces in Yugoslavia dare a bit and use any German surrender initiatives in that region to seize the prize ports of Trieste, Fiume, and Pola. In Caserta's opinion, to undertake such adventures with the tiny Western units available on the Dalmatian coast would only invite failure and usher in serious political trouble with Tito.[9] Similarly, Alexander's top staff was unwilling to listen to the suggestion of a conservative partisan leader, Pizzoni (Longhi), who urged the West to deal with the Germans on something "less than unconditional surrender" in order to save "the hydroelectric plants which are so vital to life in northern Italy." While acknowledging a deep interest in preserving the plants as well as in maintaining order in the north, General Morgan turned a deaf ear to all Pizzoni's entreaties—even the idea of bribing the Germans "with Swiss francs or gold"—and insisted that the Allies "would not consider anything" other "than unconditional surrender."[10]

After escaping from the tense, conspiratorial atmosphere of Bern, even Lemnitzer and Airey had become more skeptical about surrender deals, concluding that there was only a "slight possibility" of a Sunrise capitulation.[11] Once they learned the full story of the tensions which the affair had produced with the Soviets, their messages to Dulles reflected the political caution prevailing at Caserta. On 9 April, while Parrilli was still standing by in Bern, Lemnitzer fired off a dispatch ordering Dulles not to let the Germans have any advance indication of surrender terms. "I know you will be most careful to avoid giving [the] Germans any excuse for claiming that we are negotiating," Lemnitzer wrote. "I would also caution you against sending to the Germans through intermediaries anything in writing which they could use to suggest that negotiations are in progress."[12] Dulles was further told to give Parrilli a simple two-point verbal message for delivery to Wolff—the Allies refused to provide an advance copy of the surrender terms and, if the Germans dispatched parliamentaries, they should come with "absolute authority to act."[13] On 10 April, Dulles dutifully gave this message to Parrilli and added that speed was essential.[14] It is important to stress here that when the Italian intermediary returned to Wolff's headquarters, he only carried with him a partial response to the SS man's last communication. The German request to see the surrender terms ahead of time had been denied, however Wolff was not specifically told that his "military honor" proposals had been rejected, nor was Parrilli given any indication of how suspicious Caserta had become of the Sunrise affair.

Parrilli and Wolff were the only principles left guessing on the latter point, however, because on 12 April, Alexander sent Washington and London a sober appraisal of Parrilli's message, which also indicated that the Sunrise surrender prospects were nearly hopeless.[15] This summary of Wolff's request for an advance copy of the surrender document and for special terms respecting "military honor" reached London at the same time as the first flash that Franklin Roosevelt had died at Warm Springs, Georgia. The Bern affair, about which the British had long been nervous, thus appeared most doubtful and vulnerable at the very moment when the American government was weakest at the summit. The British moved swiftly to seize the opportunity, and on 14 April, recommended through both military and diplomatic channels that the Bern OSS contact be broken because there was no prospect for an "acceptable" surrender.[16] On the following day, 15 April, Churchill sent a personal message to President Truman reinforcing the British proposal. Stretching the facts somewhat, the prime minister contended that Roosevelt's last message to Stalin had implied that the Sunrise discussions should end.[17] In reality, Roosevelt's cable of 11 April had merely spoken vaguely of the incident fading "into the past." When Churchill summarized the political reasons why Dulles's "parleyings" should be stopped, however, he was on firmer ground. Although the prime minister still asserted that Soviet suspicions were "base," he went a fair way to granting that Russian doubts were reasonable and justified. The Soviets had been told "not to come," he admitted, yet discussions had continued, German commanders were shuffled from one front to another, and the Western powers seemed "to get a walkover" at Soviet expense. "The tale may become a legend in the Russian army," Churchill mused, and,[18] more pointedly, he noted that the removal of these "sore points" was necessary to strengthen the position of the Western powers in the East-West controversies over Poland.

Apparently without making additional inquiries of either the OSS or Caserta, the American government started the machinery into motion to accede to the British request. However, there was a six-day interval between Churchill's letter to Truman and the dispatch of a Combined Chiefs' cable to Caserta ordering that the Bern contact be broken. The delay in issuing the cutoff order, which did not reach Caserta until 21 April, seems to have been due more to bureaucratic lethargy than to disagreements over policy. In any event, the interval from 15 April to 21 April had a significant impact on the course and future of Sunrise. Instead of a clean break, there was another period in which developments on the German side were allowed to ripen, and the continued contact between Wolff and Dulles drew the OSS ever deeper into the business of surrender.

Since the message which Parrilli had brought back from Dulles had not been totally negative, Wolff had gone ahead lining up German officials in Italy to support the negotiation effort. He was successful in getting the adherence of the Luftwaffe commander, General von Pohl, although the 50,000 airmen under his command were no more able to operate independently than was the SS and police force which Wolff controlled.[19] The Obergruppenführer apparently also obtained the nominal backing of Gauleiter Hofer of the Tyrol, who had just returned from Berlin, apparently disillusioned by Hitler's unwillingness to face the desperateness of the situation.[20]

But the key to any special capitulation was, as always, the German army, and once more, Wolff failed to get commitments from the soldiers. The SS man had still retained some hope of using Field Marshal Kesselring's influence to swing over the wavering army men. But the field marshal enveloped himself in Olympian detachment and kept all overtures at arm's length with the statement that he "had no time" to discuss the situation of military forces which were not under his command.[21] Nor could Wolff obtain Vietinghoff's firm support. For the third time, the general conceded that "all clear-thinking officers" realized that the war was lost, but he still claimed that most of the troops and the broad mass of the German people clung to their faith in the Führer.[22] Vietinghoff's only practical suggestion was that they all wait until disaster had overtaken the German homeland, and then, once the Italian theater had been cut off from the north, the general would "assume full freedom of movement . . . so as to prevent a complete collapse."[23] However, until Berlin fell, or at the very least, until the East-West advance had cut Germany in two, Vietinghoff maintained that he could do nothing.

The general's estimate of his soldiers' attitude was, as usual, probably not far from the mark, but it offered little solace to Wolff, for whom extended delay was tantamount to being buried in the wreckage of the surrender project. To cap his troubles, he received a message from Himmler on 13 April, ordering him to come to Berlin immediately for consultation. Wolff initially stalled, fearing his head might be hanging in the balance, but Himmler would not be put off. Finally on 15 April—the same day on which Churchill wrote to Truman recommending the end of Sunrise—Wolff left Fasano for Berlin. Due to the rapid Allied advance, he was forced to make a wide sweep through Prague, which consumed another two days, and he did not arrive in the German capital until 17 April.[24] Although information on these meetings is sketchy—depending solely on statements attributed to Wolff—the SS general apparently first spoke with Himmler, and then with Himmler and Kaltenbrunner together, on 17 April. Aside from the fact that each talk lasted several hours, all we know about them is that Kaltenbrunner had learned of Wolff's trips to Switzerland and allegedly attacked him "furiously."[25] But once more, Wolff eluded the mortal fate which befell others who dealt with the enemy. Himmler could not decide whether to punish Wolff or to make use of his contacts with the Anglo-Americans. Paralyzed by indecision, he allowed Wolff to present his case directly to Hitler on 17 and 18 April. Wolff purportedly saw the Führer three times during these two days, and though Hitler "seemed in low spirits," he was "not hopeless."[26] Again the SS man's luck held. The Führer praised him for making a "top-level" contact with the Americans, but when Wolff tried to focus his attention on "the senseless destruction" in Italy, Hitler simply "did not react."[27] Instead, the Führer presented what he considered a clear plan for the future. He told Wolff to temporize in his talks with Dulles because it was still too early to consider a surrender, or even serious negotiation. Instead, Hitler contended, Germany "must fight on to gain time," while holding onto redoubts in the north (Berlin) and the south (the Alps). "In two more months," the Führer claimed, "the break between the Anglo-Saxons and Russians will come about and then I shall join which [ever one] approaches me first[,] it makes no difference which."[28]

On the journey back to northern Italy, Wolff pondered the lessons of his talks in the German capital. Apparently disenchanted by Hitler's willingness to jettison his anti-communism and go with whichever side offered him the highest price, the SS man was also convinced that the Führer was unable to see how close he had come to the precipice. Bidding farewell to his loyalty to Hitler with the reflection "that when the gods strike and wish to destroy someone, they strike him with blindness,"[29] Wolff arrived at his Fasano headquarters determined to make the best local deal he could. The date was 19 April; just two days before, the Combined Chiefs of Staff ordered Allen Dulles to liquidate Operation Sunrise by cutting all contact with Karl Wolff.

Now it was Dulles's turn to stumble in the dark. Unaware of the impending action of the Combined Chiefs, he had nothing in his hand except a few clipped and distorted reports of what had transpired on the German side in the second and third weeks of April. He did not obtain detailed information on some events, such as Wolff's trip to Berlin, until much later, but the Germans had sent other tidbits, carefully tailored to make the best possible impression on him. Wolff only provided guarded hints regarding Vietinghoff's surrender reservations, but his reticence made little difference, because Dulles and the OSS officials in Washington did not even relay the negative signals they did receive to higher authorities.[30]

Yet it would be a mistake to judge Wolff's relations with Dulles solely on the basis of how deftly he crafted the accounts of his surrender activities. The Obergruppenführer also made some of his points with Dulles by providing him with pieces of useful intelligence information, including the precise location of Kesselring's headquarters.[31] On 16 April, Bern was informed by Wolff that the area east of the Isonzo River, including Trieste, had been transferred to the German Army Group E stationed in Croatia. The OSS then notified the Joint Chiefs in Washington that Trieste was thereby excluded from any surrender based on Vietinghoff's Army Group C.[32] But the importance of this report simply failed to register.[33] Wolff and the OSS had tried, but the Anglo-American leaders apparently never understood that after 16 April, Trieste—the most important point in the north Adriatic— would not automatically fall into their hands, even if Sunrise was successful.

Wolff was more effective with the personal appeals which he directed to Dulles, appeals which sounded increasingly like messages from one business associate to another. He sent the OSS man a three-page handwritten condolence letter at the time of President Roosevelt's death, and then added that no matter what happened, "he was convinced of the final success of the mutual effort."[34] The SS man also begged the Allies "not [to] make useless sacrifices with their intensified offensive," because he was assuming "full responsibility" and guaranteed that "during the coming week[,] all will be surrender[ed]."[35] Even when, on 17 April, he was forced to admit that he was going to Berlin to see Himmler, Wolff still put the best possible face on things by stating, suggestively, that he was trying "to do something for the entire German people."[36]

Although Wolff's ingratiating messages clearly helped to string Dulles along, when they were relayed to Caserta, they ran into the icy doubts of the military authorities. Generals Lemnitzer and Airey seemed to be in the vanguard of those who had lost faith in Sunrise. On 11 April, the two generals had informed the OSS man that in their opinion there was "every reason to believe" that the Germans were trying to embroil the Western powers in a conflict with the Russians.[37] Lemnitzer and Airey had become so suspicious of Wolff and the Germans that they felt it was "very doubtful" that Wolff had ever visited Kesselring. They tended to hold instead that the whole operation, including the release of Parri, had been part of a "plot to prove to [the] Russians that negotiations are already in progress."[38] On 14 April, Airey informed Dulles that Wolff had inadvertently spoken recently with a confidential Allied agent and in the presence of the agent had said that he was waiting for the "inevitable disintegration in Germany," which he considered "imminent," before surrendering the German forces in Italy. Airey concluded that the SS man would only surrender "when [the] rest of Germany surrendered," but in the meantime "Wolff wants to have it both ways . . . he and other Crossword personalities feel they are insuring themselves and helping [the] general German policy of arousing Russian suspicions."[39] Lemnitzer stressed the same theme in a 13 April message to Dulles when he wrote, "We believe there is always an even chance that [the] Germans will in any case attempt to make trouble between the Allies whatever happens."[40]

When Gaevernitz and a Swiss intelligence officer suggested that they journey to Wolff's headquarters in an effort to accelerate a surrender, the idea was flatly rejected at AFHQ Mediterranean. A Lemnitzer message to Bern of 18 April indicated that Caserta was putting far more faith in military power than in clandestine contacts or the messages of Karl Wolff. "If Wolff and Vietinghoff ever needed a prod to make them act," Lemnitzer wrote to Dulles, "that prod is now being vigorously applied on our front[,] where everything including kitchen stoves are [sic] being thrown at the Germans."[41]

At this point, Dulles faced the ultimate test of his remarkable ability to bounce back and find an ever brighter lining. Returning from a short trip to Paris on 17 April, the OSS representative recognized that the course of events, as revealed in the messages from the Germans and Caserta, was running strongly against him. He nonetheless tried to convince AFHQ that Sunrise was deserving of favorable attention. In a cable of 17 April he conceded the possibility of Wolff's "eliminat[ion]" by Himmler, but still felt that Wolff could avoid this fate. If the Obergruppenführer was spared, Dulles believed, he "might still be used to help effect [a] general[,] or Italian theater[,] capitulation."[42] On 18 April, Dulles followed up this observation with a long general defense of Sunrise. Initially he put forth the well-worn contentions that the operation was necessary "to spare the lives of our troops and bring us into [the] heart of [the] German Reduit."[43] Then, while showing some caution—Wolff's trip to Berlin should make the Allies "doubly circumspect"—Dulles went on to develop a completely new argument in support of his surrender activities. He asserted that the "Russian susceptibility," about which he had obtained "additional information" while in Paris, was actually rooted in a Soviet determination "to block" the successful completion of Sunrise. Dulles knew that Trieste was outside the area covered by the project, but he contended that a surrender would give the Allies such a head start "that our forces [in] Italy would probably be the first to occupy Trieste."[44] He claimed that his Paris "sources" indicated that Trieste "now constitutes an even more important objective for [the] Russians than Berlin." Although this estimate was simply preposterous, Dulles was closer to the mark when he argued that if Sunrise failed "and [the] Germans retreat fighting[,] . . . then in all probability [the] Russians [that is, Tito's Partisans] will reach Trieste ahead of us."[45]

Surprisingly, these labored messages from Dulles seem to have had a strong impact on at least one important officer at Caserta. Showing little sign of his recent chilliness toward the project, Lemnitzer responded by urging the OSS man to get the "quickest possible" unconditional surrender of the German forces in northern Italy. While adding the totally unrealistic comment that "if [the] scope of Crossword [Sunrise] can be widened to include Kesselring's forces[,] so much the better," Lemnitzer gave Sunrise a ringing vote of confidence by declaring that it "should continue as a project of highest priority."[46]

Although it needs to be noted that Lemnitzer had always been more sympathetic to Sunrise than had General Airey,[47] it is difficult to understand why the American reversed himself so sharply on 19 April. Dulles's erroneous references to the direction of the Soviet advance were certainly not decisive with Lemnitzer; the general was better informed than Dulles on the focal point and tempo of the Soviet offensive. Nor is it certain that Dulles's cold war picture of Tito's partisans as synonymous with the Red Army was shared by the military high command in Italy. Regarding other matters, Alexander and his aides continued to dodge political issues and hide behind the principle of military necessity.

However, they did place a high value on the acquisition of Trieste, because their plans for the invasion of Austria were keyed to it as the best port of supply. With the Allied offensive in northern Italy gaining momentum, and a total collapse of Army Group C now possible, Lemnitzer and others in Caserta probably took more seriously the question of resistance in the "redoubt" and the importance of firm supply lines into Austria. Hovering along the edge of this issue was the prospect of gaining a march on Tito by seizing the positions vital for communications through Venezia Giulia. Although Dulles's political arguments for seizing Trieste may not have had a strong impact on Caserta—at least not consciously—by indirectly raising the question of the redoubt and the Trieste supply route, he seems to have rekindled the generals' enthusiasm for Sunrise.

Bern and Caserta could not have chosen a less opportune time to close ranks in support of the surrender project. With that sure touch for the ludicrous which characterized so much of Sunrise, Lemnitzer sent his encouraging cable to Dulles on 19 April. Two days later, on 21 April, the order of the Combined Chiefs arrived, demanding that the Sunrise contact be broken off immediately. Apparently all was lost and there was nothing for

Caserta to do but abide by instructions while notifying the Soviets that the contact had been cut. Trying to put the best possible face on failure, Lemnitzer sent Dulles a message in which he held out the hope that if their efforts resulted "in saving a single Allied life," it would "not have been in vain."[48] Such thoughts seemed as farfetched as they were ethnocentric on 21 April, because the sun had seemingly set without producing positive benefits for anyone.

But of course no one told any of this to Wolff and his friends, who went blithely ahead trying to make a bigger and brighter Sunrise. Confusion reigned among the German authorities of northern Italy in the aftermath of Wolff's trip to Berlin, but virtually everyone was agreed that something should be done immediately. The political situation was unclear to them, but the thrust of the Allied advance was not. The Anglo-American attack, strongly supported by partisan actions, had been pressing forward for nearly two weeks.[49] A mighty pincer movement had taken shape with the Allied Eighth Army moving against the German Tenth Army along the eastern coast, while the American Fifth Army drove against the German Fourteenth covering the western approaches to Bologna. As early as 14 April, the Polish corps had pushed the Eighth Army's front as far north as Imola, and by the twenty-second, units of the German Tenth Army holding the center of the line were forced to evacuate across the Po. Toward the west, Bologna was hard pressed by units of both the Fifth and Eighth armies, and after a partisan rising on the nineteenth, the city fell to the Allies on 21 April.

These developments marked serious reverses for General Vietinghoff's forces, but they were short of a total debacle. Most German units continued to resist fiercely, and the next few days showed that portions of both the Tenth and Fourteenth Armies could still execute the difficult maneuver of retreating across the Po. The Allied prisoner bag was substantially below 50,000 men, and although the partisans had supported Allied operations, had harassed German communications, and had risen in some cities like Turin and Genoa, as well as Bologna, there had as yet been no general popular rising.[50]

Yet a Nostradamus was not necessary to predict that the German retreat could shortly turn into a rout that would bring down the whole Axis position in northern Italy. A showdown meeting of German officials had to occur quickly, and on the initiative of either Ambassador Rahn, or Gauleiter Hofer, it took place on 22 April at Vietinghoff's headquarters at Recoaro.[51] Documentation on what was discussed at the meeting is so sparse that one German historian has characterized it as "a masterpiece of imprecise information."[52] Apparently, however, each leading participant (Wolff, Vietinghoff, Hofer) raised his own special demands, and discussion then dragged on as the group strained to find an acceptable compromise. Rahn and Wolff wanted simply to send emissaries to Switzerland without delay in order to get the best terms they could. Hofer also desired quick action, but was more interested in saving his province "from senseless destruction" and in avoiding conflicts between the German and Italian populations of the Tyrol. He even advanced the mad idea that his Tyrolean satrapy should be preserved until "a postwar peace conference" settled its future.[53]

Vietinghoff was not as unrealistic as Hofer, but he was still loath to commit himself to a capitulation until he knew the Allied terms. The general finally allowed himself to be pushed along by the others, and near the end of the meeting, he haltingly agreed to talks with the Anglo-Americans. He designated Colonel Victor von Schweinitz, a general staff officer from his command to serve as his representative in the negotiations. Vietinghoff signed a statement on 22 April giving Schweinitz power to represent him, but then the general added that this should only be done "within the limits of my instructions."[54] Obviously, the content of Vietinghoff's verbal instructions to Schweinitz is one of the critical points in the whole German surrender initiative, yet because the instructions were verbal they remain somewhat clouded. The Allies never learned precisely what Vietinghoff told Schweinitz, and the other German participants in the meeting of 22 April also seem to have been left largely in the dark. According to the statement which the general made soon after the capitulation, his directions contained three broad points. First he told the colonel that there must be no "dishonorable conditions"[55]—a phrase which actually embraced a number of subpoints. Apparently Vietinghoff was still asking for an assurance of what he later called "chivalrous treatment,"[56] some gesture indicating that the Allies respected the defeated Germans, perhaps a ceremonial withdrawal from the battlefield or the retention of sidearms by officers. He also seems to have desired a guarantee that his men would not be used as reparations labor, especially not in Siberia, and he wanted to make certain that the Italian Fascist troops under his command would receive the same treatment as the German—that they would become POWs. In addition, under the guise of honorable conditions, Vietinghoff may have been clinging to the hope that he could hold part of Army Group C intact to be used as an anti-Communist force inside postwar Germany.

Vietinghoff's second verbal instruction was more specific. It stipulated that Schweinitz should sign nothing until a "German government capable of negotiation" had ceased to exist, or until the Allied advance had progressed so far that no one could accuse Army Group C of having stabbed other units in the back by surrendering.[57] Thus Vietingoff was unwilling to move very far or very fast, but he was not lost in total fantasy. His third and final instruction to Schweinitz directed the colonel to try to preserve Hofer's Gau, but even Vietinghoff explained both to Schweinitz and Hofer, that this "might not be possible."[58]

Therefore the meeting of 22 April ended with a collective resolve to send Schweinitz and Wolff to Switzerland, but there was little agreement among the German leaders regarding what they wanted from the Allies, and even less clarity about what they were likely to receive. The hopes harbored by Hofer and Vietinghoff were totally unrealizable, and Rahn seems still to have been clinging to the illusion that Dulles would arrange terms substantially better than unconditional surrender. The Obergruppenführer was probably more realistic than the others, yet he too was still groping after some large concession, such as an "honorable" withdrawal of Army Group C after the capitulation. Even when prospects looked dimmest, Wolff counted on his "personal reputation with the Anglo-Americans"[59] to extract guarantees from Dulles that the "idealistic" and "decent" men of the army, party, and SS would be able to play an "active part in the reconstruction."[60]

Blinded by his illusions, yet determined to act, Wolff set off for Como on 22 April, accompanied by Wenner and Schweinitz. En route, the Obergruppenführer and his party skirted Milan, where Cardinal Schuster was once again trying to arrange peace discussions.[61] This time the cardinal had established contact among the partisans, the Neo-Fascists, and the local German authorities. But Wolff was no longer interested in middlemen or complicated parleying, and he did not respond to the entreaties of Schuster's representatives urging him to participate in the Milan talks. Neither the Church authorities nor the Italian Fascists had been told that a special surrender was being arranged in Bern. Wolff and Rahn had earlier given Mussolini and Graziani a few hints that the Germans might be compelled to make some arrangement with the Allies, but beyond that the Italian Fascists were kept in the dark. On the eve of his journey to Switzerland, Wolff was determined to keep it that way.

Arriving in Como on 23 April, Wolff did move quickly to protect his other flank. He sent Eugen Dollmann to Kesselring's headquarters to give the field marshal the picture "in broad outline."[62] However, Wolff "had no intention of burdening him [Kesselring] with all the facts,"[63] and Dollmann was instructed to give the field marshal the impression that contacts were being made with the Allies pursuant to Hitler's orders. Dollmann first caught up with Kesselring at his temporary headquarters, at Pullach near Munich, on 26 April. Face to face with the field marshal, Dollmann carried out his orders and "just hinted at the true state of affairs."[64] Kesselring may have received some veiled indications that a surrender was in the making, and he may even have implied that once Hitler was dead, he, too, would cooperate with such an enterprise. But the SS men realized that the field marshal "was very nervous of the whole thing," and wanted to hear nothing that smacked of treason.[65] So Dollmann did not advance beyond "general remarks," and Kesselring was left to rest quietly with his hopes and his dreams.[66]

Having slipped past the Italian Fascists and having made a move to mollify Kesselring, Wolff sent Parrilli into Switzerland on the morning of 23 April to announce that he and a German army representative "with powers" would be arriving at the frontier in the early afternoon.[67] The message, which was relayed to Dulles by the Swiss, hit the OSS representative like a morning thunderclap. Dulles had been expecting a visit from Parrilli, but thought that the Italian would simply be relaying another routine message from Wolff. In conformity with the order that he had received from the Combined Chiefs to cut the Sunrise contact, Dulles was primed to rebuff Parrilli with the explanation that he had "no further time to give to [the] matter . . . which now has dragged beyond all bounds."[68] However, when he heard that Wolff was on his way to Switzerland, Dulles's hopes and dreams about Sunrise immediately revived. He informed Caserta that he was "obeying instructions," but that he had no way of stopping the Germans from coming.[69] He would not see Wolff, Dulles averred, but he would nonetheless try to aquire "intelligence" through "our Swiss intermediaries."[70] A few hours later, Dulles informed Caserta that Parrilli had telephoned from the frontier to say that Schweinitz was accompanying Wolff, and that he was in possession of "full powers."[71] Soon thereafter, Major Waibel of Swiss intelligence phoned Dulles to report that in his opinion "Vietinghoff's representative has [a] serious mission and powers."[72]

It requires no imagination to understand how strongly all this affected the OSS man. Not only had Sunrise apparently risen once more, Parrilli had also asserted that while Schweinitz and Wolff were in Switzerland, Dollmann was contacting the field marshal in order "to advise Kesselring[,] and to endeavor [to] arrange for him to take common action."[73] Although he tried to be cautious, Dulles took the bait. The reports which he sent to Caserta granted that "confirmation" of some of the information he had received was "difficult" because details were hard to secure by telephone, but he was clearly inclined to accept both the Kesselring-contact story and the assertion that Schweinitz had full powers.[74]

His enthusiasm was intensified by the response which his messages brought forth from Caserta. Lemnitzer reported that Alexander had sent two cables to the Combined Chiefs of Staff asking them to reverse their cut-off order of 21 April.[75] Although the general also directed Dulles to abide by the order until a reply was received from the Combined Chiefs, he simultaneously instructed the OSS man to "parry for time" and allow the Germans to communicate with him through intermediaries.[76] Dulles took the ambiguity in these directives as an authorization to keep Sunrise alive. He went through the motions of telling Parrilli, Waibel, and Husmann that the "affair was no longer of interest"[77] to him, then he reported to Wolff through intermediaries that news of his arrival "had been communicated to the appropriate quarters." If Wolff "wished to wait," Dulles indirectly informed him, he would be apprised whether "his presence in Switzerland" caused the Combined Chiefs to authorize a resumption of the surrender discussions.[78]

Following Dulles's lead, Wolff and Schweinitz remained in Lucerne for two days, becoming increasingly nervous with every passing hour. Between 23 April and 25 April, while the German emissaries were "pacing like tigers,"[79] the Allies finally achieved a decisive military breakthrough in northern Italy. On 23 April, the U.S. Tenth Mountain Divison crossed the Po and numerous other bridgeheads were soon established by the Fifth Army. The main thrust took place north of San Benedetto Po, with an advance so rapid that the Mantua-Verona Highway was already cut on 25 April. Numerous German units were destroyed or isolated once the Anglo-American armor penetrated the open country north of the river. The German Fourteeneth Army was torn apart, and the Adige defense line turned, long before large units of the German Tenth Army had an opportunity to take up positions there. A broad defense of northeastern Italy by Vietinghoff's forces was thereby rendered impossible. Henceforth, the most that Army Group C could hope to accomplish in that region was a delaying defense along the approaches to the Brenner Pass and Trieste.[80]

The relatively weaker Axis forces in central and western Italy were less hard pressed by the Allied advance, but on 25 April, the CLNAI in Milan called for a general rising throughout northern Italy. Villages, towns, and cities became the scenes of pitched battles between the partisans and the Axis police and military units. The outcome of many of these conflicts was still in doubt on 25 April, but in other crucial centers, especially Turin, Genoa, and Milan, the fighting had turned decisively in favor of the partisans, and even the SS units found themselves besieged in their isolated strongholds.

Whether in the east or west, in the cities or at the front, the German situation had suddenly passed from bad to catastrophic. All parties to Sunrise were thus caught in a limbo that was both embarrassing and dangerous. They were eager to make some kind of deal with one another, but could not even discuss the situation, while the object of all their intrigue and effort— the German position in northern Italy—rapidly disintegrated. A desperate Wolff begged Waibel to hurry, and the Swiss intelligence man, in turn, pleaded with Dulles to produce the proverbial rabbit, and do it quickly. "We are in an absolutely impossible situation," Waibel said, "we will be ridiculed for centuries if we don't manage this properly."[81]

Dulles responded by doing his best to convince the authorities in Caserta, and through them the Combined Chiefs, that Sunrise prospects were favorable. All he needed was an authorization to send the Germans south, Dulles stated on 25 April, then Caserta could allow "the Russians . . . [to] be present from the beginning"[82] and further political problems would be avoided. Even if the worst happened and an "immediate surrender" was "not effected," Dulles wrote on another occasion, the very presence of Wolff and Schweinitz in southern Italy would "not fail seriously to undermine German morale."[83] But Dulles trusted Wolff and he strove mightily to convince the Combined Chiefs that Wolff and Schweinitz merited their confidence too. He passed along Wolff's claim that "a significant consolidation" in favor of surrender had occurred among German officials in northern Italy, as well as Schweinitz's assertion that he could give the Allies information about food stocks, ammunition dumps, and so on, which "otherwise might fall into [the] hands of Neo-Fascists or other disordered elements."[84] The OSS representative described Schweinitz as a man who "makes an excellent impression"; a man "said to have been active in [the] July 20 movement"; a man who had been a prewar exchange officer with a British regiment.[85] No positive piece of trivia was too tiny to go unreported. Dulles even told Caserta that Schweinitz's grandmother was an American, and that he was a "descendant of Chief Justice Jay!"[86]

The crucial point, however, was the way in which the OSS man handled the matter of the powers which Vietinghoff had given to Schweinitz. After transmitting the text of Schweinitz's powers, including the critical qualifying phrase restricting the colonel's authority to "the limits of my instructions," Dulles registered his own opinion that the "full power appears genuine."[87] Yet he failed to find out what Vietinghoff's instructions to Schweinitz actually were. Incredible as it may seem, no one on the Allied side raised a finger to explore what might be lurking behind the phrase "the limits of my instructions." Instead Dulles merely accepted the interpretation of this passage that the Swiss intermediaries gave to him. Waibel and his friends, like Dulles and Wolff, were thirsting for a negotiated settlement, and they were eager to sweep aside Vietinghoff's qualifying language. Dulles followed their lead and on 25 April, notified Caserta that "our Swiss friends have [the] impression that [the] qualifying language is more or less eyewash."[88]

This optimistic act of self-deception was Allen Dulles's ultimate effort to so reassure the Combined Chiefs that they would allow him to deal with the Germans. But even though he thereby ran roughshod over the minimal rules of caution and good sense, Dulles still failed to win the race. Wolff's patience cracked before the Combined Chiefs were roused to action. Since the Obergruppenführer's primary responsibility was for rear-area security, he could hardly continue to languish in Switzerland once the German front had been torn open and the partisans had started their rising. On 25 April, he sent word to Dulles that he was going back, claiming that the tension between "Neo-Fascists, Communists, Wehrmacht, SS, and other troops in northern Italy" might "explode at any moment."[89] Actually it had already "exploded" and that was why Wolff was leaving. The SS man also asserted that Mussolini might be "preparing a last-minute coup of some sort," and that Himmler, or even Hitler, might be arriving in northern Italy momentarily.[90] Although Wolff stated that he no longer owed allegiance to Himmler— he was silent about his feelings regarding Hitler—he claimed that the sudden appearance of any of the top Nazis would cause serious difficulties. After providing Dulles with all these bogies to worry about, the Obergruppenführer also informed him that Wenner had been given full powers to surrender the SS, and promised that Wenner and Schweinitz would remain in Switzerland for one to two more days, awaiting word from the Combined Chiefs. Finally, Wolff declared that once back at his own headquarters, he would propose to Vietinghoff that they issue a joint proclamation with Hofer and Rahn, proclaiming that northern Italy was cut off and that "independent action" would be taken "to avoid useless bloodshed."[91]

The Obergruppenführer's mission to northern Italy, which sounded so significant in these OSS dispatches, actually became a political burlesque almost immediately. Wolff only managed to travel ten kilometers or so before he discovered that the roads were being seized by partisans. Unable to find a way out rapidly enough, Wolff was trapped, and he barricaded himself in the headquarters of the SS border police, the Villa Locatelli, near Como. The SS man could not get through to his headquarters, which was now at Bolzano, nor could he discuss the situation with Vietinghoff, even though communications were still intact, because the general, for security reasons, refused to talk by telephone or radio. "Extremely pessimistic" because of this turn of events, Wolff was still determined to surrender something and decided that if all else failed, he would try to give northwest Italy to the Allies as a token of his good intentions.[92] But Wolff's lucky star was still twinkling, if dimly, and a series of developments pushed him back into the forefront of the Sunrise adventure.

Among the Axis officials trapped with Wolff in Como was Marshal Graziani, war minister of Mussolini's dying Fascist Republic. The Duce and other Fascist leaders had walked out of the Milan capitulation talks which Cardinal Schuster had arranged because they apparently first learned there that the Germans were making a surrender deal in Switzerland.[93] After forsaking Milan for Como, the Fascist chief and some of his entourage proceeded up the west side of the lake on the morning of 27 April. There, on the following day, the Duce, his mistress, and a handful of Fascist leaders met their deaths at the hands of the partisans.

Among those left behind in Como was Graziani, and though he initially reproached Wolff for betraying the Fascists, in the end he calmed down and gave the SS man his signed authorization to surrender the Fascist forces on the same basis as the German. Wolff thereby casually picked up a valuable card for his game of convincing the Anglo-Americans that he could head off anarchy and mass destruction in northern Italy. But time was short, and Wolff's initial attempts to find a way out of Villa Locatelli, by getting help from the SS authorities in Milan (who were themselves besieged), all failed.[94]

Foiled in his efforts to break out to the south, the SS man was saved by his Swiss and American partners in Sunrise. Word of his plight filtered through to Swiss intelligence operatives on the border, and they, in turn, relayed it to Major Waibel. Waibel and his colleagues had repeatedly bent, if not burst, their government's rules of neutrality during the eight weeks in which the Sunrise project had meandered along its way. In the process, dozens, perhaps hundreds, of individuals had learned of the active role which Swiss intelligence men had played in the affair. To have it peter out in total failure, while Wolff stood nearby apparently ready to capitulate, was simply impossible for Waibel to accept. Such an end would inevitably unleash a major scandal in Switzerland and might finish Waibel's career.[95] On 26 and 27 April, the Swiss major made a bold bid to guarantee that the sun rose instead of fell. He set about trying to rescue Wolff, not with Swiss forces alone, but by using the men of the OSS. First he turned to Gaevernitz and urged him to participate. Although such an enterprise was an almost incomprehensible violation of the Combined Chiefs' order to break off the Sunrise contact, Gaevernitz agreed and informed Dulles of what he intended to do. The chief OSS representative mumbled something about the cutoff order to Gaevernitz, but as he later conceded, he then purposely turned a blind eye so that his subordinates could carry on with the rescue attempt.[96]

How completely Dulles and his companions had been carried away by their involvement in Sunrise is revealed most glaringly by this incident. Surely the OSS man, as well as Waibel, and perhaps even Wolff, were drawn along by a desire to save lives and limit destruction. But most of all, they were pulled in ever deeper by their egos, their mistakes, and the deceptions they had practiced on one another. Ultimately, they became members of a kind of Sunrise Club, in which their obligations to each other, and their determination to make the enterprise prosper, outweighed their obligations to their own governments. On the night of 26 April, Allen Dulles put more faith in the intentions of Karl Wolff than he did in the judgment and authority of the Combined Chiefs of Staff. Gaevernitz was allowed to join Waibel, and the race to rescue Wolff, and to save Sunrise, was on.

At the border town of Chiasso, the two intelligence men met a second OSS agent, Donald Jones, who had been serving as an American consul in Lugano, and directing OSS operations in support of the Italian partisans along the Swiss frontier. Waibel, Gaevernitz, and Jones quickly assembled a mixed rescue team including Swiss intelligence men, Italian partisans, and two SS men. Led by Jones, who was well known among the partisans, the little force set off in three cars on the night of 27 April, headed for Como.[97] It was hoped that the different nationalities and affiliations of the men on board would allow the party to persuade and conjole its way to Villa Locatelli. The plan worked smoothly, and in the middle of the night they found Wolff at the Villa, resplendent in his SS Obergruppenführer's uniform, ready to toast his rescuers with scotch whiskey which itself had been liberated from British forces in North Africa two years before.

Wolff, who was immediately persuaded to change into civilian clothes, was then secreted in one of the cars, and the caravan headed back to the Swiss border. When it arrived at Chiasso in the wee hours amid much rejoicing, Gaevernitz was embraced by the Obergruppenführer, a man with whom—according to the Combined Chiefs of Staff—he was not even supposed to be in contact. "I will never forget what you have done for me," Wolff told Gaevernitz, and the OSS agent, as well as his chief in Bern, concluded that by this rescue they had put Wolff forever in their debt.[98] As usual, they failed to recognize that Wolff put a rather different interpretation on the events of 27 April. To his mind, Dulles, by going to such lengths to save his life, had merely given new evidence of how much the OSS man valued and trusted him. Wolff was more ready than ever to arrange a capitulation, but henceforth he seems to have looked upon himself chiefly as a bosom colleague, or friendly companion, of the men who made up the OSS Sunrise team.[99]

Following the rescue, Gaevernitz and Waibel took Wolff to Lugano, where in a small hotel room, the three discussed what to do next. Without hesitation Wolff agreed to send orders to Milan forbidding all action against the partisans. After some discussion, they then decided—apparently with Dulles's concurrence by telephone—that before proceeding through eastern Switzerland to his new headquarters in the Tyrolean city of Bolzano, Wolff should sign over to Wenner the authorization which Graziani had given him to surrender the Italian Fascist forces. Since Vietinghoff had also moved his army headquarters to the Bolzano area, it was hoped that Wolff would be able to pull the loose threads together and implement a capitulation, and on the morning of 27 April, accompanied by Waibel, he headed for Feldkirchen.[100]

Actually, with every passing day there was significantly less to surrender. During the forty-eight hours which had passed since Wolff first attempted to leave Switzerland for northern Italy, the Allied armies had crossed the Adige River in force. Verona fell on 26 April, and in western Italy, the partisans had delivered Genoa to the Anglo-Americans with its vital harbor installations intact. From every section of northern Italy reports poured into Allied headquarters indicating that partisans were seizing control without heavy destruction or large casualties. Furthermore the combination of partisan restraint and Anglo-American control (such as the Rankin B system) obviated any possibility that a revolution might erupt out of the final struggle against Nazis and Fascists. With sighs of relief, Allied observers noted that "anti-scorch was most successful," and that in town after town there were "no excesses" and "no disorder." As early as 26 April, four thousand partisans in Bologna held a "ceremonial parade" which was reviewed by the American commander of the Fifteenth Army Group, Mark Clark. After the ceremony, the partisans handed their weapons over to the Allied authorities, an incident which helped incline the British ambassador in Rome, Sir Noel Charles, to the conclusion that the north Italians were "an eager, self-respecting," and above all, "a docile population."[101]

Thus by 27 April, two of the major reasons why the Western Allies had sought a Sunrise surrender had been overtaken by events: Army Group C was no longer a formidable fighting force, and German cooperation was not necessary to prevent mass destruction, or a partisan revolution, in northern Italy. Aside from saving lives (at this point, primarily German lives), and eliminating the need for extensive mopping-up operations in the mountains, such a capitulation might benefit the Allies only if it rapidly opened up the Brenner and Trieste routes into the Austrian Alps. But with Anglo-American forces racing toward the Brenner from north and south, and the Eighth Army, as well as Tito's forces, moving in on Trieste, the surrender of even these points was no longer critically important for subsequent military operations.

At this stage of the campaign, the frenzied pursuit of Sunrise by Anglo-American officials was primarily a mere reflex action by men who had not grasped the suddenness and scope of the victory. This was especially true of those participating directly in the clandestine operation; for them the appearance of a successful conclusion of the game had become as important, if not more important, than the winning of the war itself. In light of this passionate devotion to gamesmanship, the actual performance of the star player on the OSS team was somewhat less than stunning. For if Allen Dulles had gone to his office in Bern on the night of 26 April, or even early in the morning of the twenty-seventh, much of the guesswork and a good bit of secret scurrying about could have been avoided. The OSS representative, however, apparently did not go to work until mid-morning, and only then did he discover that a copy of cable number 710 from Caserta, dated 26 April, contained an authorization by the Combined Chiefs to send the German emissaries to Alexander's headquarters, was lying on his desk.[102] The whole operation to rescue Wolff, as well as the decision to have him go to Bolzano, had occurred at a time when the Combined Chiefs had already authorized Dulles to send Wolff and Schweinitz to Caserta. But no one involved knew this. They had bemoaned the slowness of the authorities in Washington, when the latter had actually reacted rather promptly. Considering all the circumstances surrounding the incident which inclined the Combined Chiefs to be suspicious and cautious,[103] as well as a communications blunder that delayed the arrival of Dulles's first dispatches,[104] the military authorities did well to reverse their cutoff order and notify Caserta as quickly as they did. At a time when the top government authorities in Washington were fencing with mortal issues, such as whether to initiate a showdown with Russia regarding Poland, the Sunrise affair looked far more important to the Bern group than it did in the American capital.[105] Yet within seventy-two hours, the Combined Chiefs routinely ordered Caserta and Dulles to avoid all negotiation or bargaining in Switzerland, while sending Schweinitz and Wolff south immediately.

On 27 April, Dulles had to work swiftly to fulfill the terms of this order, and especially to make sure that his tracks were covered. He had informed Caserta early on the previous day that Wolff was leaving Switzerland on his way to Como. Later in the same day he told Alexander's headquarters that Wolff had arrived in Como but could get no further because "all roads were blocked by partisans."[106] Now Dulles had to explain how Wolff had returned to Switzerland, without thereby revealing to Caserta and the Combined Chiefs that he, and other OSS officials in Switzerland, had violated the cutoff order. His solution to the problem was to say as little as possible and he therefore cabled Caserta on the twenty-seventh: "According to [a] report from Waibel[,] Wolff succeeded in working his way back to Switzerland from Como and when your message [was] received[,] he was on his way to [the] Feldkirch frontier."[107] By this deliberate misrepresentation, Dulles managed to pacify his superiors and gained enough elbow room to save the remains of the Sunrise project once more.

The OSS man then rushed about, pulling the pieces together. Wolff was intercepted just before he crossed the border and was told that the cutoff order had been rescinded and that the surrender undertaking was going ahead.[108] The SS man was directed to continued to Bolzano so that the capitulation could be implemented and the no-destruction orders obeyed. Dulles also arranged for an OSS radio operator to follow Wolff to Bolzano to establish communications with Caserta and Bern.[109] Gaevernitz was summoned back to Bern so that he could join Dulles in briefing Schweinitz and Wenner. Caserta had just been informed that Wolff was being allowed to go to Bolzano, and that Wenner, not the Obergruppenführer, would be going to Allied Mediterranean headquarters. Speaking for Alexander, General Lemnitzer agreed to the switch, because, like Dulles, he wanted Wolff on the spot in Bolzano to insure surrender implementation.[110] But Lemnitzer was troubled by the prospect of the two Germans setting off for Caserta in the company of Allied officers whom they did not know. He wanted nothing to panic them at the last moment and urged Dulles to arrange for Gaevernitz and Waibel to accompany the German emissaries on their trip to southern Italy.[111]

Dulles tried to accede to Lemnitzer's request, but the effort to include Waibel produced further delay, and was ultimately unsuccessful. Gaevernitz, Schweinitz, and Wenner first waited in Bern until Waibel returned from Feldkirchen; then the four-member Sunrise team set off for Annemasse where they were to cross into France and meet the plane which was to take them to Caserta. The OSS man and the two Germans crossed easily, but Waibel—the Swiss superspy—became so embroiled in the red tape of his own government that he was not able to get clearance to leave the country![112] On the morning of 28 April, his three companions spent a couple of nervous hours waiting for him on the French side of the border. But to no avail. Waibel was still unable to join them and even Gaevernitz could see that time was running out on Sunrise and that further delay was impossible. He decided to leave Waibel and rushed on to meet the C-47 which was standing by at Annemasse. In mid-morning the OSS man and the two Germans finally took off for Caserta, only to be plagued again by bad luck in the form of stormy weather. Fighting through a dangerous downpour of rain and snow, the Sunrise plane did not manage to arrive at Marcianese Airport, outside Caserta, until 3:15 P.M. on 28 April.[113]

Once on the ground, the confusion appeared to end, and the exhausted Germans found themselves in the middle of a well-organized and well-oiled surrender machine. Officials at Caserta had been developing and refining an "Instrument of Local Surrender of German Forces in Italy" for more than a month, and by 28 April they had a voluminous twenty-page document ready for Schweinitz and Wenner.[114] During the preceding week, they had also constructed a special small camp for the German plenipotentiaries, and on

27 April, Alexander's chief of staff, General Morgan, had prepared a detailed plan for "the Reception and Conduct of Parleys with German Emissaries."[115]

Furthermore, the fourth week of April had produced an answer to the question of Soviet participation in surrender talks, a question which earlier had heavily beclouded Sunrise. On 21 April, the Combined Chiefs of Staff forwarded a recommendation to the Soviets which was brilliant in its simplicity.[116] Under the plan, the three Allied powers would immediately appoint officers to serve as surrender representatives at each others' military headquarters. Then, for example, if the commander of German forces in Austria wanted to surrender to the Soviets, there would be Anglo-American officers attached to Soviet army headquarters, who could act as observers during the capitulation proceedings. Similarly, Soviet officers assigned to SHAEF and AFHQ Mediterranean could act as Russian representatives if any special capitulations were engineered by the Anglo-Americans.

The Soviet government accepted the Western recommendation with alacrity, and on 25 April Moscow designated General Kislenko—who was already serving as military advisor in Rome—to be the Russian surrender representative in Caserta.[117] On the following day, as soon as the Combined Chiefs of Staff rescinded the cutoff order for Sunrise, both Alexander and Churchill told the Russians that a German surrender in Italy was taking shape and that the Soviet observer should immediately proceed to Caserta.[118] On the following day, another notification, urging speed, was sent directly to Kislenko, and shortly after, the Russian general arrived at Allied military headquarters.[119]

The Anglo-American generals were only eager to have Kislenko present, however, they were not willing for him to play any meaningful role in the proceedings. Although the Soviet general told an AFHQ representative that he was "most anxious to be invited to take part at the very beginning of any negotiations,"[120] the surrender procedure developed by General Morgan specifically barred the Soviet general from the first Anglo-American talk with the Germans.[121] This action may in part have arisen from a fear that an initial Soviet presence could scare off the Germans, but it was primarily a clumsy effort to show that the Western military leaders were in charge of this capitulation and that they could prevent Soviet attendance at a session designed to check the credentials of the emissaries.[122] The decision to bar Kislenko was a pointed rebuff, wounding and gratuitous. The Soviet general dutifully stayed away from the opening session and sat dumbly through two others which the Anglo-Americans had with Schweinitz and Wenner. But even as he did so, Kislenko bitterly protested his exclusion from the first session, and in subsequent months, he, and other Soviet authorities, bombarded the Western Allies with protests regarding the terms and the implementation of the Sunrise surrender.[123]

The Caserta generals felt themselves on the eve of triumph, however, and as on previous occasions, they gave little thought to the political consequences of their actions. Their minds and eyes were rigidly fixed on making their surrender machine roll. Less than three hours after Schweinitz and Wenner reached Caserta, the Anglo-Americans summoned them to the first meeting. The Allied team in this session was led by General Morgan, and included generals Lemnitzer and Airey, plus an air force general and an admiral. Although Schweinitz spoke excellent English, Gero von Gaevernitz served as interpreter.[124]

Morgan opened the meeting and began to march briskly through the points he had laid out in his program. In response to his first question, Schweinitz obediently replied that the two Germans present were indeed Major Wenner representing Wolff, and he himself, representing Vietinghoff. When Morgan then asked "if the officers had full powers to act" on behalf of their commanders, the Allied scenario immediately ran into trouble. Schweinitz replied, according to Gaevernitz's rather inelegantly paraphrased translation, that he could act for Vietinghoff only "within the orders he had got."[125] To underscore his point, Schweinitz added that "it was possible however that propositions might be made to him which would be outside his orders and would therefore have to be referred to his commander." Morgan was in no mood to be put off by such complications, or even by the facts, however, and routinely asked again if Schweinitz had "full powers." The German colonel tried a new tack this time. Averring that "within his orders" he had full powers, he handed over the authorization from Vietinghoff, which, as we know, gave Schweinitz authority "to make binding commitments . . . within the frame of instructions given by me." At the same time Wenner gave Morgan the full powers covering the SS which he had received from Wolff, and Graziani's authorization, which Wolff had relayed to him.

In possession of the German credential documents, Morgan, like others before him, failed to raise any question regarding Vietinghoff's special instructions. Perhaps the general held back because of the delicacies of surrender decorum, but it seems more likely that the "go-ahead" mood which gripped Caserta made it only possible for him to perceive what he wished to perceive. He was primed for an unconditional surrender. He heard Schweinitz say "full powers" and he read that Schweinitz could make "binding commitments" on Vietinghoff's behalf; beyond that, he did not want to see or hear anything. Instead of questioning further, he raced on to the third point in his surrender procedure and gave the Germans three copies of the "Instrument of Surrender." Morgan told Schweinitz and Wenner that they would be given three hours to examine the twenty-page document and at the end of that time they would again meet with Allied representatives. At the second session they could ask questions, but they would also be expected to declare "whether the terms were accepted or not."

Morgan seems to have closed the first session content that he had blocked the side doors and left the elusive Germans no choice but surrender or annihilation. What he had actually done was to hand the capitulation terms to German officers without making certain that they had the authority to agree to, or implement, an unconditional surrender. For weeks, Lemnitzer and others had been striving to avoid just such a development. The Germans had received the conditions in writing under circumstances which could arouse Soviet suspicions, especially if any hitch developed in the acceptance or fulfillment of the terms. At a time when a victory free of political liabilities seemed finally within their grasp, the Anglo-Americans had, through this fifteen-minute session at Caserta, pumped new life into the hazards which had plagued Sunrise from its beginning.

To Schweinitz and Wenner, however, the first meeting with General Morgan seemed to provide many grounds for despair and few for hope. When they returned to their quarters to study the capitulation document, they found it composed of a simple two-page unconditional surrender statement, plus eighteen pages of detailed appendices. The cold, matter-of-fact language of the unconditional surrender portion was a "deep shock"[126] to the Germans, who still harbored dreams that a face-saving formula would be included.

The appendices did contain one point to allay a major German fear. Since the Allies did not want large quantities of German arms to fall into the hands of the partisans, paragraph 6 directed the Germans to "stay put" until they were disarmed by Anglo-American forces.[127] Obviously this gave the Germans some comfort—no one in Axis uniform wished to surrender to the partisans—but it did not obviate the grave dangers to their mission and the safety of their comrades, which Schweinitz and Wenner found elsewhere in the appendices. Paragraph 8 of the instructions for German naval forces called for the surrender of Trieste, although ten days previously it had been explained to Washington and Caserta that the territory east of the Isonza River was no longer under Vietinghoff's command.[128] The provisions also included a ban on radio communication and all German troop movement after the capitulation. Transmission of surrender information to isolated units, as well as the acquisition of even basic food and medical supplies for the German army, was thereby rendered impossible.

The most serious threat, however, seemed to lie in paragraph 8 of the "Orders for German Land Forces," which read:

All personnel of the German Armed Forces shall be subject to such conditions and directions as may be prescribed by the Supreme Allied Commander. At the Supreme Allied Commander's discretion, some or all of such personnel *may*° be declared to be prisoners of war.[129]

What did this mean? Did the Allies intend to deny POW status to "all," or "some," of the men of Army Group C so that they could be exterminated, sterilized, or used as forced labor in Italy, America, or worst of all, in Siberia? Were the Allies planning to exclude large categories of men, such as the whole SS, from the prisoner of war protections of the Geneva Convention, to facilitate their punishment as war criminals? The language of the appendices gave no clue as to what lay behind the ominous statements in paragraph 8. They did not seem to be aimed especially at the Italian Fascist forces, because paragraph 1 stated that whenever the term "German land forces" was used in the document, it would be taken to mean all "Italian Republican military or paramilitary forces" as well.[130] So what was the point of paragraph 8?

With little time even to compare the German and English texts, Schweinitz and Wenner were forced to dash off to the second meeting with General Morgan at 9:00 P.M.[131] Schweinitz's suspicions were thoroughly aroused, however, and he was determined to discover at this session what fate the Anglo-Americans had in store for the men of Army Group C. In the meeting, the Germans faced the same Allied officers who had been present previously plus three additional Anglo-American generals, two secretaries, General Kislenko, and a Russian interpreter. Morgan explained that Kislenko and his interpreter were attending the meeting "as observers on behalf of the Russian staff." He then asked Schweinitz directly whether the Germans "accepted the terms of surrender or not." Schweinitz replied that "they had some important questions to raise in regard to the appendices," but, under prompting from Morgan and Lemnitzer, he granted the acceptability of the "General Instrument," that is, the two-page unconditional surrender statement.

Even as he did so, however, Schweinitz continued to press for explanations and changes in the appendices. The crucial item was paragraph 8, and Schweinitz immediately asked why such tortured language had been used. Speaking for Alexander, General Sir Brian Robertson, chief administrative officer at AFHQ, replied that although most of the men in the German

° Italics added.

armed forces "were soldiers pure and simple," the Germans had also used other "paramilitary personnel" and these persons "would be considered as displaced persons rather than prisoners of war." The first scruffy cat was thereby let out of the bag. The Anglo-Americans were going to seize the men in the auxiliary forces which the Germans had gathered up in Eastern Europe and send them back to their homelands. What awaited these Cossacks, Ukrainians, and Croatians once they were handed over to Soviet authorities did not require much imagination from anyone. But the Allies draped the sordid reality under the polite phrase "displaced persons." The Germans raised no objections, and Kislenko, of course, said nothing.

Schweinitz, however, did not believe that the Anglo-Americans had composed paragraph 8 merely to facilitate the transfer of a few Slavic auxiliary troops to Russia. He pressed Morgan by asking if every German and Italian man who was "regarded as a soldier" would also "be treated as a prisoner of war." Morgan replied that this was "what it would probably amount to but the Allies did not wish to tie themselves down at present." Schweinitz, echoed by Wenner, countered with the assertion that the German troops had been ordered to fight to the end, and if they were denied POW status, or even if they were given POW status only to be sent off "to America or some other place for an indefinite length of time," many of them would disobey the surrender order and carry out a fighting retreat into the mountains.

The German emissaries wanted an assurance that the troops "were not going to be sent away," that they would be kept in Italy for a short period and then returned to Germany. This was precisely what the Allies were not prepared to give them. Alexander and his staff knew that policies regarding postwar treatment of German troops had not been settled. At various levels, the Allied governments were considering the use of German troops as "labor reparations" for rebuilding areas devastated by the Nazis.[132] If a labor reparations system materialized, the bulk of the captured Germans might go where most of the damage had been done—to the East and into the hands of Soviet authorities. Morgan and his colleagues thus had to answer Schweinitz in a way that would be reassuring without closing the door on the possibility that the troops would be sent out of Italy. The Anglo-American generals gave Schweinitz one answer after another, while managing to tiptoe around the threatening words "forced labor," "the East," and "Russia." During it all, Kislenko sat among them silently watching.

First, General Lemnitzer attempted to get through the thicket by observing that "the detailed contents of these appendices" would not reach the German troops. The soldiers would only be told that "they would be treated honorably and well"; they would therefore probably obey, and the surrender would be effective.[133] What the Allies did with the German soldiers subsequently was not Schweinitz's problem and, Lemnitzer suggested, it should not trouble his conscience. General Morgan chimed in to say that the Allies would treat the troops "fairly . . . and would handle the affair correctly and properly." In Morgan's opinion Schweinitz need only leave the matter to "the well-known generosity and good faith of the British and Americans in such matters," and all would be well. Alexander's chief of staff went so far as to assert that even General Vietinghoff should not be concerned about what the future held in store for his soldiers, because if he did his best to carry out the surrender, "the Allies would not blame him if certain troops did not follow his orders."

To their credit, Schweinitz and Wenner refused to accept this Allied invitation that they shrug off their reponsibilities. They persisted with their questioning, and just as persistently, General Morgan and his colleagues refused to provide solid assurances. Alexander's chief of staff said that he "did not know where any individual soldier would go" after capitulation. It was possible that German soldiers "might go to England, North Africa, France, the United States, or might stay in Italy." Morgan did not include the ominous word Russia in his list, but he was also unwilling "to give a guarantee or make . . . promises" of any kind. If the German troops refused to capitulate, the Allied generals predicted that "they would merely be slaughtered." Their only choices were to be killed or to surrender, and in Morgan's view, "they would be well advised to surrender."

Still Schweinitz and Wenner were not silenced, and the SS man asked rhetorically what good it would do the Allies if they obtained "the signature of General von Vietinghoff on an instrument, the conditions of which he could not fulfill because his troops would not follow his orders." Schweinitz then came back to raise the earlier question, namely, did the Allies "have any real interest in sending the personnel captured in Italy away to somewhere else." Faced by this double assault, Morgan gave a bit of ground. He declared that the "prisoners would eventually be returned to Germany," and added the observation that "he would be surprised if it was a matter of years before they were repatriated." Beyond that, however, Morgan would not go, and he presented the Germans with the choice of either accepting paragraph 8 as it was written, or breaking off the surrender discussions. After consultation with Wenner, Schweinitz stated that "the conditions were accepted." Morgan thereupon made a "personal statement" declaring that:

> He believed, and he thought all the other Allied officers present believed, that owing to the shipping situation it was unlikely that any large number of German

prisoners would be transported far from Italy. That was not a promise but a statement. The German officers could use the statement as they liked.

On this reassuring note, the most serious altercation over the surrender terms came to an end. The Germans still harbored some fears; the question of deportation to Russia had not been faced, and the ominous topic of war criminals was not broached by either side. Apparently, Schweinitz deferred to Wenner on the latter point, and the SS man, following the lead of Wolff, held that it was best to allow the matter to slumber while hoping for the best. The Allies did not want to tie their hands or frighten the Germans on this question any more than they did on forced labor, so not a word was exchanged regarding German atrocities and no provision referring to the SS, Gestapo, or SD were included in the surrender terms.

Once the problems of paragraph 8 were circumvented, even though not clearly resolved, the remainder of the discussion in this session went swiftly. Schweinitz asked for, and received, permission for officers and military police to retain their side arms in order to "maintain discipline" up to the time when the troops would be made prisoners of war. The emissaries thereby obtained one of the token symbols of "honorable" treatment which were so important to General Vietinghoff. Schweinitz also convinced the Allies that they should relax some of the restrictions they had imposed on German use of the radio and Morgan further conceded that the German army had to have a limited right of mobility in order to obtain supplies. Consequently, "in clear" radio communication relating to the surrender was allowed and only "large-scale" troop movement was prohibited. Even the Trieste question was disposed of expeditiously, though Rear Admiral H. A. Packer, representing the British navy, was "visibly disappointed" that the ports of Trieste and Pola would not immediately fall into Anglo-American hands.[134] Bowing to the obvious, the Allies agreed that only the area under the authority of Army Group C could be covered by the surrender, and therefore the region east of the Isonzo River was excluded.

After tentative agreement had been reached on the appendices, Schweinitz asked permission to notify Vietinghoff of the main points in the surrender document. General Morgan instructed the colonel to send the introductory two-page unconditional surrender statement to Bolzano as quickly as possible so Vietinghoff could set the time at which hostilities would end. Morgan added that as soon as Vietinghoff had established a time for capitulation, Schweinitz and Wenner would be allowed to sign the surrender and the war in Italy would be over. Schweinitz agreed with this procedure, but added that he also had to inform Vietinghoff of certain points in the appendices, especially those "relating to prisoners of war and [the] retention of small arms." Morgan reluctantly acceded to this request but admonished Schweinitz to hurry, because long messages would delay the final surrender, and with the German front broken open, such delays were hardly "in the interests of the Germans themselves."[135]

When the meeting ended, Wenner and Schweinitz returned to their camp, accompanied by Gaevernitz. The OSS man urged the Germans to swallow their doubts and quickly dispatch a brief summary of the terms to Vietinghoff.[136] Wenner was ready to follow Gaevernitz's advice, but Schweinitz insisted that he had to inform his commander of all the points within the document that clashed with the verbal instructions he had received. Schweinitz's basic problem—one that he was not about to disclose to anyone—was that he had not been authorized to sign until Berlin fell or Italy had been cut off from the Reich.

Gaevernitz advanced one argument after another trying to wear down the colonel's resistance. Finally he appealed to Schweinitz's conscience by observing that every minute which passed would "cost the lives of hundreds of soldiers" and might mean "further destruction . . . further death" and "further air raids on German cities."[137] At this, Schweinitz weakened and near 4:00 A.M. on 29 April agreed to join Gaevernitz in hammering out a compromise message. The two-page telegram which resulted from their efforts contained a clipped summary of the unconditional surrender terms, leaving blank the time at which the capitulation would become effective. In the last paragraph, Schweinitz added a few brief "comments" for Vietinghoff. He reported that the men of the army group would go into captivity *(Gefangschaft)*—the complexities of the POW issue were not raised—and that he had failed to obtain a commitment that they could "remain in Italy." However, Schweinitz added that "due to the shortage of shipping," it was "doubted here" that they would be "transported" outside the peninsula. The only other solace that he could offer Vietinghoff was the clause which authorized officers and military police "to retain their side arms."[138]

Their main work done, and exhausted by the toil and strain, Wenner and Schweinitz went to bed. While the Germans slept, Gaevernitz took the draft telegram to General Lemnitzer who was "greatly encouraged" by it. Instructions were given to encode the message for transmission to Bern, and then Gaevernitz and Lemnitzer also tried to squeeze in a little nap. But hardly had they closed their eyes when they, together with the two Germans, were up again and off to meet with General Airey.[139]

What followed was, in Gaevernitz's words, an "informal meeting"; an especially appropriate phrase, because the surrender procedure was about to move from gravity to farce. After they had argued with the Germans for hours about the content of the message which should be rushed to General Vietinghoff, the Allied authorities discovered that they had no way to transmit it. They could not send it in the clear, because premature exposure would, in all probability, wreck the complicated arrangements before Vietinghoff had an opportunity to signal his acceptance. A message sent in German code was impossible—even presuming that Schweinitz knew the details of such a code and was authorized to use it—because the Allies, eternally suspicious, would be unable to check its actual content. Since the Allies' own radio communication with German headquarters was not yet established—the OSS operator who was scheduled to join Wolff at his headquarters had not yet reached Bolzano—no alternative remained except to send the message to Bern and have couriers deliver it overland to Vietinghoff. Given the chaos engendered in northern Italy by the Allied advance, a reply could not be expected from Vietinghoff for two or three days "at the earliest."[140]

Once these simple realities penetrated the consciousness of the Allied military leaders, they immediately scrapped the arrangements so laboriously made the day before. Airey bluntly told Schweinitz on the morning of 29 April that the game had been changed and that he would have to sign the surrender that very day without receiving his commander's prior approval.[141] The colonel was weighed down by his responsibilities and undoubtedly numbed by depression and lack of sleep. Late in the morning he resignedly agreed to end the tension and confusion by signing the capitulation.

Consequently at 2:00 on the afternoon of 29 April, the final surrender meeting took place in the special camp at Caserta.[142] The cast was substantially the same as for the previous formal session, except that three secondary Allied generals had been cut from the roster while another admiral, four more generals, and a colonel had been added. There was also present a small army of reporters and photographers who were allowed to record the event but were sworn to hold their stories until the terms of the surrender had been implemented. The capitulation instrument had been amended to state that hostilities would end on 2 May at 12:00 noon, Greenwich time. General Morgan, once more in charge, opened the proceedings by asking Schweinitz and Wenner if they were ready to sign the documents. The German plenipotentiaries, who were "shocked" by the Hollywood stage set on which they found themselves, still replied, matter of factly, that they were. With that, Morgan signed on behalf of Alexander. Before taking his turn to sign, Schweinitz declared that he wished to make a statment, repeating what he had said "at previous meetings." He reiterated that he had "received powers from General von Vietinghoff," but these were only valid within certain limits. "I am taking it on my own responsibility to exceed the limits set by General von Vietinghoff," the colonel declared, adding that, although the general would probably approve his action, he could not "give an absolute assurance to this effect." General Morgan replied, "We accept that." The two German plenipotentiaries then signed the capitulation.

With that act, the Sunrise surrender ceremonies were finally over, and in the eyes of the Allied military authorities, the war in Italy ended with them. Alexander reported to the Combined Chiefs that the capitulation formalities had proceeded with hardly a hitch. The field marshal conceded that Schweinitz had made a statement indicating that "in some respects"[143] he had exceeded his powers, but Alexander did not think that this "would affect the results."[144] The German army was broken, plenipotentaries had signed an unconditional surrender, and hostilities were to end on 2 May. Against all odds, the sun had actually risen, and within three days all the fruits of victory would fall into the hands of the Anglo-Americans.

Or so it seemed.

CHAPTER 7

Somewhere Between Sunrise and Sunset

W HETHER OR NOT the Sunrise surrender document would stop the fighting depended primarily on the ultimate course taken by the waves of intrigue, fear, and indecision which washed over German officials in northern Italy during the last week of April, 1945. When Wolff, Schweinitz, and Wenner first went to Switzerland on 23 April, they had been spokesmen for a reluctant coalition of German authorities, some of whose participants had lodged serious reservations when they agreed to cooperate. Vietinghoff and Hofer, in particular, had only gone along under pressure from the others and because they were led to believe that a deal with the Allies would protect their special interests. But the six days which elapsed between 23 and 29 April destroyed whatever bargaining position the Germans had and produced a capitulation document bearing little relation to the fantasies of Vietinghoff and Hofer. The partisan risings and the Allied advance had shredded the Axis zone of occupation. Then, in a series of downward steps, beginning with the discovery of the Combined Chiefs of Staff's cutoff order, and passing through Wolff's confinement in Villa Locatelli, Schweinitz and Wenner finally found themselves isolated and alone in Caserta. There, Wolff's negotiated surrender scenario evaporated, and the German emissaries were forced to accept whatever the Allies chose to give them.

These were the hard facts of life in the closing days of World War II, but many Germans in northern Italy were not ready to face them. The war had gone on too long, and there had been too many military and paper victories for Nazi officials to easily reconcile themselves to the notion that all was lost and that their dreams, their titles, and their offices were soon to be as nothing. They grasped at every straw and threw themselves with redoubled vigor into the customary Nazi game of factional squabble and intrigue. Nor were all their plots and maneuvers based solely on fantasy, for there were still a few real power factors left in the Nazi system. Substantial, if battered, combat units continued to fight desperately in Italy and elsewhere. The SS and Gestapo terror apparatus was also still intact and continued to freeze the hearts of civilians and soldiers alike. Throughout western Germany, soldiers who retreated too enthusiastically were being summarily executed, and their bodies were strung up on trees and telephone poles as warnings to those who believed that nazism had lost its bite. It was all very well for Karl Wolff to claim that his SS and SD subordinates would dutifully support a local surrender initiative, but other Germans knew that Wolff might be eliminated or overruled. Then these same SS and SD units would not hesitate to carry out orders to gun down those favoring capitulation as traitors to the Third Reich. As long as Hitler lived, his brutal fanaticism meant that countless directives commanding death and destruction could still come from Berlin. Until the Führer breathed his last, the old magic of his name and the charisma of his person would fire some men to implement any order.

In addition to terror and propaganda, the Nazis had also been careful to make more specific preparations for a fight to the finish. Among these was an order of 15 April from the High Command of the Armed Forces (OKW) establishing a system to continue resistance once the Allied advance cut Germany in two.[1] In this eventuality, Field Marshal Kesselring would take command over all military forces in the southern sector, including the Balkan, Italian, and Western fronts. On 25 April, spearheads of the U.S. First Army made contact with advance Russian units near Torgau on the Elbe, slicing Germany in half. The OKW notified Field Marshal Kesselring on the following day that the command structure laid out in the directive of 15 April had thereby become operative and all forces in the south, including Vietinghoff's Army Group C, were henceforth subject to his orders.[2]

Six weeks previously, those favoring a capitulation in northern Italy would have rejoiced at this development, but not on 27 April. Kesselring's conduct in the forgoing month and a half had not been such as to inspire confidence in his willingness to oversee a surrender operation. Many people had swapped surrender hints with the field marshal during this period, but all that had emerged was a note of wonder at Kesselring's ability to be coy and sphinxlike. If there was any real chance of rousing Kesselring to action, or at least to benign forbearance, it lay in a direct personal appeal from Wolff to the field marshal. The SS man, however, had gone off to Switzerland four days before, and those left behind had received no clear indication of what had happened to him, or whether a capitulation was actually in the making. Uncertain which way to turn, the four most prominent remaining Sunrise participants—Rahn, Dollmann, Hofer, and Vietinghoff—scurried off to Innsbruck early on 27 April to see if a meeting with their new military commander would produce an answer to the dilemma.[3] But none of them was ready to say frankly that the Obergruppenführer was, at that very moment, in Switzerland trying to surrender the Italian front in his name and theirs. They told the field marshal that Wolff had gone to Switzerland, but they enveloped the purpose of his trip in the now customary clouds of mumble about the need to explore a negotiated settlement via Dulles. In the course of the meeting, Gauleiter Hofer also seems to have attempted to enlighten everyone present by dancing nimbly about among various political and surrender possibilities. The Tyrolean Gauleiter was well suited for such a role because he was due to receive Hitler's appointment as political chief of the redoubt within the day, and was simultaneously participating both in Wolff's surrender project and Kaltenbrunner's scheme of releasing an "Austrian" capitulation balloon.

By the end of the conference, the Sunrise group had managed to elicit Kesselring's assent to the idea that Dollmann should go to Switzerland to talk with Dulles and discover what had happened to Wolff. But the many innuendoes and labored explanations which had surfaced during the meeting had also awakened the field marshal's suspicions, and henceforth he was less coy and more distrustful.[4] The Innsbruck gathering had, conversely, provided some of the surrender advocates with grounds to wonder how firmly Gauleiter Hofer was wedded to the Sunrise cause.

More confused and discouraged than when they had left, Vietinghoff, Dollmann, and Rahn returned to the ambassador's headquarters at Meran on the evening of 27 April and made another attempt to find some way out of the corner.[5] They were joined there by Vietinghoff's chief of staff, General Roettiger, who had long supported Wolff's surrender initiative and now emerged as the strongest military advocate of capitulation. General Vietinghoff, on the other hand, had lost most of his earlier modest enthusiasm for the project. While Rahn and Eugen Dollmann sank into the background, the two generals apparently engaged in a violent argument over whether to continue with the operation by sending Dollmann to Switzerland, or whether it was better to try abandoning it altogether. Ultimately Roettiger seems to have prevailed, and just as Dollmann was about to leave for the border with Vietinghoff's reluctant blessing, word came that Wolff had returned from Switzerland and was on his way to meet them.

At 2:00 A.M. on March 28, the German Sunrise group assembled in

Bolzano, and Wolff reported on his adventures.[6] He explained that although he was not sure of the precise terms which Schweinitz and Wenner would face in Caserta, there was little likelihood that they could obtain much of importance beyond unconditional surrender. Despite his efforts to portray this as the inevitable consequence of the many delays, the Allied advance, and the partisan risings, a number of Wolff's listeners were still bitterly disappointed. All but one of them, however, agreed to hold to their surrender commitment at least until Schweinitz and Wenner arrived with the capitulation document.

Gauleiter Hofer, though, found such a course unacceptable. Believing with some justice that he had been deceived by Wolff, he quarreled with most of those present and clung to his dream of establishing what the Obergruppenführer contemptuously called his "Maria Theresia Reich" in the Tyrol.[7] Hofer's fantasies were extreme even by Nazi standards, but he was still a force to be reckoned with. His appointment as political chief of the redoubt made Kesselring his immediate colleague, and he had retained close ties with the ever-dangerous Kaltenbrunner. Unable to obtain satisfaction from the supporters of the Sunrise project, Hofer angrily walked out of the Bolzano meeting in the early morning hours of 28 April.

For a day and a half, the remaining members of the Sunrise group gritted their teeth while waiting for the return of Schweinitz and Wenner. In this same period Hofer sat simmering in Innsbruck. Then in the course of 29 April, the Gauleiter received another report indicating that Vietinghoff and Wolff were working against his interests, and he exploded. The incident which ignited Hofer was an outgrowth of the activities and fears of an Italian partisan leader in the Tyrol named Dr. De Angelis.[8] Although partisan forces in most sections of the north had already achieved substantial domination over the towns and countryside by 28 April, this was not true in the Tyrol. SS and German army units were unusually strong there and the Allied offensive had not penetrated the region in force. De Angelis was afraid that the Nazi occupation authorities, backed by the large German-speaking population, might seize this last opportunity to massacre the Italian citizenry, thereby establishing a Germanic claim to the region by murderous default. In order to head off a possible bloodbath after clashes between the police and Italian civilians, and perhaps also to establish a precedent for partisan participation in the future administration of the region, De Angelis offered the Germans a deal. If the Nazi authorities would agree to the formation of a temporarily mixed partisan-German administration, he promised to hold off massive partisan attacks on German installations and lines of communication. To insure that both the partisans and the Germans played fair, De Angelis proposed that their joint rule be supervised by a representative from the Fifteenth Army Group, the Allied force which would soon control the region.

On 27 April, De Angelis had presented his plan to a representative of the top police official in Innsbruck, SS Brigadeführer Brunner, a man who had close connections with many of the major figures in our story, including Wolff, Kaltenbrunner, and Hofer. Brunner was favorably impressed by De Angelis's suggestion and sent him on to Wolff. During the afternoon and evening of 28 April, the Obergruppenführer and the partisan leader explored the possibility of a joint administration. Wolff, irritated by De Angelis's assertiveness and wary of additional deals with the enemy, initially rejected the idea. Only when De Angelis warned that he would bear the responsibility for any bloodshed, did Wolff forward the idea to the army authorities. This time, paradoxically, General Vietinghoff's caution produced decisive action. The general was afraid that the army could not maintain its line of communication or its rear area installations if the Tyrolean partisans launched an all-out assault. In order to avert such a catastrophe, and also to prevent "racial strife,"[9] Vietinghoff urged Wolff to agree to the mixed administration proposal. On the morning of the twenty-ninth Wolff did so, after stressing that the army bore "full responsibility" for the arrangement, while he only wanted to meet their wishes and "save blood."[10]

This was all very well, but apparently due to a series of oversights, no one remembered to inform Hofer. When the Gauleiter, who now saw himself as the political potentate of the whole redoubt region, learned of the arrangement in the course of 29 April, he believed that the Sunrise gang had tricked him twice in thirty-six hours—first in the Bolzano talks, and then by this deal with De Angelis. Understandably, his anger and desire for revenge were boundless, and he struck out in all directions. He apparently ordered repressive measures taken against any of De Angelis's supporters who ventured into the open, and on the following day, this tough stand seemingly caused the German police in the Tyrolean town of Merano to shoot down Italian civilians, among them some children.[11] Hofer also phoned Kaltenbrunner and informed him of all "the secrets" of Sunrise, including the fact that Wenner and Schweinitz had gone to Caserta to sign a capitulation.[12] Kaltenbrunner relayed the message to Hitler's bunker in Berlin, but due to some unexplained communications failure, the message was never received, and Hitler's suicide on the next day spared Wolff the dire fate which would surely have followed if the cable, or a confirming message, had reached its destination.

Hofer's thirst for revenge was nonetheless amply satisfied. When he reported to Field Marshal Kesselring that General Vietinghoff had made a deal with De Angelis, and that the Sunrise group was trying to conclude a separate peace at Caserta, the field marshal was furious. Kesselring had become increasingly suspicious about developments in Italy since the Innsbruck meeting two days earlier, especially because Army Group C had retreated precipitously, failing to obey his orders to coordinate its movements with those of Army Group E to the east.[13] Believing that he had been deceived by the Sunrise plotters, the field marshal immediately ordered Vietinghoff to have no dealings with the enemy. Then, still on the evening of 29 April, without pausing to talk with either Wolff or the general, Kesselring peremptorily sacked Vietinghoff and Roettiger and replaced them with two new generals, Schulz and Wenzel.[14]

On the following morning, Hofer, Vietinghoff, Schulz, and Wenzel were summoned to confer with Kesselring at Innsbruck.[15] At this meeting, the field marshal and a gloating Hofer were in full charge. Kesselring extracted the whole story of Sunrise from Vietinghoff, including the information that Wenner and Schweinitz had gone to Caserta to sign a secret surrender and were momentarily expected to return to northern Italy with a signed capitulation document. Flatly rejecting the whole proceeding, Kesselring placed Vietinghoff under house arrest and told Schulz and Wenzel to go to Italy, to make Army Group C fight, and to have no dealings with the enemy. The field marshal then notified both Kaltenbrunner and the OKW of what had transpired and of the corrective actions which he had taken.

On any other day such a report surely would have produced an instant order for the arrest, and perhaps the summary execution, of all those involved, but 30 April was no ordinary day. Hitler had finally recognized that the battle of Berlin was hopelessly lost and had spent the morning and early afternoon winding up his affairs and preparing for his suicide. Compared with the impending death of the "chief," all other business seemed of minor importance in Berlin, and action was delayed on many vital matters—including Kesselring's report—until after Hitler's Walther pistol and the poison finally did their work at 3:30 P.M.

While this momentous development unfolded, Sunrise was allowed to remain an Italian affair. Generals Schulz and Wenzel went to take charge of the remains of Army Group C in Bolzano, where they were welcomed and briefed by General Roettiger, who had been minding the store while Vietinghoff met his end at Innsbruck. After informing the incoming generals of the military situation, Roettiger was scheduled to follow in Vietinghoff's footsteps to Innsbruck, and then presumably on to house arrest and an ominous future. But apparently no direct order demanding that he immediately go to Innsbruck arrived, and Roettiger was obviously not in any particular hurry. He lingered in Bolzano hoping that some miracle might save Sunrise and its devotees, and in the course of the afternoon of 30 April, the first bugle blast from the relief party was heard: Schweinitz and Wenner had crossed the border and were on their way to Bolzano.[16]

Wolff tried to use this information as a bridge to start working on the new leaders of Army Group C, generals Schulz and Wenzel, but they refused to talk with him.[17] So throughout the evening of 30 April, Roettiger and Wolff could do nothing except to sit and wait until Schweinitz and Wenner reached Bolzano. Shortly after midnight the exhausted emissaries arrived, and in the early hours of 1 May they described for their colleagues what had happened in Caserta as well as their slow and frustrating 1½-day return trip from Allied headquarters. Wolff and Roettiger were hardly overjoyed by the harsh terms of the surrender agreement, but they were even more disconcerted by the news that the capitulation was supposed to go into effect in less than thirty-six hours.

Wolff had thereby reached the ultimately ironic crisis of his surrender endeavors. After maintaining Anglo-American interest through every conceivable twist and turn for seven weeks, he had actually managed to entice the Western command into accepting the capitulation of the tattered remains of Axis northern Italy as if they were the real thing. Then, at the final moment, he appeared unable to get the agreement fulfilled on schedule by his German colleagues. No public announcement of Hitler's death was made in the thirty hours following 3:30 P.M. on 30 April due to the intrigues of Goebbels and Bormann, and in the interim the Nazi system held together, freezing everyone in his existing position. Vietinghoff no longer held his command, Hofer had turned openly hostile to Sunrise, and the generals in direct charge of Army Group C would not even speak to Wolff. Worst of all, Field Marshal Kesselring, the man once heralded as a miracle worker, was in command, but he had now revealed himself as vehemently opposed to Wolff's capitulation adventures. It is a measure of Wolff's presence of mind and belief in his mission that he—and Roettiger—did not give up at this point and either kill themselves or run for their lives. The very uncertainty of the final days of the Third Reich made every action potentially more dangerous, yet the two men, supported by Schweinitz and Wenner, resolved to try to push the secret surrender through to its end.

Wolff took the first step along this route by trying to persuade the commanders of the two main constituent units of Army Group C, generals Lemelsen and Herr, of the Fourteenth and Tenth armies respectively, to support the Sunrise capitulation. In a predawn telephone conversation, Wolff apparently obtained the generals' agreement to the proposition that the military situation was hopeless, but he did not receive carte blanche to take any action necessary to get the surrender fulfilled.[18] Yet that was what the situation actually called for, because Roettiger had decided on the extreme step of arresting Schulz and Wenzel in order to force through the capitulation. Accordingly, at 7:00 A.M. on 1 May, Schulz and Wenzel were taken into "honorary custody" by an army unit, and communications between northern Italy and the Reich were cut by General Kempf, one of Roettiger's colleagues on the staff of Army Group C.[19] Roettiger then telephoned Lemelsen and Herr and asked them to help him implement the surrender, only to discover that these two were so paralyzed by the rules of obedience and good form that they would not act so long as their superior, General Schulz, was under arrest. This apparently baffled Roettiger, but Wolff was undismayed, and he shoved General Pohl of the Luftwaffe forward to work on Lemelsen. But this failed too, and though Roettiger and Pohl seem to have lost their nerve at this point, Wolff kept pushing on. For two hours he urged Schulz and Wenzel to help him implement the capitulation, but even though the generals were compelled to speak with him since they were prisoners, his eloquence did not make them drop their demand that they be released before they entered into serious discussions. Finally Wolff managed to get them grudgingly to admit that he had acted on the basis of "honorable motives," and that if released, they would participate in a general conference to explore what should be done.[20]

This was not much to go on, but Wolff had no other choice, and following the release of Schulz and Wenzel, a meeting was held in Schulz's Bolzano office at 6:00 P.M.[21] The commander of Army Group C chaired the marathon session, which included among its participants Wolff, Wenzel, Pohl, Roettiger, and the commanders of the Tenth and Fourteenth armies, generals Lemelsen and Herr. The latter immediately reported that the situation at the front was catastrophic—Herr's Tenth Army having been virtually destroyed—and that something had to be done quickly. Schulz and Wenzel conceded that there remained no rational military reason to prolong resistance, but they still contended that they could not order the troops to lay down their arms in conformity with the Sunrise surrender agreement without Kesselring's approval. The others present argued passionately that the surrender had to be implemented in less than twenty-four hours and that it should be done with, or without, Kesselring. But Wenzel and Schulz refused to budge; unless the field marshal agreed, they would not order the army group to capitulate.

Under Wolff's prompting, a series of telephone calls was made in an effort to reach Kesselring, who was away from his headquarters. As if to round out the Sunrise drama, the only person in the office of commander in chief south, with whom Schulz and Wenzel were able to make contact, was Kesselring's chief of staff, General Westphal. Westphal was sympathetic to the aims and motives of the callers, but as on every other occasion since the beginning of Sunrise, he refused to take any surrender responsibility. After advising the Bolzano group to wait patiently until the field marshal returned to headquarters, Westphal rang off. Wolff and the others then tried again to persuade Schulz to act on his own initiative, but in vain.

At this juncture Wolff apparently came up with the idea of completing Sunrise's journey back to its origins by calling General Blaskowitz (at this point commander of the Twenty-fifth Army in Holland) in hope that he would persuade someone or other to allow the implementation of a surrender in Italy.[22] Blaskowitz succeeded in keeping his behavior as consistent as had Westphal, and only took a brief moment to tell Wolff that he would not get involved in the question of an Italian surrender at all.

Having come back to ground zero by 9:30 P.M., the group received a jolting reminder that time was running out. A message arrived from Alexander addressed to General Vietinghoff which stated that his emissaries had signed an honorable capitulation and urged him to fulfill its terms at 2:00 P.M. on 2 May.[23] Actually, after twenty-four hours of euphoria following the signing of the capitulation, Caserta had begun to worry, and on 30 April this message had been sent to Bolzano. But there had been no reply, except a couple of cryptic messages from Wolff asserting, among other things, that "centers of resistance" should not be attacked, because the "surrender will be arranged from here."[24] Becoming more anxious, Alexander had therefore repeated the message to Vietinghoff, and this was the communication which arrived in the middle of the Bolzano meeting on May 1. The Germans' failure to reply directly to Caserta's earlier message was due to another Allied communications breakdown. An OSS operator had reached Wolff's headquarters as early as 29 April, long before Schweinitz and Wenner returned to Caserta, and through this line of communication, the Germans were able to send messages to Alexander. But because of an almost incredible oversight, the radio operator had not been provided with keys to the code which Caserta was using to send messages to Bolzano, and until Schweinitz and Wenner arrived, the Germans were unable to decipher Alexander's dispatches.[25] Not until Alexander's prodding reminder reached them at 9:30 P.M. did Wolff and the others understand what Caserta was saying. Less than seventeen hours were left until the capitulation was supposed to go into effect, and the Allies were demanding to know whether the Germans were going through with the deal or not.

The message goaded Wolff into action once more, and he fired off a reply to Caserta thanking Alexander for his patience and stating that "a decision will follow within the hour."[26] The SS man then telephoned General Westphal and demanded that the chief of staff either act himself or authorize someone in Bolzano to issue an order that the troops should lay down their arms by the 2:00 P.M. deadline. Westphal promised that Kesselring himself would call by 10:00 P.M. with an authoritative answer and then hung up. But 10:00 P.M. came and went without word from the field marshal, and the tension continued to mount in Bolzano.[27]

The old arguments for capitulation were dragged out once more, and Wolff added that it was essential, in the moment of defeat, that the Allies not be given new cause to believe that Germans always broke their word or failed to fulfill their commitments.[28] Still no reply came from Kesselring, and with only sixteen hours now left until the deadline, the Bolzano group sat frozen in an impasse. Finally, shortly before 10:30 P.M., General Herr turned to his adjutant and matter of factly directed him to order the men of his decimated Tenth Army to lay down their arms at 2:00 P.M. on the following day. With that the dam was broken and a flood of similar orders flowed through as Wolff, Pohl, and Lemelsen directed their units to meet the capitulation deadline of the Sunrise surrender.[29]

For a moment Generals Schulz and Wenzel hung back, still claiming that they could not approve such a course without Kesselring's permission. But then, like an act of deliverance, a report arrived that Admiral Doenitz, Hitler's successor designate, had just announced that the Führer was dead. Wolff expressed the feeling of the whole group when he later stated that at the news of Hitler's end "we breathed a sigh of relief."[30] All those present had followed Hitler through thick and thin. The generals had sworn an oath of personal loyalty to him, and Wolff was still wearing a beltbuckle inscribed with the SS motto, "My honor is loyalty." But in April–May, 1945, Hitler had become a roadblock in the way of those seeking to lay the basis for a German future, and even his closest followers greeted his death less with sorrow than with a sense of liberation.

Having been freed from their oath by the Führer's death, and also in consequence, less afraid of reprisal, Schulz and Wenzel acknowledged that it was a "necessity" for someone to take immediate action to implement the surrender.[31] They still refused to do it themselves without Kesselring's consent, but they made no effort to prevent the secondary commanders from doing so. With harmony fairly well restored by this arrangement, the conference broke up at approximately 11:30 P.M. and Wolff, Roettiger, Pohl, Lemelsen, and Herr drifted over to the SS man's headquarters. There, shortly before midnight, they learned that the Luftwaffe High Command had ordered Pohl seized, and a few minutes later a message arrived calling for the arrest of Vietinghoff, Roettiger, Schweinitz, and General Kempf, the officer who had cut communications with the Reich when Schulz and Wenzel had been put in confinement.[32] Wolff and his companions assumed that they had been betrayed and that this action was engineered by Schulz, Wenzel, and Kesselring. Actually, it was only the delayed response of Kesselring's headquarters and Berlin to the discovery of the original surrender plot and to the coup which Roettiger had carried out when he arrested Schulz and Wenzel. But no one in Bolzano was in a position to know this, and Wolff, Lemelsen, and Herr assumed that since they, along with Pohl, were the ones who had actually sent out surrender implementation orders, directives for their arrest would soon follow. Believing there was no time to delay, they agreed to try to put through the surrender in any case, and then they scattered, each man heading for the safety of the guard units in his own headquarters.

From behind the shield of a small SS contingent, Wolff sought to save the operation and its supporters by a direct appeal to the Allies. In a cable to Alexander, he reported that "in consequence of a betrayal by Hofer,"[33] Vietinghoff had been arrested, and that Pohl, Lemelsen, Herr, and Wolff himself had been compelled to order the "cessation of hostilities" on their own responsibility. Consequently an order "for our arrest" had been issued, and the SS man appealed to Alexander for "an action with parachute and/or armored troops in the area [of] Bolzano" to save the surrender as well as the "approximately 160 prominent hostages" held there, and, of course, Wolff and his Sunrise friends.

Aside from producing momentary consternation in Caserta, this message had no significant effect. Events on the German side were moving so rapidly that the Allies could not have influenced them even in the unlikely event that they had been willing to undertake new Sunrise adventures. Shortly after sending his appeal to Caserta, Wolff received a telephone call from an angry Marshal Kesselring who had just returned to his headquarters to discover that Hitler was dead and that the secondary commanders in Italy had bypassed Schulz and ordered a surrender. For two hours, Kesselring poured out all his bitterness and rage on Wolff, the man he rightly concluded was primarily responsible for the latter development.[34] He castigated the SS man for stabbing other German units in the back by arranging a special surrender, but at the start of the prolonged argument he asked Wolff if the terms of the capitulation would allow Army Group C "to return to the Reich, and together with Anglo-American units continue the fight against Russia?" The Obergruppenführer dismissed such notions as "entirely out of the question" at this stage of the war, and hammered back at the field marshal with his usual contention that the most important consideration at the moment of defeat was for the Nazis to act in a way that would help them find a soft spot in the hearts of the Anglo-Americans. To drive this point home, the SS man stressed that it ill behooved any of them to be forced to capitulate in a few days after repudiating another solemn German promise such as that made by Schweinitz and Wenner in Caserta. In Wolff's view, Kesselring might bemoan the fact, but he was stuck with the choice of either allowing the German forces in Italy to surrender honorably, or trying to quash the order and risk chaos—that frightening word—while convincing the victorious Allies that they had been tricked once more by the dastardly Germans.

Perhaps by the end of this conversation, Kesselring had made up his mind, but if so, he did not give Wolff the satisfaction of telling him that he had won. Not until a half hour later, at approximately 4:30 A.M., and only after General Schulz had also urged him to sanction the capitulation, did the field marshal formally yield and give the Sunrise surrender his blessing.[35] He then restored General Vietinghoff to his command in order to smooth the surrender implementation, but even so, he asked that the public announcement of the capitulation be withheld for forty-eight hours, presumably because he wanted time to ease his relations with the other German commanders and with the new head of the Third Reich, Admiral Doenitz. At 10:00 A.M. a message was sent from Bolzano to Caserta over the OSS radio link, informing Alexander that no "parachute troops" were needed because Kesselring had confirmed the surrender.[36] This message also forwarded the field marshal's request that the capitulation be kept secret for two more days. Immediately thereafter, Vietinghoff notified Allied headquarters that he had been restored to his command, and with a self-confidence bordering on brazenness, asked why the Allies were "still shooting."[37]

Alexander and his aides were not about to be put off by the tone of the German communications, or by any special requests. The Allied supreme commander went through the motions of trying to obtain the Combined Chiefs' approval for a forty-eight-hour delay for publicity, but he was so enraptured by the news that the surrender would actually be implemented that nothing else really mattered to him.[38] When, shortly before noon, Caserta radio began to pick up uncoded commands from German officers to their troops, ordering them to lay down their arms at 2:00 P.M., Alexander quickly dropped the idea of a delay for publicity. Afraid that the Western powers might lose a "press scoop" if someone else heard the German messages, Alexander decided to release the news of this first major capitulation of a German army group at 6:00 P.M. on 2 May.[39]

In the early evening, the capitulation was announced simultaneously in Washington and London. Churchill interrupted a session of parliament to proclaim that secret diplomacy had capped Alexander's heroic struggle, and the long-sought victory had finally been realized. In Washington, amid public announcements and accolades, Secretary of War Stimson noted hopefully in his diary that the capitulation had set "a tremendous example for the rest of Germany . . . and cannot help having a tremendous effect on the people who are trying to hold out."[40]

In Berlin on this same day, another capitulation struck an equally sharp blow at the German will to resist. After weeks of bitter fighting, the battle which Hitler had predicted would determine the course of the war was over. During the early morning hours the garrison laid down its arms and the German capital passed into the hands of the Red Army. The surrenders in Caserta and Berlin produced an immediate wave of new German capitulation proposals. Doenitz dispatched Admiral Freideberg to Montgomery on 2 May, offering to surrender to the Anglo-Americans all the German forces facing the Russians. But the Western powers were unwilling even to touch so politically volatile a proposal, and the admiral was firmly rebuffed. Then on the next day, Kesselring inquired of Alexander what procedure he should follow to surrender all German forces on the Western front. Nothing came of this query either, but on 4 May, Admiral Friedeberg returned to Montgomery's headquarters and surrendered the Nazi units in northwest Germany, Denmark, and Holland. Doenitz was forced to deal decisively with the general disintegration, and bowing to the inevitable, on 6 May he authorized the German High Command to surrender all forces unconditionally. In hastily arranged ceremonies at Rheims on 7 May, and in Berlin on 9 May, the capitulation formalities were performed to the satisfaction of the Anglo-Americans and the Soviets respectively, and the Second World War in Europe was ended.

The Grand Alliance had managed to outlast nazism, but as the twin capitulation ceremonies of 7 May and 9 May made clear, common action had been very difficult. Much hauling and tugging was required during the closing days to maintain even an appearance of Allied unity. Some of the hottest spots in the coming cold war had begun to flare up in the no-man's land being overrun by Allied armies in April–May, 1945. As the forces of East and West drew closer to each other, serious political issues arose at one point after another in central Europe. There were bitter thoughts and often bitter words over Berlin, western Czechoslovakia, and the occupation zone lines for Germany and Austria.

In Italy too, the Sunrise surrender did not enable the Anglo-Americans to avoid all East-West territorial controversies. Although there were no serious problems over the political future of the lands directly occupied by Army Group C—this whole region obviously belonged to the Italian state—the territory immediately to the east was another matter. During the last days of April, while the German participants in Sunrise were concentrating on how to implement the surrender, the focus of many Anglo-Americans had already swung toward the Adriatic seaport of Trieste.[41]

The knotted and tangled question of Trieste, and the surrounding territory of Venezia Giulia, extended far beyond the scope of Operation Sunrise, but its fate was closely interwoven with the Bern talks and the Caserta surrender. The region had been sought by Italy every since the Risorgimento, and was ultimately acquired after World War I. The population of the region was mixed: largely Italian in the towns and western coastal areas, predominantly Slovene and Croat in the east and the interior. During the interwar period, the Yugoslav government had laid claim to most of the territory, and later when the Germans came to occupy it, Tito's partisans infiltrated the zone, at times clashing with the Italian partisan bands operating in the same area. Venezia Giulia thus presented a special problem for any Allied occupation system. The Anglo-Americans feared that Italian partisans might get out of control everywhere in Italy at the moment of liberation, but they were doubly concerned to gain quick military authority over Venezia Giulia, in order to avoid clashes between Italians and Yugoslavs. The strategic position of Trieste also dictated a speedy occupation, because one of the main Allied lines of communication for the advance into Austria ran through the port. The other route to the north, crossing the Brenner Pass, was easier for the Germans to defend and would require supplies to make long journeys overland, even after it had been secured by the Allies. The Anglo-American military leaders therefore believed that once the bulk of Italy was in their hands, it was imperative that they get immediate control of Trieste and the Venezia Giulia communications route.

If the surrender document signed by Schweinitz and Wenner had given Trieste to the Western powers, as all those involved in the Sunrise operation ardently desired, there would have been little problem. But as we have seen, the region east of the Isonzo River had been transferred to the command of Germany's Army Group E in mid-April, and was therefore excluded from the Sunrise capitulation. To get the prize, the Allies needed to exploit the vacuum left by the capitulation of Vietinghoff's Army Group C and run for Trieste, as well as for the Brenner Pass. No sooner had the German emissaries signed the capitulation on 29 April than Alexander issued directions to General Mark Clark's Fifteenth Army Group saying that if the "Germans intend to carry out the surrender . . . the earliest possible seizure of [the] whole Brenner Route and [the] occupation of Trieste . . . remain tasks of [the] highest priority. . . ."[42] Clark needed little prompting, because the major German forces left in northeastern Italy lay along these same routes, and in the three days that elapsed before the surrender became effective on 2 May, units of the Fifteenth Army Group moved to the edge of both the Brenner Pass and Trieste.

On the day the surrender became effective, Clark's men, who were approaching the Brenner Pass from the south, were met by advance forces from Eisenhower's command which had struck through the pass from the north. The whole Brenner route was thereby in Allied hands, and the great Anglo-American nightmare of a last-ditch Nazi stand in an Alpine stronghold was laid to rest.

A simple military operation had solved the clearly defined military problem of the Brenner Pass. The Trieste issue, however, was neither clearly defined nor purely military. Before the German emissaries had signed the capitulation, in fact before they had even arrived in Caserta, the American diplomatic representative at Allied Mediterranean headquarters began pointing toward political advantages which could accrue from a dash to the head of the Adriatic. While stressing the need for tact in order to avoid "giving the impression that we are attempting to interfere in purely military matters," Alexander Kirk urged Acting Secretary of State Joseph Grew° on 27 and 28 April to press for a rapid advance on Trieste.[43] "If negotiations ... should be brought to a successful conclusion in the next days," Kirk cabled on the 27th, "the release of Allied forces in Italy for other tasks could be conducive to implementing the position we have been maintaining in regard to Venezia Giulia." Kirk not only wanted the Fifteenth Army Group to seize Trieste because it was a major strategic prize but also because quick military action might offset one of the more serious Anglo-American political blunders of World War II. Despite the importance of the area—the serious Italo-Yugoslav rivalries there and the broader question of Western relations with Tito—virtually nothing had been done to smooth the way for an Allied occupation at the end of the war. There had been no serious negotiations with the Soviets or the Yugoslavs about the fate of Venezia Giulia, and what is even more remarkable, the British and Americans had not even agreed among themselves on what they desired in the area, or how they proposed to get it. Kirk wanted Clark to head for Trieste with extra speed on 29 April, because the general's major task was more to create an Anglo-American policy than it was to implement one.

This dangerous state of affairs had arisen directly from the difficulty of making the labyrinthine Anglo-American command system provide clear answers to political-military problems. During the early stages of the occupation of Italy, State Department officials had recognized the explosiveness of the Venezia Giulia question and recommended that the region be put

° Secretary of State Stettinius was at the San Francisco United Nations conference during this whole period.

under an Allied military government as soon as possible, leaving its ultimate fate to be settled at a postwar peace conference. Speaking for the British government, Churchill hesitantly agreed to this proposal in the fall of 1944;[44] but the directives for its implementation were left hanging for months, primarily because of latent British opposition.[45] The government in London preferred not to approach the problem as an offshoot of Anglo-American operations in Italy but on the basis of the special relationship it was trying to develop with Tito. By providing military aid for his forces, and by favoring Yugoslav territorial demands against Italy, Britain hoped to woo Tito to the Western side, or at least to a position of neutrality between East and West.[46] Building on the so-called "fifty-fifty" agreement which Stalin and Churchill reached in Moscow in October, 1944, whereby their two countries would share equal influence in postwar Yugoslavia, Britain attempted to make a proposal on Venezia Giulia favorable to Yugoslavia at the Yalta conference of January, 1945. But the heavy agenda at Yalta thwarted the British effort, and Foreign Secretary Eden's suggestion that Yugoslavia be granted all territory east of the Italian border of 1914 was not even discussed by the delegations of the Big Three.[47]

Balked at the summit, and wary of American opposition to any Western political agreement which would prejudice the final disposition of Venezia Giulia, the British government charged Field Marshal Alexander with the task of reaching a direct understanding with Tito. If the field marshal could get Tito to agree that Alexander should occupy the areas necessary for his operations, while leaving the remainder of the region to Yugoslavia, Britain's pro-Yugoslavian policy could be implemented in the familiar form of military necessity.[48] State Department opponents of a political division of Venezia Giulia would find it difficult to object should the military authorities in the field produce a de facto division of the territory as part of their operational planning.

Pursuant to orders from London, Alexander met with Tito in Belgrade in February, 1945. But the field marshal was reluctant to plunge headlong into the political thicket. He made no mention of Eden's idea that Venezia Giulia be divided to benefit Yugoslavia, nor did he make it clear to Tito that the British and American governments had agreed in principle that the entire region should be placed under Allied military government pending a final postwar settlement. All Alexander told Tito was that the Western powers would need the use of Trieste and the lines of communication into Austria— a requirement which "at first sight" would apparently involve the occupation of all territories west of Italy's 1939 frontier.[49] When Tito objected and tried to raise the question of who would ultimately possess the region, Alexander backed away, stressing that he was only concerned with military operations, and that in any event, his talk with Tito was purely "explora-tory."[50]

This muddled encounter was the only wartime occasion on which the Western powers attempted to deal with Tito over Venezia Giulia, and as a result, there would be much future difficulty arising from the confusion and misunderstanding generated there. Tito was not left with an impression of British generosity or support for Yugoslavia; rather, he gained a sense of London's hesitancy and caution. The Yugoslav leader seems to have conclud-ed that the Western Allies expected the final disposition of the region to depend chiefly on whose forces occupied it at the time of German withdraw-al, and that they would yield to Yugoslav claims, if confronted with a fait accompli. For his part, Alexander returned to Caserta believing that he had "made a deal"[51] with Tito. He seems to have felt that he had tiptoed past the political issues tormenting London and Washington and obtained Tito's agreement to the proposition that the Anglo-Americans should secure what-ever territory they thought necessary for their military operations. Actually, the vague fencing in Belgrade gave Alexander no legitimate grounds to believe that he had obtained Tito's consent to anything, and no sooner was he back in Caserta than he learned that the Anglo-American political controver-sies over Venezia Giulia were far from over. Members of his own staff, including Harold Macmillan, decried the field marshal's readiness to make a purely military agreement with Tito, and the State Department representa-tive, Alexander Kirk, was most outspoken in his criticism. Contending that there was no evidence to suppose that the USSR would back Yugoslavia, Kirk opposed any "special facilities" being offered to Tito in Venezia Giulia. "Instead of asking Tito what he would like," Kirk contended on 2 March that "we should tell Tito what we intend to do in that area and state that we expect his cooperation."[52]

The call for a tough stand on Venezia Giulia made by Kirk and his State Department colleagues came at a time when the British government was having second thoughts about its policy of championing Yugoslavia. During February and March, London received much evidence of anti-British feeling among Yugoslav leaders. In his public statements, Tito consistently played down the importance of British support, while strengthening his ties with the Soviet Union, and in April, Yugoslavia and the USSR signed a treaty pledging close postwar cooperation for twenty years. In this same period, the royalist members of the united Yugoslav government, men who had only been accepted by Tito after long negotiations promoted by London, were gradually deprived of their authority, thereby completely undermining Britain's efforts. To cap matters, Belgrade became more overtly expansionist, not only in Venezia Giulia, but also by asking for a zone of occupation in Austria and for the transfer of some Austrian territory to Yugoslavia.

So adversely did these developments affect the mood in London that on Churchill's prompting, the Cabinet began to discuss the advisability of cutting off all military aid to Yugoslavia. By the second week of March, Churchill confided to Eden that he had lost his "relish" for Yugoslavia and wondered whether it would not be better "to back Italy against Tito," thereby trying to "save Italy from the Bolshevik pestilence."[53] For the moment cooler British heads prevailed and supplies continued to flow to Yugoslavia until 2 May.[54] But even so, London's honeymoon with Tito was clearly ending by the second week of April, and the British shift at last made it possible for an Anglo-American coordinating committee to complete a draft directive for Allied military government in Venezia Giulia. The plan called for Alexander to have authority over nearly all of the area, with actual administration left to the "local authorities found in these regions[,] of whatever nationality." Soviet and Yugoslav acceptance and cooperation were to be secured by the Anglo-American governments, but in the meantime Alexander was to go ahead and establish military government "if military reasons require implementation of the plan before Yugoslav and Soviet concurrence has been obtained."[55]

Only if the Western Allies had acted rapidly and resolutely would this scheme have had a chance of success. The planning committee did forward its recommendation expeditiously, but the Combined Chiefs dallied, and in the interval, events in Italy moved with lightning speed. On 20 April, Tito's forces reached the 1939 Italo-Yugoslav frontier, then moved in the direction of Fiume. When confronted by strong German resistance before that city, they altered course and struck toward Trieste. Further to the west, the Anglo-American forces crossed the Po on 23 April, and on the same day, the German Sunrise team of Schweinitz and Wolff arrived in Switzerland claiming that Army Group C was ready to lay down its arms.

The decisive moment had come, and Alexander was forced to face it without instructions from the Combined Chiefs. In emergency meetings held at Caserta on 24 and 25 April, his deputy chief of staff, the American general Lyman Lemnitzer (a man who played a major role in many aspects of Sunrise) proposed that all Venezia Giulia be occupied, and an Allied military government be established "in the usual way."[56] This suggestion paralleled the recommendation of the Allied coordinating committee which was at that moment awaiting action by the Combined Chiefs. But Lemnitzer's proposal was flatly rejected by Alexander and his British political adviser, Harold Macmillan. Supported by some of his American, and all of his British, staff officers as well as Macmillan, Alexander concluded that the risks of such a course were too great, and that everything possible had to be done to avoid offending Tito or "drifting into a state of war" with him. Once again, a senior British official tipped toward Yugoslavia rather than Italy—conceding de facto control of most of Venezia Giulia to the Yugoslavs—but in this case it is not possible to say with certainty whether Alexander's decision was based solely on the fluid military situation, or whether a lingering dream of British influence in postwar Yugoslavia helped to guide his hand.

In any event, on the day following these meetings, 26 April, Alexander reported to the Combined Chiefs that unless he received instructions to the contrary, his forces would only seize those portions of Venezia Giulia vital to his operations, namely Trieste, Pola, and the lines of communication into Austria. All the remainder would be left to Tito, who would be informed of this arrangement in advance.[57]

On the heels of Alexander's cable, a message from Churchill to President Truman reached Washington on 27 April. As on other occasions, the prime minister tried to win Truman's support by invoking the spirit of FDR, stating in this case that the late president had "always attached great importance to Trieste."[58] Churchill urged the president and the Combined Chiefs to decide quickly in favor of Alexander's proposal, because it was important to get Trieste "in the easy manner proposed" without taking the large risks often "inherent in these kinds of political-military operations." While voicing his support for Alexander, the prime minister made clear his own motivation and also revealed that on one crucial point he was not in agreement with the field marshal. Churchill was only willing to concede de facto Yugoslav occupation of most of Venezia Giulia because he could not prevent it, but all his previous sympathy and support for Tito had evaporated. Unlike Alexander he did not wish to give the Yugoslavs advance warning of Allied occupation plans; instead, he wanted the Anglo-Americans to exploit the Sunrise surrender initiative by dashing for Venezia Giulia and seizing Trieste and as much other territory as possible. "The great thing is to be there before Tito's guerrillas are in occupation," the prime minister emphasized to Washington. "The actual status can be determined at leisure . . . possession is nine points of the law."[59]

Therefore, when the Combined Chiefs began discussing Trieste and Venezia Giulia on 27 April, they were faced with two sharply different policy recommendations and two equally divergent proposals for communicating with the Yugoslavs. The plan of the inter-Allied committee, backed by the State Department, called for the establishment of Anglo-American military government in the whole region, while Alexander desired merely to take possession of Trieste and the communication route into Austria. The inter-Allied committee recommended that Yugoslavian and Soviet acceptance of Allied military government be secured through regular diplomatic channels without a communication by Alexander. On the other hand the British commander proposed that the way should be smoothed for the more limited operation by notifying Tito directly. Given the dominance of the military necessity principle in wartime Washington, Alexander's plan should have had good prospects of acceptance, especially since time was short and the issue could not be eased through diplomatic channels before Tito took over much of the region. In addition, there was a real danger of a collision between Anglo-American and partisan forces.

However, Alexander's recommendation clashed with the position that Italy's 1939 frontiers should not be prejudiced prior to a postwar peace conference. In the immediately preceding months the Italian government had been assured by the Allied Control Commission that Tito would not be allowed to administer Italian territories, and these pledges could only be fulfilled if Allied military government was extended to all Venezia Giulia. With hostilities drawing to a close, devout appeals to military necessity made little sense, and if the fact that time was running out could be disregarded—a very big if!—the proposal for a large zone of military government offered a hope of shelving the political issue for the time being. Under strong pressure from the State Department, both Stimson and General Marshall came to support this position. The secretary of war found the plan for Allied military government of Venezia Giulia "sensible," "clear," "authoritative," and with little investigation or deliberation, the Combined Chiefs followed Stimson's lead.[60] Alexander was instructed not only to secure Trieste and the communication route into Austria, but to establish Allied military government over the whole of Venezia Giulia. This order was transmitted to the field marshal on 28 April, at a time when the Fifteenth Army Group was over the Adige in force, but portions of Venezia Giulia were already in the hands of Tito's partisans.[61] On this same day, Mussolini was strung up in Milan, and the German surrender emissaries—Schweinitz and Wenner—arrived in Caserta.

Despite the rapidity of his advance and the bright prospects for a capitulation of Vietinghoff's army. Alexander was convinced that the Combined Chiefs' directive was completely out of touch with reality. He feared that whatever happened in Italy, Tito would clear the Germans from most of the territory east of the Isonzo, and once in possession, would not evacuate if only faced by a polite request from a British field marshal. Alexander therefore cabled Washington that he could not carry through the Combined Chiefs' directive without the concurrence of Soviet and Yugoslavian authorities, and his only feasible course was to limit himself to immediate military objectives.

OPERATION SUNRISE

It was in this state of limbo that Alexander ordered Clark and the Fifteenth Army Group to strike for Trieste and the communication line into Austria on 29 April. On the following day, in an effort to stay within hailing distance of the Combined Chiefs' directive, the field marshal told Clark, "Concurrently with operations indicated . . . you will continue operations against the enemy until you have completely cleared Venezia Giulia or linked up with regular armed forces." To show that he put prudence before expansion, Alexander emphasized to Clark that "in linking up with regular Yugoslavs, maximum care will be exercised to avoid armed clashes."[62] On the same day, he also informed Tito of his intention to seize Pola and Trieste, plus the supply route into Austria, and asked him to subordinate all Yugoslav forces already in that area to the Anglo-American Command. Having settled for limited objectives, cautioned Clark, and notified both Tito and the Combined Chiefs of his intentions, Alexander believed that he had done what he could. From this point forth, the fate of Trieste and Venezia Giulia lay largely in the hands of Clark, Tito, and the Anglo-American governments.

While the two military commanders rushed forward on a collision course, the Western political leaders struggled to reach agreement on some common Anglo-American policy. Their clumsiness and ineptitude rivaled that of the German leaders in northern Italy who, at this moment, were playing out their own comic melodrama over fulfillment of the Caserta surrender. Winston Churchill was the first Western leader on stage. He cabled President Truman on 30 April that it would be a "delusion" to suppose that the Yugoslav and Soviet governments would agree to Allied control of Venezia Giulia, because these two powers would certainly try to "overrun" it themselves.[63] Although the prime minister gave lip service to the implementation of the Combined Chiefs' policy, he was really advocating a covert dash for Trieste. "We are as much entitled to move freely into Trieste if we can get there as were the Russians to win their way into Vienna," he asserted, and added that Alexander should be allowed to advance "as quickly and as secretly as possible."[64]

In a confidential message to Alexander on the following day, the prime minister spoke more directly.[65] Although he knew that Alexander had chosen to direct his advance solely at military objectives and was notifying Tito of his plans, Churchill still told the field marshal that he had been "urging President Truman not to let the Combined Chiefs of Staff give you orders to tell Russia and Yugoslavia of what you are going to do beforehand." The prime minister went on to reveal the considerations which were at this point uppermost in his nimble mind:

I think it highly important that we and the Americans should get control of Fiume,

Trieste, Pola, and the Istrian Peninsula, and that your communications into Austria should be safeguarded. There is also of course going to be a frightful outcry between the Italians and the Yugoslavs for these territories. I am in favor of backing up the Italians because that will split their Communist forces and will also fit in with the very friendly interest the Americans have in Italy and which I should like also to share. I imagine the Italians care more about Trieste and Istria than about Communism, and it would be a good thing to have a settled government in Italy which was united to the two Western democracies.[66]

Churchill was so carried away building these political sand castles that he failed to note how much confusion he was adding to an already muddled situation. Not only was he challenging the Combined Chiefs' policy, he was also urging a secret assault on Trieste after Alexander's message to Tito meant that there was no secret.

The American government leaders were not privy to all Churchill's hopes and schemes—his ruminations about Italy, communism, and Trieste were not communicated to Washington—but Secretary of War Stimson saw enough to be perplexed and apprehensive. Although the prime minister's telegram to the president of 27 April had been routinely answered,[67] the second message from London (that of 30 April) awakened Stimson's latent fears that the British were trying to involve the United States in imperialistic adventures in the Balkans. Actually Churchill had already been forced to give up his grandest scheme—substantial British influence in postwar Yugoslavia—but the language he used in urging a secret seizure of Trieste sounded assertive, if not aggressive, to Stimson. The secretary of war told General Marshall that with President Roosevelt dead, Churchill "was seeking to take a more active part in the direction of matters of grand policy in central Europe," and the War Department had to do what it could to block him by advising the new president "as to the background and past differences between Britain and America on these matters."[68]

Stimson also discussed his concern over the dangers of being embroiled in the Balkans by the British with Acting Secretary of State Joseph Grew. In a long telephone conversation on 30 April, Stimson told Grew that he had supported the State Department view on the matter of Trieste and Allied military government for all Venezia Giulia against the advice of the Joint Chiefs. The generals were worried, since they felt Tito was backed by the Russians, and clashes were likely to occur when Alexander tried to advance into Venezia Giulia. Preaching caution, the secretary of war pointedly reminded Grew that President "Wilson's hand was forced last time in the same locality."[69]

Heeding Stimson's warning, Grew used his next conference with President Truman to urge that a precautionary reply be sent to Churchill. The new president seems to have been without a firm opinion of his own on Venezia

Giulia at this point, and he was willing to be led by his strongest advisors.[70] Once Stimson persuaded Grew that British ambitions should be held in check, Truman readily agreed that a message appropriate to this position should be sent to London.[71] The resulting cable conceded that there was no need to obtain prior Russian agreement to the establishment of Western control of Trieste and Pola, but it gave no encouragement to Churchill's wish that an all-out clandestine effort be made to seize the two cities. Stressing that Alexander had "all the guidance" he needed because the Combined Chiefs' directive ordered him to consult Washington if he ran into trouble with the Yugoslavs, Truman's message ended with the significant declaration that the United States was unwilling to commit its forces to combat in "the Balkan political arena."[72]

Two days later, on 2 May, Stimson accidentally learned that in the recent Anglo-American policy discussions on Venezia Giulia, British representatives had emphasized that they wished to avoid all risk of clashes with Tito. Totally perplexed by this information, Stimson telephoned Grew in an effort to discover what position the British government was actually maintaining.[73] Despite much questioning and hypothesizing, neither man hit on the right answers—that Britain was gradually moving away from its pro-Yugoslav stance, and that Churchill and Alexander were at loggerheads about whether to inform Tito regarding Western operations in Venezia Giulia. But Stimson learned enough from his inquiries to see that the primary force behind the effort to establish a large Allied military government in Venezia Giulia did not come from London but from the State Department, and he concluded that it was essential to prevent "these younger men" in the department from "doing dangerous things."[74] Since the attainment of an extensive Allied military government in Venezia Giulia was not even supported by the British, the secretary of war pressed the view that this policy objective had to be abandoned forthwith. On 2 May, he told both Grew and the president that unless something was done immediately to ease the dangerous situation, "Alexander and the Yugoslavs would be shooting at each other before we could get between them."[75]

Stimson's belated effort to clarify Anglo-American policy had come much too late, and his fear of an immediate military collision with Tito was actually exaggerated. Alexander and Clark were on their own, but the field marshal was deeply concerned to avoid an armed conflict with Yugoslavia. Churchill's pressure notwithstanding, he had decided not to expose his men to unnecessary danger by asking them "to turn away from the common enemy to fight an ally."[76] Alexander not only took it for granted that Tito would push the Yugoslav frontier westward, he personally believed that Trieste should immediately be ceded to Yugoslavia when the Western powers no longer required it as a port of supply for their operations in Austria. Rather than make a great leap forward, Alexander and Clark took caution as their watchword and moved eastward with all deliberate speed.

The Second New Zealand Division, under General Freyberg, had been entrusted by Clark with the task of leading the advance on Trieste. German resistance was scattered and the partisans had seized the crucial bridges, so by 1 May the New Zealanders crossed the Isonzo River and entered Monfalcone, a few kilometers west of Trieste. There they came in contact with an advance Yugoslav partisan detachment which had entered the town in the morning. Following Alexander's orders. Freyberg halted and tried to make contact with the Yugoslav commander. Two appointments were arranged for the New Zealander to meet with his Yugoslav counterpart, but Tito's representative failed to appear on either occasion. The Yugoslavs probably assumed that it was in their interest to occupy all the territory they could before being forced to recognize the presence of the Anglo-Americans. But even as Freyberg vainly sought other commanders' meetings, his troops pushed further eastward and entered Trieste in the late afternoon of 2 May.[77]

Once inside the city, the New Zealanders faced an extremely confusing situation. Two days previously, on 30 April, the Italian resistance leaders had called for a rising and had managed to seize the municipal government buildings. Almost immediately, Yugoslav partisans in the city also rose, while the German garrison retreated into a series of strong points including the law courts building and an old castle near the center of the city. Despite some friction, the Yugoslav partisans in Trieste and the forces of the CLNAI carried out a number of joint military actions against the Germans on 30 April and in the early hours of 1 May. But the situation was rapidly altered when the Twentieth Yugoslav Division, the advance unit of Tito's Fourth Army, entered the city on the morning of 1 May. This Yugoslav force quickly disarmed the Italian resistance fighters and occupied the government buildings, but it was too weak to compel the capitulation of Trieste's German strongpoints. Most of the Germans had made the prudent decision not to surrender to the Yugoslavs but to await the arrival of the Western armies. The largest force, seven hundred men, was barricaded in the old castle and easily resisted the efforts of the lightly armed Twentieth Division to dislodge them. But when Freyberg's New Zealanders arrived, the Germans quickly indicated their willingness to capitulate, and almost all immediately laid down their arms.[78]

Interpreting this to be the formal surrender of the city, the Anglo-Americans congratulated themselves on having won the race. On the following day, New Zealand forces moved through scattered Yugoslav units in the neighborhood of Trieste and took possession of the nearby town of

Gorizia. In Washington, Secretary of War Stimson exulted that it was a good thing that Tito had "talked bigger" than he could "make good on." [79] But the Western powers were rejoicing too soon; Tito had lost the first heat, but had not given up the race. He had pushed his regular units toward Trieste with such haste that the German defensive "Ingrid" line was flanked and important cities including Fiume, Lubiana, and Zagabria were temporarily left in German hands. [80] When he saw that the advance of the bulk of his regular army would fall short, he had used local partisans and the Twentieth Division strike force to stake out a claim in Trieste. It was easy for Freyberg to brush off these units as insignificant, but on their heels came the rest of the Fourth Yugoslav Army, well equipped and battle tested, and certainly no laughing matter. While Freyberg was limiting his occupation to the points of military importance in Trieste, such as the docks and the communications route into Austria, regular Yugoslav forces swept into the city, taking possession of everything in their path. The Yugoslav commander, General Petar Drapsin, immediately made clear to Freyberg that he considered the Western troops intruders, and stressed that he was determined to take control of the city. A Yugoslav administration was immediately established both within and without Trieste, and Tito's men began indiscriminately arresting prominent Italians, including members of the Italian resistance, on the grounds that the region had to be purged of fascism.

Without orders from Alexander, and taken by surprise by the Yugoslavs, Freyberg had not yet tried to establish Allied military government in Trieste or any other area east of the Isonzo. Confused and conciliatory, the New Zealander even turned over to the Yugoslavs the prisoners he had made when the German garrison surrendered. By 7 May, the day of the general German surrender at Rheims—the day the Second World War in Europe came to an end—the Western troops in Trieste found themselves badgered by the Yugoslav authorities and nearly encircled by the Yugoslav army. Confined within the few strong points which they had occupied, they could only look on helplessly as Tito's officials introduced harsh repressive measures and began stripping Italian civilians of their possessions.

This situation was clearly untenable, and the Anglo-American governments would soon be faced with the choice of withdrawing or using force to secure complete control of the city and lines of communication. They were face to face with a Communist seizure of power, and since the war in Europe was officially over, they could no longer choose a course of action by appealing to the fabled magic of military necessity. Before the month was over, the conviction that the Soviet Union was supporting Tito in a strategic land grab would lead Washington to get tough and to demand that Tito withdraw his troops in favor of an Anglo-American military government for Trieste.[81]

Through the Caserta surrender, Western forces had blundered into a political–military confrontation with the East, but it was their rising suspicion of the Soviet Union which ultimately made the Anglo-Americans dig themselves in. Operation Sunrise was what brought the Western powers to Trieste, but early cold war winds were what made them dig in and stay.

CHAPTER 8

Conclusion

"In two years from now all these things will
look quite different."
                    Karl Wolff, June 1945

OPERATION SUNRISE is a classic instance of how difficult is the task
of drawing sharp lines between war and peace, and it would be tempting to
allow this narrative to flow on into the postwar world. But the stream would
quickly go underground, and even where it seemed to resurface, it would
soon be lost in a new landscape. What happened at Bern was an incident
which had consequences, but did not have its own distinct future, and
therefore the story cannot be moved forward. Despite the temptation to push
it along, especially in Trieste, we have no choice but to stop in May, 1945,
and try, as best we can, to take stock of the whole incident and to measure its
most important effects.

The majority of those involved in Operation Sunrise saw it as an attempt to
immediately end the destruction and carnage of the world's most murderous
conflict and, at the same time, to shape postwar conditions in northern Italy.
Certainly these were not the only motivations of Dulles, Wolff, and the
others, nor do these questions have the emotional charge or importance for
us that they had for contemporaries, but in fairness they need to be
examined briefly before we pass on to the broader issue of Bern's impact on
the cold war. Since World War II ended everywhere in Europe within a
week after the capitulation in Caserta, the number of lives actually saved by
Sunrise should probably be measured in hundreds, or thousands, rather than
in tens of thousands. Certainly the life and property of some Italian civilians

was spared, as were a larger number of German troops who, in the first week of May, were exposed to the full destructive force which Allied air and artillery power could apply to a broken army. In addition, some special property, such as the Uffizi art treasures, was turned over to the Allies intact, and certain categories of prisoners, including Count Stauffenberg's relatives, were freed, while in other theaters of war similar art works were destroyed and such special enemies of the Third Reich were liquidated. On the other hand, probably few Allied lives were actually saved, because in the course of its final offensive, the Fifteenth Army Group absorbed very low casualties. Of course one may hypothesize that without Operation Sunrise the general German disintegration could have taken longer and the death and destruction in Europe might have been greater, but such questions belong to the further regions of speculation and "if-history."

Operation Sunrise also seems to have had very little special impact on immediate postwar conditions in northern Italy. German and Italian Fascist prisoners of war there were treated the same as other Axis personnel who fell into Allied hands in Western Europe.[1] All were kept in internment camps for varying periods, a few were held for war-criminal prosecution, and most were used for reconstruction labor. Those auxiliary forces from Eastern Europe attached to the German army who were covered by the clauses of the Yalta agreement obligating the Western powers to turn them over to Soviet authorities, were in fact shipped east, just as happened in all other regions controlled by the Anglo-Americans.[2] Thus the enemy rank and file received no special benefits from Sunrise,* nor on the other hand did the Italian partisans. The CLNAI did not gain political power or have extensive political influence in the immediate postwar period, but neither did any other partisan organization in Western or Eastern Europe, with the sole exception of Yugoslavia. In postwar Italy, as everywhere else, the conquering Allies seized, and held, the political authority.

Whatever hopes were harbored by participants, one may conclude that Operation Sunrise had a very modest humanitarian impact, and that its direct effect on postwar Italy was meager. Only in regard to the question of the origins and course of the cold war did the affair have significant consequences, and these were both subtle and complex. In order to chart them clearly, a number of points should be borne in mind. There was no Anglo-American attempt at Bern to make a separate peace with Nazi Germany; the triple policy of military necessity, unconditional surrender, and alliance with the USSR stayed in place until the end of the European war. Yet there also existed a deep Anglo-American suspicion of the Soviet Union held by much of the public and many government officials, and this

*For the case of Karl Wolff see p. 188.

had not been eliminated by the wartime partnership.[3] In the spring of 1945 these feelings were aggravated by a rising sense of American power and by what appeared to be Soviet intransigence and possible aggressiveness in regard to the future of Poland and other issues. Furthermore, the anti-Soviet inclination of some of the main participants in Sunrise, especially Dulles and Gaevernitz, was combined with a strong sympathy for Germany. These men worked well with Germans, supported "the other Germany," and hoped to see a denazified Germany play an important role in postwar Europe. With such people in the lead, the Western powers were willing to stretch the meaning of unconditional surrender so that they might obtain an easy victory in Italy and, if Kesselring had cooperated, along the whole Western front. This was not an exercise in separate peace-making, or a technical violation of the principle of unconditional surrender, but it was something short of full Allied openness and joint action.

The angry exchanges which occurred over Bern did exacerbate East-West mistrust and hostility further, and in the next quarter century cold warriors on both sides would find it a perfect hook on which to hang their suspicions. Starting in 1945, Gaevernitz repeatedly intimated (without substantiating evidence) that the Soviets had carried out dark plots to sabotage Sunrise,[4] and as recently as the present decade Russian television has used a popular serial to dramatize what it views as Dulles's diabolical dealings with the SS in Switzerland.[5] Traditionalist historians have stressed the purity of Western deeds in Bern and have decried what they consider the paranoia and spiteful obstructionism of the Soviet response.[6] Revisionist historians, on the other hand, have defended what they see as a reasonable Soviet reaction to an attempted Western double-cross of the USSR.[7]

Even when all of this is added together, it would be too much to say that Sunrise was a major factor in producing the cold war. But Bern clearly played a part in sharpening the tone of East-West animosity and, in their turn, a number of its side effects also helped to chill the international atmosphere. Foremost among these was the Anglo-American presence in Trieste, for as we have seen, Sunrise was what caused the Western powers to be there, and Trieste was the setting for the first armed confrontation between East and West. Only there had no inter-Allied demarcation line been drawn, and in 1945 this spot was where the two sides came closest to an armed clash—a sobering reminder for those who condemn inter-Allied territorial agreements such as those made at Yalta. After a tense month in which both the Western powers and the Yugoslavs massed military forces in the area, Tito yielded—apparently because the Soviet Union would not support him in a showdown on this issue—and the crisis passed. But the incident left more bad feelings between East and West as well as in Russian-

Yugoslav relations. In addition, it was Harry S. Truman's first exercise in using the threat of military force to wring concessions from what would soon be known in Washington as the Soviet Block. In Trieste, political-military brinksmanship worked, and it is likely that the incident encouraged the new and inexperienced president to believe that his predilection for drawing lines and standing tall offered the brightest prospect for success in foreign policy. It is just this aspect of Truman's foreign-policy stance which has drawn the sharpest criticism in recent literature on the cold war.[8] Again, neither the face-off in Trieste, nor the Sunrise events which made it possible, may reasonably be credited with causing Truman to be a tough cold warrior, but the affair may well have been important in increasing the president's enthusiasm for confrontation as the best means of dealing with the Soviet Union.

Another man prominent in the direction of American policy during the harshest cold war period seems to have been even more significantly affected by the Sunrise experience. Allen Dulles considered the Bern affair his most noteworthy covert operational success of the Second World War, and it seems to have heightened both his pleasure in playing spy and his belief that espionage and covert operations were inherently meritorious.[9] One must be cautious in drawing conclusions about the cold war and the development of the CIA from this, because Sunrise alone obviously did not make Allen Dulles an anti-Communist or an espionage enthusiast, and Dulles did not single-handedly create the CIA nor did he solely shape the agency into the instrument which perpetrated the great cold war excesses of the 1950s and early 1960s. But Sunrise did enhance Dulles's reputation as an espionage expert, and it did strengthen his basic confidence in himself and in his ability to use covert operations to get things done. For nearly ten years he was able to call the CIA's tune with little outside interference, shielded and supported by his brother, Secretary of State John Foster Dulles, and a host of friends and associates, including his old Sunrise partner, General Lyman Lemnitzer, who, in the late 1950s, was chief of staff of the Army.[10] Behind this protective wall of relatives, personal associations, and his own reputation, Allen Dulles and the CIA were allowed to run amok. Sunrise did not cause this to happen, but it played a part by helping to provide Dulles with the credentials to obtain that position and in strengthening his belief that unrestricted covert intelligence activity was desirable and efficacious.

Therefore it is fair to say that Operation Sunrise, and its offshoot in Trieste, played a circumscribed part in speeding Dulles and other American leaders on their journey to that confined state of mind where the world was made up of "us" and "them," and where there were few reservations about what it was permissible to do to "them." This development not only necessitated a shift in the American image of the Soviet Union, it also required an alteration in the prevailing view of the defeated enemy states, especially of Germany. Implicit in the cold war evolution was a shift from the picture of Germany as an evil and aggressor nation to that of a comrade in the struggle against Communism. This process has often been alluded to in discussions of the coming of the East-West struggle, but almost exclusively as if the West unilaterally changed its mind about Germany. What Operation Sunrise demonstrates is that individual Germans were eager to do what they could to push the Western powers into a cold war stance as quickly as possible. The case of Karl Wolff is especially instructive because he grasped sooner than most of his contemporaries that the best way to get the Western powers to lessen their hostility to Germans—and Nazis—was to be as cooperative as possible and to wait for the realities of power politics to build a bridge from Nazi anti-Communism to Anglo-American anti-Communism. The chronicle of Wolff's life after the capitulation on 2 May is highly enlightening concerning this process.

In the days immediately following the capitulation, Wolff tried to hold on to his position as SS and police chief for as long as possible, while doing his utmost to convince the Allies that German participants in Sunrise should be treated not as defeated enemies, but as partners in the cause of peace. By picking "up the political threads . . . and playing on the old discrepancy between Russia and America," the SS man sought to snuggle up to the Anglo-Americans and to throw a protective blanket around his subordinates in northern Italy.[11] He went so far as to ask Alexander to grant POW status to all SD and Gestapo men, an action which made the field marshal recoil and caused him to warn Allied officials involved in the Bern affair, including Dulles and Gaevernitz, to be more cautious about making any commitments to Wolff.[12]

Despite the latter incident, it is obvious that if the members of the Anglo-American Sunrise team had been allowed to follow their hearts, Wolff would have won his game right there. Dulles, Lemnitzer, and the others were prepared to let bygones be bygones and to treat Wolff like a regular fellow as a reward for his surrender services.[13] But the wishes of both Wolff and the western Sunrise people were thwarted by the great rush of popular anti-Nazi feeling, as well as the horror generated in the immediate postwar period by the revelations regarding German atrocities. Anglo-American policy in the spring of 1945 was dominated by a desire to implement a tough occupation program for Germany, one which would make that country atone for its sins and at the same time render it harmless in the future. Foremost among the means through which this was to be accomplished was a stringent and comprehensive action against alleged war criminals.

As soon as the pursuit of Nazi war criminals assumed the central place in Allied policy, Wolff's dreams of immediately playing an independent political role were doomed. His rank, position, and previous services to the party and the SS guaranteed that he would be in the front rank of those accused. After ten days of postwar quasi-freedom in Bolzano, he was taken into custody on his birthday (13 May) by members of the American Eighty-eighth Division.[14] Initially confined in a prison in Rome, he spent the summer being shuttled from one Allied detention camp to another. In August he narrowly missed being included on the defendant list for the main Nuremberg trial. With both Himmler and Heydrich dead, Ernst Kaltenbrunner had been designated the major defendant for the SS and the Gestapo, but in light of the enormity of the accusations against these two organizations, they were underrepresented, and other prominent SS men could have been placed in the dock. During one of the final preparatory meetings of the chief prosecutors on 24 August, an effort was made to expand the list of defendants, but after a lively discussion, the Allied prosecutors decided to hold the list of the accused at two dozen, and to go after other top Nazis in a second trial. Of those held to be most worthy of inclusion as defendants in such a follow-up proceeding against major Nazi criminals, four individuals were named, and one of these was Karl Wolff.°[15]

Although the Obergruppenführer was unaware of what had happened, he was actually saved from serious harm through this decision. By the time the first major war-criminal trial ended, the tensions of the cold war had developed to such a point that the plans for a second four-power trial were scuttled, and each of the Allies went ahead to deal independently with the top Nazis in its hands. The Americans prosecuted twelve groups of Nazi defendants between late 1946 and 1949 (the so-called "little" Nuremberg trials), including four cases in which SS men were prominent defendants. Since Wolff was in American hands, one would suppose that he would have been caught in this net, but he was saved again, in part by a combination of lucky circumstances.

After having held out against the mental pressures of his situation for a year, Wolff succumbed to a feeling of betrayal by his Sunrise colleagues, and a paranoid anti-Semitic fantasy that he was pursued by Jewish demons. Diagnosed as suffering from extreme paranoia, he was confined in a mental institution during the late winter and spring of 1946.[16] Once released and back in ordinary detention, he quickly came under the scrutiny of the American war crimes prosecutors who interrogated him repeatedly throughout the rest of 1946 and all of 1947. Although he was a model of cooperation,

---

°The other three were Luftwaffe Field Marshal Milch, Army Field Marshal von Brauchitsch, and former Agriculture Minister Darré.

Wolff did not fit neatly into the defendant categories for any of the American cases tried in 1948 or 1949. In addition, the prosecutors were not certain how to deal with his Sunrise experiences, and they were leery about using him as a defendant or a witness due to his unstable mental condition. Thus when the British asked that Wolff be turned over to them so that he could be prosecuted together with Field Marshal Kesselring for crimes committed during the Italian campaign, the American chief prosecutor, General Telford Taylor, agreed with alacrity.[17]

Once the British had Wolff in their hands, however, they too decided that he was not very suitable for service in a major proceeding, certainly not in one as controversial as the Kesselring case turned out to be. So instead of sending him off to Venice for an examination of his actions in Italy, the British held Wolff in confinement until 1949 and then quietly prosecuted him in a little-publicized trial in Hamburg. With the cold war then in full swing, it was easier for Wolff to play down his Nazi past and to gain merit for his surrender services. All his major Anglo-American Sunrise associates now came forward to assist him; Lemnitzer, Airey, and Dulles wrote affidavits in his behalf and Gaevernitz actually appeared as a defense witness. In the face of a half-hearted effort by the prosecution, this high-level endorsement of Wolff's activities in the cause of peace and the interest of the Western world was enough, and he was acquitted.[18]

For thirteen years Wolff was at liberty while the increasingly close relations between the NATO powers and the new West German state seemed to confirm his predictions in 1945, that ex-Nazis would find an easy resting place in an American dominated postwar Europe. Then in 1962 the furor produced by the Eichmann trial prompted the West German government to launch an extensive investigation and prosecution of ex-Nazis who had been involved in the wartime extermination programs. Wolff was placed on trial and charged with extermination planning during his years as Himmler's adjutant and SS liaison officer at Hitler's headquarters. The most damaging piece of evidence against him was a 1942 letter he had written to a state secretary in the Transportation Ministry, expressing his "special joy (*besondere Freude*) that now five thousand members of the Chosen People are going to Treblinka every day."[19] This time none of his Sunrise friends appeared as character witnesses, and although Wolff squirmed and wiggled while asserting that he really did not know what had gone on at Treblinka, the German court sentenced him to fifteen years confinement.

If one subtracts the elements of accident and luck from the course of Wolff's life between 1945 and his final release from prison in the mid-1970s, there is a clear line running over this whole tale. From the beginning of the

Sunrise dealings, the Obergruppenführer placed himself on the side of anti-Communism and played down Nazi ideology and the atrocities, while pledging himself to be useful to the West. With the exception of a few lapses, due to discouragement and mental instability, he did not deviate from that stance. It was not enough to save him from a prison sentence in 1962, but it surely helped to keep him out of an Allied courtroom in the mid-1940s, when the stakes were most mortal. Most other Germans, including the majority of those who participated in Sunrise, also discovered that if they were not too tainted and showed themselves understanding of the needs and sensitivities of the cold war, they too could enjoy a new life in the post-war world. A man such as Rudolf Rahn easily blossomed during the late 1940s as a prosperous businessman, a confidant of the French intelligence service, and a moderately successful conservative politician.[20] But it is Wolff's case which shows most graphically how the wartime and postwar attitudes of the Western powers smoothed the transition from collaboration with Hitler to a pleasant existence in the anti-Communist West. Since the execution of Ernst Kaltenbrunner in 1946, Karl Wolff has been the highest ranking SS man alive; today he is living a comfortable life in Munich and appears on British and American television as a respected witness to the events of the Second World War.

Wolff's survival is an appropriate symbol for the ultimate meaning of Sunrise. The Western Allies thought they could gain a cheap victory via a covert operation in Bern, but they discovered that the price was higher than they had imagined. They gained a formal, if belated, capitulation to be sure, but it brought them few tangible benefits and put another nail in the coffin of the wartime alliance. Many members of the defeated Wehrmacht, on the other hand, owed their lives to the early end of hostilities, and Sunrise eased the postwar road for a number of its German participants. Most of all, the operation foretold the political lineup of the next epoch in European history: West Germany would cease to be an outcast and would quickly become a respected, if not always highly honored, member of the Western coalition. What happened in Bern was not the dawn of a new era of peace, but a twilight between hot war and cold war that offered a glimpse of a world order in which the roles of allies and enemies would be reversed. The Soviet Union would soon symbolize dangerous and aggressive power, while West Germany would become a European bastion against communism.

In the fourth week of May, soon after his arrest, Karl Wolff had spoken confidentially to two of his SS subordinates about his own vision of the future. "We'll get our Reich back again," the Obergruppenführer assured them. "The others will begin to fight amongst themselves eventually and then we'll be in the middle and can play off one against the other."[21] Events were to show that the first part of this prediction was wrong. The Germans would not be allowed to build a Reich once more, and the East-West blocks would be too rigid to permit much independent action by either of the postwar German states. But Karl Wolff had based his actions on the assumption that the Grand Alliance would inevitably break up. In the end, this assumption, which the SS man had shared with many German leaders from Hitler to Doenitz, would prove to be correct.

Guide to Frequently Cited Sources

AFHQ—Allied Forces Headquarters Mediterranean Records, RG 331, Federal Records Center, Suitland, Maryland.

Allied Control—Allied Control Commission Records, RG 331, Federal Records Center, Suitland, Maryland.

CAB 21 Crossword—Crossword File 1602/7953, CAB 21, Cabinet Offices, Public Records Office, London.

CCS-387 Germany—Combined Chiefs of Staff, 387 Germany, 9-21-44 Germany, RG 218, Modern Military Branch, National Archives, Washington, D.C.

Churchill—Winston S. Churchill, *Triumph and Tragedy* (Boston, 1953).

Coles and Weinberg—Harry L. Coles and Albert K. Weinberg, *Civil Affairs, Soldiers Become Governors* (Washington, D.C., 1964).

Cox Race—Geoffrey Cox, *The Race for Trieste* (London, 1977).

Crossword—Memorandum "Crossword" AFHQ Reel 21, RG 331, Federal Records Center, Suitland, Maryland.

Deakin—F. W. Deakin, *The 600 Days of Mussolini* (Garden City, NY, 1968).

Dollmann—Eugen Dollmann, *Dolmetscher der Diktatoren* (Bamberg, Germany, 1963).

Dulles/Gaevernitz—Allen Dulles and Gero von Gaevernitz, "The First German Surrender," *Allen Dulles Papers*, Princeton University (Princeton, New Jersey).

Dulles Secret—Allen Dulles, *Secret Surrender* (New York, 1966).

FO—Foreign Office Records, Public Records Office (London).

FRUS—*Foreign Relations of the United States* (Washington, D.C.), varying years, special topics, and dates of publication.

Kesselring—MS #T-123, Part III, vol. 3, Commander in Chief West, RG 338 Foreign Military Studies, Modern Military Branch, National Archives (Washington, D.C.).

Kimche—Jon Kimche, *Spying for Peace* (London, 1961).

Lanfranchi—F. Lanfranchi, *Le Resa degii Ottocentomila* (Milan, 1948).

OSS Reports—OSS Reports, Entry 2, Box 131, RG 331 Federal Records Center (Suitland, Maryland).

Post and Counselor Files—Post and Counselor Files, RG 84, Federal Records Center, Suitland, Maryland.

President's Secretary's File OSS—President's Secretary's File, OSS Files, Boxes 170-171, Franklin D. Roosevelt Library (Hyde Park, NY).

Rahn—Rudolf Rahn, *Ruheloses Leben* (Düsseldorf, Germany, 1949).

Roosevelt and Churchill—Francis L. Loewenheim, Harold D. Langley, and Manfred Jonas, eds., *Roosevelt and Churchill: Their Secret Wartime Correspondence* (New York, 1976).

Secret Surrender Files—"Secret Surrender Files," *Allen Dulles Papers*, Princeton University (Princeton, New Jersey).

Selected CSDIC Reports—Selected CSDIC Reports referring to SS Obergruppenführer Wolff, RG 331, AFHQ, Reel 21M, Federal Records Center (Suitland, Maryland).

Stimson Diary—Diary of Henry L. Stimson, Roll 9, Yale University (New Haven, Connecticut).

Stuhlpfarer—Karl Stuhlpfarer, *Die Operationszonen "Alpenvorland und Adriatisches Kustenland" 1940-1945* (Vienna, 1969).

Toland—John Toland Collection, Box 9, Library of Congress (Washington, D.C.).

Toland, Last 100—John Toland, *The Last 100 Days* (New York, 1967).

Wolff's Interrogations—Nuremberg Interrogations, RG 1019, Roll 80, Modern Military Branch, National Archives (Washington, D.C.).

Notes

Introduction: First Light

1. Allen Dulles, *Secret Surrender* (New York, 1966), hereinafter cited as *Dulles Secret*.

2. Perhaps the most influential is Gabriel Kolko, *The Politics of War: The World and United States Foreign Policy, 1943–1945* (New York, 1968), p. 375f.

3. The bibliography of this volume indicates the range of OSS materials which we succeeded in declassifying. Selected CSDIC Reports referring to SS Obergruppenführer Wolff, RG 331, AFHQ, Reel 21M, Federal Records Center, Suitland, Maryland (hereinafter cited as *Selected CSDIC Reports*). For a general discussion of the documentary sources related to Karl Wolff, see chapter 3, note 52.

4. OSS Reports, Entry 2, Box 131, RG 331, Federal Records Center, Suitland, Maryland (hereinafter cited as *OSS Reports*).

5. "Secret Surrender Files," *Allen Dulles Papers*, Princeton University, Princeton, New Jersey (hereinafter cited as *Secret Surrender Files*).

6. Primarily the three following sources: "Post and Counselor Files, Caserta," RG 84 (hereinafter cited as *Post and Counselor Files*); Allied Forces Headquarters Mediterranean and Allied Control Commission Files, RG 331 (hereinafter cited as *AFHQ* and *Allied Control*). All three groups of documents are in the Federal Records Center, Suitland, Maryland.

7. We drew documents from a number of collections in the Public Records Office, but the principal source was a file marked "Crossword," number 1602/7953 CAB 21, Cabinet Offices, Public Records Office, London (hereinafter cited as *CAB 21 Crossword*).

8. Although we did not obtain access to the OSS central files, we were able to examine the OSS reports on Sunrise sent to the Joint Chiefs of Staff and the president. The former are in Combined Chiefs of Staff CCS 387 Germany, RG 218, Modern Military Branch, National Archives (hereinafter cited as *CCS 387 Germany*), the latter in President's Secretary's File, OSS Files, Boxes 170-171, Franklin D. Roosevelt Library, Hyde Park, New York (hereinafter cited as *President's Secretary's File OSS*).

9. *CCS-387 Germany* and Diary of Henry L. Stimson, Roll 9, Yale University, New Haven, Connecticut (hereinafter cited as *Stimson Diary*).

10. See chapter 5, note 19.

Chapter 1: Creators of a Sunrise

1. The general remarks that follow owe a broad debt to the work of John Lewis Gaddis, *The United States and the Origins of the Cold War 1941–1947* (New York, 1972) and Daniel Yergin, *Shattered Peace, the Origins of the Cold War and the National Security State* (Boston, 1977), but while both authors stress the importance of military primacy in American wartime international policy, the books are actually written on the basis of State Department, not War Department, records. Significantly different impressions emerge from specific studies done on the basis of military records. See, for example, Brian L. Villa, "The U.S. Army, Unconditional Surrender, and the Potsdam Proclamation," *The Journal of American History* LXIII, no. 1 (June, 1976), pp. 66–92, and Elena Agarossi, "La Politica estera americana e l'Italia nella seconda

guerra mondiale" in Giorgio Spini et al, eds., *Italia e America dalla grande guerra a oggi*, Venice 1976.

2. See p. 288.

3. Psychological warfare is not a significant theme in this volume. For a comparative view and a bibliography see Gordon Wright, *The Ordeal of Total War* (New York, 1968) pp. 66f and 285–286.

4. Books such as Edward Hymoff's the *OSS in World War II* (New York, 1972), R. Harris Smith, *The OSS, the Secret History of America's First Central Intelligence Agency* (New York, 1972), Leonard Mosley, *Dulles: A Biography of Eleanor, Allen, John Foster Dulles and their Family Network* (New York, 1978), William R. Corson, *The Armies of Ignorance* (New York, 1977), and especially Anthony Cave Brown, ed., *The Secret War Report of the OSS* (New York, 1976) throw some light on the origins and early stages of the OSS. We also drew information from the M. Preston Goodfellow papers at the Hoover Institution, Stanford University and the *Final Report of the Select Committee to Study Governmental Operations with Respect to Intelligence Activities*, Supplementary Detailed Staff Reports on Foreign and Military Intelligence, Book IV, Senate Report no. 94–755 (Washington, 1976). But until the CIA sees fit to declassify the relevant documents, there will be much "airy" speculation on the subject.

5. R. Harris Smith, *The OSS, the Secret History of America's First Central Intelligence Agency* (New York, 1972), p. 35.

6. Much of this interaction may be followed in Francis L. Loewenheim, Harold D. Langley, and Manfred Jonas, eds., *Roosevelt and Churchill: Their Secret Wartime Correspondence* (New York, 1976), hereinafter cited as *Roosevelt and Churchill*.

7. Documentary sources for the establishment of a control agency in Italy are located in various archives including: Franklin D. Roosevelt Library, Hyde Park, NY, "Allied Control Commission for Italy," Map Room, 210; National Archives—(1) Diplomatic Branch, "Matthews Files," RG 59, Box 1, (2) Modern Military Branch, (a) "Records of the Office of the Secretary of War," RG 107, ASW 370.8 Italy, (b) "Leahy Papers," RG 218, Folder 127. See also *Foreign Relations of the United States, 1943*, vol. 1 (Washington, 1963) (hereinafter cited as *FRUS*); Harry L. Coles and Albert K. Weinberg, *Civil Affairs, Soldiers Become Governors*, (Washington, D.C., 1964) (hereinafter cited as *Coles and Weinberg*); and G. Warner, *Italy and the Powers, 1943–1949* (London, 1972).

8. These records are currently being declassified—Interservice agencies, Military Mission Moscow, RG 334, Modern Military Branch, National Archives.

9. See notes to chapter 5.

10. Bradley F. Smith, *Reaching Judgment at Nuremberg* (New York, 1977), pp. 21–22.

11. Donovan to the President, March 6, 1945, *President's Secretary's File-OSS*, Box 171. An early treatment of the redoubt question is in Rodney G. Minott, *The Fortress That Never Was* (New York, 1964).

12. Naval Aides Files—Germany, Map Room, Box 167, Franklin Roosevelt Library, Hyde Park, New York.

13. MS no. T–123, Part III, Volume 2, Commander in Chief West, p. 342, RG 338, Foreign Military Studies, Modern Military Branch, National Archives (hereinafter cited as *Kesselring*).

14. Summary of events preceding Operation Sunrise, entry of March 3, 1945, *OSS Reports*.

15. See for example Donovan to the President, March 28, 1945, *President's Secretary's File OSS*, Box 171.

16. Eisenhower to CCS, SCAF 279, 14 April 1945, German Armistice File, *Post and Counselor Files*. See also Dwight D. Eisenhower, *Crusade in Europe* (New York, 1948), p. 397f.

17. David Irving, *The Destruction of Dresden* (New York, 1963), p. 122.

Notes

Chapter 2: The Italian Setting

1. For Anglo-American discussions on the policy to follow in Italy in this period see E. Agarossi, "La politica degli alleati verso l'Italia nel 1943," in R. De Felice, ed., *L'Italia tra Tedeschi e alleati* (Bologna, 1973).

2. See the files 3858, Italy (10-19-42) Section 1, Combined Chiefs of Staff Records, RG 218, Modern Military Branch, National Archives.

3. "The Elimination of Italy," *FRUS, The Conferences at Washington 1941-'42 and Casablanca, 1943,* pp. 747–749.

4. E. Agarossi, "La politica degli alleati verso l'Italia," pp. 189–190.

5. F. M. Deakin, *The 600 Days of Mussolini* (Garden City, New York, 1968) p. 189. (hereinafter cited as *Deakin*).

6. "CCS Directive, Organization and Operation of Military Government for Husky," 28 June 1943 in *Coles and Weinberg,* pp. 177–178.

7. Ibid., p. 177.

8. For British objections, see ibid., p. 185.

9. For the introduction of this formula as the relief criterion for the population and for its application see the following files: ASW, 370.8 Italy, RG 107, Secretary of War, Modern Military Branch, National Archives and the records quoted in *Coles and Weinberg,* p. 150f. See also C.R.S. Harris, *Allied Military Administration of Italy, 1943-1945* (London, 1947), p. 240f.

10. For conditions in Allied occupied Italy, see E. Aga Rossi, "La situazione politica ed economica dell'Itali nel periodo 1944-1945: i governi Bonomi," in *Quaderni dell'Instituto Romano per la storia d'Italia dal fascismo alla Resistenza,* no. 2, 1971.

11. On the chaotic situation of the Salò armed forces, see *Deakin,* p. 82f.; Adolfo Scalpelli, "La formazione delle forze armate di Salò attraverso i documenti dello Stato Maggiore della RSI," in *Il Movimento di Liberazione in Italia,* no. 72–73, (July–September, 1963), p. 19f and 38f. On their composition at the end of the campaign see Enzo Collotti, "Dati sulle forze di polizia fasciste e tedesche nell'Italia settentrionale nell'aprile 1945," in *Il Movimento di Liberazione in Italia,* no. 71 (April–June, 1963), p. 51f.

12. On the two zones see Enzo Collotti, *L'administratione tedesca dell'Italia occupata 1943-1945* (Milan, 1965), pp. 101–104; E. F. Moelhausen, *La carta perdente* (Roma, 1948), pp. 390–391; Karl Stuhlpfarer, *Die Operationszonen "Alpenvorland und Adriatisches Küstenland" 1940-1945* (Vienna, 1969), (hereinafter cited as *Stuhlpfarer*). The *Operationszone Adriatisches Küstenland* included the Italian provinces of Udine, Gorizia, Trieste, Pola, and Fiume, plus the province of Lubiana annexed by Italy after the Italian invasion of Yugoslavia. The *Voralpenland* included the provinces of Bolzano, Trento, and Belluno.

13. John Ehrman, *Grand Strategy* (History of the Second World War, United Kingdom Military Series, volume 5) (London, 1956), pp. 399–402. See also the report presented to the Combined Chiefs of Staff at the Quebec conference in which it was stated that German resistance was "unlikely to continue beyond 1 December 1944," and might end "even sooner." "Prospects of a German Collapse or Surrender" September 9, 1944, *FRUS, The Conference at Quebec 1944,* p. 244.

14. See Dulles/Gaevernitz, "The First German Surrender," p. 16, Allen Dulles Papers, Princeton University (hereinafter cited as *Dulles/Gaevernitz*).

15. Ibid.

16. Winston S. Churchill, *Triumph and Tragedy* (Boston, 1953), p. 62 (hereinafter cited as *Churchill*).

17. This mood shows clearly in the Roosevelt/Churchill correspondence preceding the Quebec conference as well as in the papers approved at Quebec by the Combined Chiefs. *FRUS, The Conference at Quebec 1944,* pp. 221f and 471f.

18. *Churchill,* pp. 224–225. This message was actually prepared by Admiral Leahy as spokesman for the Joint Chiefs of Staff and dispatched to Churchill with only minor deletions.

The draft as well as the Joint Chiefs' supporting arguments may be found in the Leahy papers, Folder 127, RG 218, Modern Military Branch, National Archives.

19. Memorandum of Major General Clayton Bissel, G-2, to the Chief, Strategy Section, Operations Division, on "estimate of German Forces and Capabilities in Italy," 25 December 1944, OPD 381, TS 1945, Case 599/3–4, RG 165, Records of the War Department, General and Special Staffs, Modern Military Branch, National Archives. As late as April 1945, there were still twenty-four German divisions on the Italian front, and, according to an Allied appraisal, they were "stronger and in better condition than those on any other front." Memorandum, "Expected Developments of April 1945 in German-occupied Italy," 2 April 1945, OPD, 350.05 TS, Sec. Case 19, Records of the War Department General and Special Staff, RG 165, Modern Military Branch, National Archives. This same report noted that probably due to lack of fuel, as well as Allied disruption of lines of communication, only three German divisions had been withdrawn since January.

20. Maurizio (Maurizio was Ferruccio Parri's underground covername) "Il Movimento di Liberazione e gli Alleati," *Il Movimento di Liberazione in Italia*, no. 1 (July, 1949); Franco Catalano, *Storia del CLNAI* (Bari, Italy, 1956), pp. 84–86; Charles F. Delzell, *Mussolini's Enemies, The Italian Anti-Fascist Resistance* (Princeton, New Jersey, 1961), pp. 312–313; and a recent volume that surveys the history of the Italian resistance, Geoffrey Cox, *The Race for Trieste* (London, 1977), pp. 122–131 (hereinafter cited as *Cox, Race*.)

21. Delzell, *Mussolini's Enemies*, pp. 319 and 362f; Massimo Salvadori, *Resistenza e Azione* (Bari, 1951), pp. 235–237. Salvadori, an antifascist who chose to go into exile, enlisted in the British army and was sent to northern Italy by the SOE as a liaison officer with the resistance movement.

22. Caserta (MacMillan) to Foreign Office, no. 308, 14 September 1944, Foreign Office 371/43877/13079/8267 Public Records Office, London (hereinafter cited as *FO*).

23. On these aspects, see the following OSS reports: "The Radical Trend in German-occupied Italy," OSS Research and Analysis, no. 1681, undated (prior to June 1944), RG 59, Modern Military Branch, National Archives; "Report on political conditions in occupied Europe," 8 January 1944, Cordell Hull Papers, Correspondence files, Library of Congress. The latter report was also presented to the Joint Chiefs as an informational memorandum, Map Room, Box 171, Franklin D. Roosevelt Library, Hyde Park, New York.

24. "War Report, Office of Strategic Services, OSS" volume 2, pp. 107–108, P.O. 314.7 TS, 16 December 1949, Record of the Army Staff, RG 319, Modern Military Branch, National Archives. This report was written after the war, as an official report, at the request of the Joint Chiefs. It contains no facts or names which could have constituted a security danger in 1949; most of its importance therefore lies in some scattered information and its description of the organization of the OSS. The report has recently been edited and published by Anthony Cave Brown (see chapter 1, note 4, on p. 195.), who has, inexplicably, made many deletions and changed the order of the chapters.

25. Ibid.

26. Report to William W. Schott, Vice President, political section, HQ, Allied Commission, WO 204, 7293, X/L 03413, Public Records Office, London. Already in September, the Allies had decided that the CLNAI had to be regarded as the "central authority" and should be used "for the purpose of government," in case a German collapse left certain areas devoid of troops for two or three weeks. For the instructions to Rankin missions see: *Allied Control* 10000/125/32; "Instructions Governing Employment of Special Operations Personnel in Occupied Countries under Conditions of Enemy Withdrawal or Collapse," 20 September 1944, WO 204 7293 X/L 03413, Public Records Office, London.

27. On early Allied policy toward the partisans see the following files in *Allied Control*: 1000:125/320; 10000/125/244; 10000/125/32. Also the files of ASW 370.8 Italy, RG 107, Modern Military Branch, National Archives and *Coles and Weinberg*, p. 538f.

28. Copy of minutes, Minister of Economic Warfare (Shelborne) to Prime Minister,

Notes

annexed to report of War Cabinet Chiefs of Staff Committee, 29 October 1944, on SOE Operations in Italy, CAB 80, 88/8267, Public Records Office, London.

29. Medcos 205, AFHQ to BCS and JCS, 24 October 1944, Map Room 300, Warfare, Box 86, Franklin Roosevelt Library, Hyde Park, New York. The decision to divert available aircraft from Italy to Yugoslavia was taken notwithstanding the fact that four days before Major General D. Noce, Assistant Chief of Staff, G 3 at AFHQ, had presented Wilson's conference with a note urging the opposite conclusion (Supreme Allied Commander's Conference, 20 October, 1944, SAC (44) 110, "Diversion of Available Special Operations aircraft from Italy to northern Yugoslavia." 800 SAC, *Post and Counselor Files*). In the meeting at which it was decided to dispatch Medcos 205, there was only a marginal discussion of the content of the dispatch. However, the conference had available a summary of the conclusions reached at meetings held three days earlier between Wilson and Churchill. The latter apparently had stopped on his way back from Moscow, and it is possible that he influenced Wilson's decision. For the minutes of the meeting of 24 October 1944, see SAC (44) 103, 800 SAC, *Post and Counselor Files*.

30. Donovan to the President, 1 November 1944, *President's Secretary's File, OSS*, Box 170.

31. Minutes (copy), Minister of Economic Warfare to the Prime Minister, 24 October 1944, annexed to the report of the War Cabinet Chiefs of Staff Committee, "SOE Operations in Italy," 29 October 1944, CAB 80, 88/8267, Public Records Office, London.

32. Ibid.

33. Ibid. (Copy of minutes dated 26 October 1944, Minister of Economic Warfare to the Prime Minister).

34. Ibid.

35. Ibid. (Minutes from Prime Minister to General Ismay for Chiefs of Staff Committee, 28 October 1944).

36. Chiefs of Staff (44) 352, 30 October 1944, CAB 79, 82/8267, Public Records Office, London.

37. Ibid.

38. "Special Operations Air Supply to North Italy," SAC (44) 118, 5 November 1944, 800 SAC, *Post and Counselor* Files, Box 615.

39. Ibid.

40. "Minutes of a meeting of the Supreme Allied Commander's conference," SAC (44) 107, 7 November 1944, 800 SAC *Post and Counselor Files*, Box 615.

41. Ibid.

42. War Cabinet Chiefs of Staff Committee, "SOE Operations in the Mediterranean," Minute by the Prime Minister, 5 November 1944, COS (44) 360, 7 November 1944, CAB 80, 89/8267, Public Records Office, London.

43. Copy of Minutes, 7 November 1944, General Ismay to the Prime Minister, COS (44) 360, 7 November 1944, CAB 79, 82/8267, Public Records Office, London.

44. For the text of the message see Pietro Secchia and Filippo Frassati, *La resistenza e gli alleati* (Milan, 1962), pp. 151–152. For the reactions to it, see Delzell, *Mussolini's Enemies*, pp. 451–456.

45. See for example the report of Allied intelligence on the neofascist press for the week ending 27 November in "Weekly Intelligence Summary," PID, Italian Region, 27 November 1944, OWI papers, Entry 367, Italy 8–C, RG 208, Federal Record Center, Suitland, Maryland.

46. Medcos 210, General Wilson to War Department, 22 November 1944, Map Room, 300 Warfare, Box 87, Franklin D. Roosevelt Library, Hyde Park, New York.

47. Ibid.

48. Cosmed 198, CCS to AFHQ Mediterranean, for Wilson, 2 December 1944, Map Room, 300 Warfare, Box 87, Franklin D. Roosevelt Library, Hyde Park, New York; General Mark W. Clark to Generals McCreery and Truscott, 20 December 1944, OPD files, 381 TS 1945, Case 599/3–4, RG 165, Modern Military Branch, National Archives; Mediterranean Joint Planning

Theater Operational Directive, Winter and Spring 1944–1945, 14 December 1944, Caserta Joint Planning Staff, Box 624, RG 84, Federal Record Center, Suitland, Maryland.

49. Medcos 228, General Alexander to CCS, 8 January 1945, Map Room, 300 Warfare, Box 87, Franklin D. Roosevelt Library, Hyde Park, New York.

50. Memorandum for Assistant Chief of Staff OPD from Clayton Bissel, "German Intentions in Italy," 13 January 1945, OPD files 381, TS Sec. 1, Case 9/5, RG 165, Modern Military Branch, National Archives; Fan 801, CCS to General Alexander, 2 February 1945, Map Room, 300 Warfare, Box 87, Franklin D. Roosevelt Library, Hyde Park, New York.

51. Alexander to CCS, Naf 863, 15 February 1945, Map Room, 300 Warfare, Box 87, Franklin D. Roosevelt Library, Hyde Park, New York.

52. Donovan to the President, 29 November 1944, *President's Secretary's File*, OSS, Box 170, now published in Ennio Di Nolfo, "L'Operazione 'Sunrise': spunti e documenti," *Storia e Politica*, vol. XIV, no. 3, p. 360.

53. See for example Kirk to Secretary of State, #1022, 22 February 1945, 740.0011 EW/2–2245, Diplomatic Branch, National Archives; SOE Report on the Garibaldi bands, 5 January 1945, *FO* 371/48810/4709.

54. Extensive documentation on Allied actions and intentions regarding the agreement are in the British document collections, especially FO 371/43879/20502f and CAB 122, 888/8032, Public Records Office, London.

55. "Support of Italian Resistance North Italy" from AFHQ to 15th Army Group, 4 February 1945, 822.3 Italian Partisans, *Post and Counselor Files*.

56. Ibid.

57. Ibid.

58. Ibid.

59. Ibid.

60. Ibid.

61. "Interim Report on Measures to deal with Patriot problems in Northern Italy," AFHQ Mediterranean Joint Planning Staff, 18 February 1945, ACC Files 10000/136/262, *AFHQ*.

62. *Coles and Weinberg*, p. 547.

63. Ibid and "Interim Report" cited in note 61 above.

64. For the mood of the time, see *Cox, Race*, p. 20f.

Chapter 3: The Senders

1. See, for example, Himmler's handling of this theme in the post-July-20th period, Bradley F. Smith and Agnes F. Peterson, eds., *Himmler Geheimreden* (Frankfurt, 1974), p. 213f.

2. Ibid., p. 195f, for Himmler's emphasis on this theme during the war. The closer he came to the end, the more important the idea became to Hitler; see John Toland, *Adolf Hitler* (New York, 1976), p. 844f.

3. MS No. B583, T-1b, chapter 12, "Der Feldzug in Italien, die Kapitulation," by General der Panzertruppe, Röttiger. RG 338, Foreign Military Studies, Modern Military Branch, National Archives.

4. General von Vietinghoff's Diary Notes, 11 and 13 April 1945. Portions of this diary are appended to *Dulles/Gaevernitz*, which was written in Bern in May 1945.

5. See MS No. T-123, Part III, vol. 3, Commander in Chief West, p. 406f, RG 338 Foreign Military Studies, Modern Military Branch, National Archives (hereinafter cited as *Kesselring*). Other German participants in surrender approaches recognized Kesselring's attitude. See "General Wolff's Story of Events" attached to *Dulles/Gaevernitz*, p. 47.

6. General von Vietinghoff's Diary Notes, April 11 and 13, *Dulles/Gaevernitz*, p. 52.

Notes

7. Ibid.

8. For an example of the effects of this propaganda, see p. 163.

9. Wolff told his story a number of times (see note 52 in this chapter), but perhaps the clearest version is the record of the "monitoring" of his cell done by Allied Intelligence after he became a prisoner, *Selected CSDIC Reports*, p. 60. See also *Kesselring*, p. 400f.

10. See for example the OSS report on Gauleiter Kaufmann of Hamburg (Defeatism Among North German Leaders), sent to the Joint Chiefs on 17 April 1945, *CCS 387 Germany*.

11. Albert Speer, *Inside the Third Reich* (New York, 1970), p. 291.

12. Three very good collections of documents which show the sweep of German surrender approaches are: (1) The OSS Material in *President's Secretary's File*, OSS; (2) *CCS 387 Germany;* (3) *OSS Reports*.

13. *Kesselring*, p. 259.

14. Statement by SS Sturmbannführer Dr. Klaus Huegel, *OSS Reports*.

15. William Friend report to Colonel Hall, Psychological Warfare Branch, AFHQ, Rome, 5 May 1945, German Armistice File, *Post and Counselor Files*.

16. Cheston to Deane, 13 September 1944, *CCS 387 Germany*.

17. Ibid.

18. Donovan to JCS and attachments, 21 October 1944, *CCS 387 Germany*.

19. Donovan to JCS, 27 March 1945, p. 5, *CCS 387 Germany*.

20. *Dulles/Gaevernitz*, pp. 1–3; *Dulles Secret*, p. 41.

21. Cheston to Joint Chiefs, 24 January 1945 and attachment, *CCS 387 Germany*.

22. Massimo Ilardi, "Nuovi documenti sugli interventi tedeschi nell 'industria italiana tra il 1943 e il 1945," *Il Movimento di Liberazione in Italia*, vol. 26, no. 106, January–March, 1972.

23. Ferruccio Lanfranchi, *La Resa degli Ottocentomila* (Milan, 1948), p. 56f (hereinafter cited as *Lanfranchi*); *Dulles Secret*, pp. 44–45.

24. The text of the document is published in I. Schuster, *Gli Ultimi tempi di un regime* (Milan, 1946), p. 35. See also *Lanfranchi*, p. 22f; Deakin, pp. 263–265; E. Di Nolfo, "L'operazione 'Sunrise': spunti e documenti," *Storia e politica*, nos. 3–4, 1975.

25. *Dulles Secret*, p. 46.

26. Donovan to the President, 2 December 1944, *President's Secretary's File*, OSS, Box 170.

27. War Office Report, M.O. 1, 1 December 1944, *FO* 371/43879/20351.

28. Donovan to the President, 5 and 7 December 1944, *President's Secretary's File*, OSS, Box 170.

29. Donovan to the President, 8 December 1944, *President's Secretary's File*, OSS, Box 170.

30. Donovan to the Joint Chiefs, 9 February 1945, *CCS 387, Germany*. That Neurath had the confidence of OSS officials in his contact efforts is shown clearly by Gaevernitz to General Sibert, 23 February 1945, John Toland Collection, Box 9, Library of Congress (hereinafter cited as *Toland*).

31. Donovan to Joint Chiefs, 9 February 1945, *CCS 387 Germany*.

32. He still held on to this dream in late April 1945, see *Selected CSDIC Reports*, pp. 41 and 74 and Albert Kesselring, *Soldat bis zum Letzten Tag* (Bonn, 1953), pp. 409 and 419.

33. *Selected CSDIC Reports*, p. 41.

34. Ibid.

35. Cheston to Joint Chiefs, 26 February 1945, *CCS 387 Germany*.

36. Ibid.

37. Cheston to Joint Chiefs, 24 February 1945 (Germany: Kesselring and Rahn reported ready to quit). *CCS 387 Germany*.

38. Cheston to Joint Chiefs, 26 February 1945, p. 3, *CCS 387 Germany*.

39. Cheston to Joint Chiefs, 24 January 1945, p. 1, *CCS 387 Germany*.

40. Ibid. (attachment entitled "RSHA Attempt to Obtain Papal Intervention for Peace").

41. Donovan to Joint Chiefs, 9 February 1945, *CCS 387 Germany*.

42. Donovan to Joint Chiefs, 27 March 1945, *CCS 387 Germany.*
43. Ibid.
44. Ibid., attachment entitled "Approaches from von Epp."
45. Summary of approaches reaching OSS in Italy as background to Sunrise, *OSS Reports.*
46. Ibid.
47. Ibid.
48. Ibid.
49. Ibid.
50. Carlo Cornia, *Monterosa, Storia della Divisione Alpina Monterosa della RSI* (Udine, Italy, 1971), p. 181f.
51. Summary of approaches reaching OSS in Italy as background to Sunrise, *OSS Reports;* Giorgio Bocca, *Storia dell'Italia partigiana* (Bari, Italy, 1966), p. 572.
52. The sources for Wolff's actions are various and difficult to evaluate. Published materials include passages in John Toland, *The Last 100 Days* (New York, 1967), p. 315f (hereinafter cited as *Toland, Last 100*) and Karl Wolff, "Ecco la Verità," *Tempo* (Milan), February–March, 1951. Summaries of what Wolff told Allied officials at the time are in *OSS Reports.* Immediately after the capitulation Wolff made statements to an American psychological warfare officer ("Local Surrender in Italy" file) in *Post and Counselor Files* and preapred a summary of some of the Sunrise events for Gaevernitz which is appended to *Dulles/Gaevernitz.* In June 1945, as a prisoner in camp 209, Rome, Wolff's cell was "bugged" by Allied intelligence officers. This material (*Selected CSDIC Reports*) seems to give a fairly balanced account of Wolff's actions and motives because he was trying to convince his fellow prisoners that he had not betrayed the Third Reich, and at the same time he was aware the conversations were probably monitored by the Allies (at one point a participant said, "Don't speak so loudly."). In 1946–47, Wolff made many statements about Sunrise when he was interrogated at Nuremberg (Nuremberg Interrogation records, RG 1019, Roll 80, National Archives, hereinafter cited as *Wolff Interrogations*), and in March 1948 wrote a three-page paper entitled "Die Kapitulation der deutsch-italienischen Streitkrafte in Italien am 29.4/2.5.1945" for a German archive, but stipulated that it could not be quoted or cited (it will be referred to as "Wolff's uncitable statement" in these notes). Finally, in 1963 Wolff granted John Toland an interview, *Toland*, Box 9. Although the following text account depends heavily on Wolff's statements and those of other German participants, we have been especially cautious in their use because in the winter of 1945–1946 Karl Wolff was confined in a mental institution suffering from paranoia. The instability of his mental condition in 1946–47 was a major reason why he was not made a defendant or used as a witness in the Nuremberg trials (*Wolff Interrogations*, 14 December 1946, Frame 944 and 957; 25 February 1947, Frame 979; Personal Communication from General Telford Taylor, June 1, 1978). In the light of this mental question mark, readers and historians should be especially careful when dealing with all Wolff's declarations.
53. Personnel Files of Karl Wolff, Berlin Document Center.
54. *Selected CSDIC Reports*, pp. 31–32. Even the Italian Fascists had hard going with Wolff; see Albe Mellini Ponce de Leon, *Guerra Diplomatica a Salò Ottobre 1943-April 1945* (Bologna, 1950), p. 95.
55. *Selected CSDIC Reports*, p. 25; Karl Wolff, "Ecco la Verità," *Tempo* (February–March, 1951).
56. *Selected CSDIC Reports*, p. 25.
57. Ibid., p. 60. Variations of this explanation appear in virtually all of Wolff's statements, but see also E. F. Moelhausen, *La carta perdente* (Rome, 1948), p. 440.
58. Again, nearly every one of Wolff's statements cited above contains the assertion that he was approached by the Allies. Furthermore the secret Caserta history of Sunrise, composed after VE Day, states that following the surrender, Allied forces found a "political precis of the German position" which Wolff had written in longhand during the third week of March. In that document—which unfortunately has not yet been found—Wolff expressed hope for a breakup of the Alliance. But even here he stated that the Allies, rather than he himself, had initiated the

Notes

contact. Clearly, even though the wish was father to the thought, Wolff believed that he had been sought out by the Western powers. Memorandum "Crossword," AFHQ, Reel 21M, RG 331, Federal Record Center, Suitland, Maryland (hereinafter cited as *Crossword*).

59. *Selected CSDIC Reports*, p. 60; *Wolff Interrogations*, 16 December 1947, Frame 1192. Fritz Hesse's claim that Himmler ordered Wolff to make the contact is too vague and too full of errors to carry much weight. Fritz Hesse, *Das Spiel um Deutschland* (Munich, 1953), p. 427.

60. *Selected CSDIC Reports*, p. 60.

61. Ibid., pp. 60–61.

62. Ibid., p. 5.

63. See OSS dispatches no. 1197 and no. 497 (?) 110 (Dulles) to Caserta and Washington, 9 March 1945 and 110 to Glavin, 13 March 1945, *OSS Reports*.

64. Later, in the cold war, the allegedly idealistic anti-Communist thread in German Sunrise motivation received heavy emphasis in accounts appearing in West Germany. See for example Erich Winhold, "Kapitulation in Italien," *Das Dritte Reich/Zweiter Weltkrieg*, no. 51 (no date), pp. 500–501.

65. Wolff to Toland, 12 July 1963. *Toland*, Box 9; OSS dispatch no. 211, Glavin to Newhouse, 15 March 1945, *OSS Reports*.

66. General Airey Interview, July 1963, Box 9. *Toland*.

67. OSS dispatches no. 494 (?) 110 to Glavin, 13 March 1945, and unnumbered McKneeley (General Airey) to 110, 18 April 1945, *OSS Reports*.

68. Ibid.

69. OSS Summary dated 5 March 1945; Statement by SS Sturmbannführer Dr. Klaus Huegel, *OSS Reports*.

70. *Dulles Secret*, p. 68f. Eugen Dollmann, *Dolmetscher der Diktatoren* (Bamberg, Germany, 1963) p. 216f (hereinafter cited as *Dollmann*); Statement by SS Standartenführer Dr. Klaus Huegel, *OSS Reports*. See also *Lanfranchi*.

71. E. F. Moelhausen, *La carta perdente* (Rome, 1948), p. 442.

72. *Dulles Secret*, pp. 70–73; *Dulles/Gaevernitz*, p. 4.

73. The first reference to the Parrilli mission is a summary entry dated 5 March 1945, *OSS Reports*.

74. Parrilli and Zimmer may have fostered the impression that the Allies contacted him, not vice versa. See E. F. Moelhausen, *La carta Perdente* (Rome, 1948), p. 444; *Lanfranchi*, p. 133f; Erich Winhold, "Kapitulation in Italien," *Das Dritte Reich/Zweiter Weltkrieg* no. 51, p. 501.

75. That the Allies approached him because they thought he was a moderate is an idée fixe in Wolff's later accounts; see for example *Selected CSDIC Reports*, p. 61. In part, at least, Wolff was right; Gero von Gaevernitz told the German court which tried Wolff on 1 June 1949 that he had only agreed to listen to the SS man because Wolff had "protected" certain people. Gero von Gaevernitz File 1-25, Allen Dulles Papers, Princeton, New Jersey.

76. *Dollmann*, p. 218; Rudolf Rahn, *Ruheloses Leben* (Düsseldorf, 1949), p. 282 (hereinafter cited as *Rahn*).

77. *Selected CSDIC Reports*, p. 95.

78. "An Interview with SS Obergruppenführer Wolff" ("Local Surrender in Italy" file), *Post and Counselor Files*.

Chapter 4: Parleying in Bern

1. The crosscurrents in the SS show up clearly throughout Heinz Höhne, *The Order of the Death's Head* (New York, 1970).

2. OSS Summary, entry of 5 March, *OSS Reports*.

3. See Friedrich Karl von Plehwe, *The End of An Alliance*, translated by Erich Mossbacher (London, 1971), pp. 64–65 and Walter Hagan (Wilhelm Hoettl) *Unternehmen Bernhard* (Wels and Starnberg, 1955), p. 129. Ambassador Rahn also had harsh things to say about Dollmann in his interrogation by the U.S. Army on 31 October 1946. This interrogation, with its mixture of fact and fantasy, is a rather typical example of the unreliable "memoirs" of the German participants in Sunrise. Interrogation of Ambassador Rudolf Rahn, 31 October 1946, Freedom of Information Center, United States Army Intelligence Agency, Fort Meade, Maryland.

4. The following account is drawn chiefly from: *Dulles Secret; Toland The Last 100; Dollmann;* and *Dulles/Gaevernitz.*

5. See for example Jon Kimche, *Spying for Peace* (London, 1961), pp. 150–151 (hereinafter cited as *Kimche*), and *Dulles/Gaevernitz*, p. 13.

6. OSS Summary, entry of 5 March, *OSS Reports.*

7. Ibid.

8. *Dulles Secret*, p. 76.

9. Ibid.

10. Report by Obersturmführer Zimmer, Secret Surrender Background Material File, Dulles Papers, Princeton, New Jersey. On Husmann see also E. F. Moelhausen, *La carta perdente* (Rome, 1948), p. 444.

11. Gaevernitz Report, p. 33, Box 9, *Toland.*

12. *Selected CSDIC Reports*, p. 33.

13. In addition to scattered references in Wolff's various statements, the following account is based on *Dollmann*, pp. 222–224; *Rahn*, pp. 283–285; and *Kimche*, pp. 129–131. Mellini's claim that Mussolini had learned of Parri's release and protested to Wolff by 5 March is highly unlikely. Alberto Ponce de leon Mellini, *Guerra Diplomatic a Salò, Ottobre 1943–Aprile 1945* (Bologna, 1950), pp. 102–103.

14. *Lanfranchi.*

15. *Rahn*, p. 284.

16. Ibid.

17. See especially Rahn himself and *Dollmann*, p. 221, plus *Selected CSDIC Reports* p. 61. An uneven German account, which, nonetheless, is obviously based on some information from German participants, says that at this point "not a word was spoken about capitulation." Erich Winhold, "Kapitulation in Italien," *Das Dritte Reich/Zweiter Weltkrieg*, No. 51, p. 501.

18. Allen Dulles and Hamilton Fish Armstrong, *Can We Be Neutral?* (New York, 1936), p. 103. In addition to the specific references on Dulles cited below, see Leonard Mosley, *Dulles* (New York, 1978).

19. Communication from John Toland, September, 1977, reporting an observation of Gero von Gaevernitz.

20. A. Dulles to Cordell Hull, 8 January 1944, Correspondence, Box 53, Cordell Hull Papers, Library of Congress.

21. Donovan to the President, 1 November and 29 November 1944, *President's Secretary's File OSS*, Box 170.

22. Donovan to the President, 24 July 1944, *President's Secretary's File OSS*, Box 168; Allen Dulles, *Germany's Underground* (New York, 1947), p. 164. The precise role of the OSS in encouraging the July 20 movement is still very clouded. Gaevernitz's view at least peeps through in Fabian von Schlabrendorff, *They Almost Killed Hitler* (New York, 1947), which was "prepared and edited" by Gaevernitz. The whole question of the German resistance is covered in Peter Hoffmann, *The History of the German Resistance 1933–1945* (Cambridge, Mass., 1977).

23. Donovan requested authority to give immunity to individual Germans in December 1944, but the request was vetoed by FDR. Donovan's request is in Box 733, "Memos for the Secretary" and the negative reply which Stettinius drafted on FDR's orders is in Box 734, "Memos for the President," Edward Stettinius Papers, University of Virginia.

Notes

24. See p. 56.
25. *Dulles Secret* pp. 35 and 55; Gaevernitz to Toland, 25 July 1963, Box 9, *Toland*.
26. *Dulles Secret* p. 37f; *Dulles/Gaevernitz*, passim.
27. OSS Summary, entry of 5 March, *OSS Reports*.
28. Ibid.
29. In addition to Wolff's statements, this section is primarily based on: *Dollmann*, pp. 224–227; *Dulles Secret*, pp. 87–102; *Dulles/Gaevernitz*, and Dulles's first three dispatches to Caserta, No. 110 (Dulles) to Glavin, 8, 9, 10 March 1945, *OSS Reports*.
30. Dollmann plays down the importance of Husmann's lecture (*Dollmann*, p. 225), while Kimche claims that Waibel did the lecturing (he wasn't even present), *Kimche*, p. 131. However, Wolff's "Uncitable Statement" of March 1948 emphasizes Husmann's lecture, and that seems conclusive. Wolff later confessed that his conscience was troubled when he told Husmann that he was not speaking for Himmler or Hitler, presumably because he believed that on 6 February Hitler had tacitly agreed that Wolff should try his hand at negotiation contacts. Wolff Interrogations, 16 December 1947, Frame 1191.
31. No. 110 (Dulles) to Glavin, 10 March 1945, *OSS Reports*.
32. *Dulles/Gaevernitz*, p. 6.
33. No. 110 (Dulles) to Glavin, 10 March 1945, *OSS Reports*.
34. Ibid.
35. Ibid. When he returned to Italy, Wolff did order an end to offensive action against most Italian partisans, but he commanded continued aggressiveness toward all units associated with Tito. Note, c. 12 March, RFSS, T-175, EAP 170-b-10-18/12, Frame 3864, Modern Military Branch, National Archives.
36. No. 110 (Dulles) to Glavin, 10 March 1945, *OSS Reports*.
37. No. 110 (Dulles) to Glavin, 9 March 1945, *OSS Reports*.
38. No. 110 (Dulles) to Glavin, 10 March 1945, *OSS Reports*.
39. Ibid.
40. Ibid.
41. No. 110 (Dulles) to Glavin, 8 March 1945, *OSS Reports*.
42. Ibid. Donovan's reports to the Joint Chiefs, the Secretary of State, and the President are, as far as can be ascertained, identical. Those to FDR and the Joint Chiefs of Staff are as cited above. Those to the Secretary of State are filed under the appropriate dates in 740.00119 EW, Diplomatic Branch, National Archives.
43. Ibid.
44. Alexander to CCS, Naf 878, 11 March 1945, *OSS Reports*. Significantly, this message repeats Dulles's first statement that an OKW representative was in Wolff's party; doubly significant because copies of Dulles's messages of 9 and 10 March, which had no reference to an OKW man, are in the same file marked "seen by SAC," that is, by Supreme Allied Commander (Alexander). Although the official British history of the foreign policy of the period is rather critical of American handling of the whole Sunrise affair, it too repeats the error that an OKW representative was present. E. L. Woodward, *British Foreign Policy in the Second World War* (London, 1976), 374f.
45. Alexander to CCS, Naf 878, 11 March 1945, *OSS Reports*.
46. Sir A. Brooke to PM, 10 March 1945, PREM 3 198/2, Public Records Office, London.
47. CIGS to Alexander, 10 March 1945, *OSS Reports*.
48. *Stimson Diary*, 11 March, 1945. See also Henry L. Stimson and McGeorge Bundy, *On Active Service in Peace and War* (New York, 1947) and William D. Leahy, *I Was There* (New York, 1950).
49. *Stimson Diary*, 11 March 1945.
50. Ibid. The wording of Stimson's diary entries fits the subsequent course of events so perfectly, that one must wonder if they were written later.
51. Ibid. JCS 1288, 12 March 1945, *CCS 387 Germany*.

52. General McFarland to Admiral Leahy et al. 12 March 1945 and A. T. Cornwall Jones to General McFarland, 12 March 1945, *CCS 387 Germany.*

53. Harriman to the Acting Secretary, 12 March 1945, *FRUS*, 1945, vol. III, p. 725.

54. A. T. Cornwall Jones to General McFarland, 13 March 1945, *CCS 387 Germany.*

55. *Stimson Diary*, 12 March 1945.

56. Harriman to Secretary of State No. 728, 13 March 1945, 740.00119 EW/3-1345, Diplomatic Branch, National Archives. This significant document is not published in the *FRUS* series.

57. Deane to the War Department, No. 23187, 13 March 1945, *CCS 387 Germany.*

58. Ibid.

59. Charles Bohlen Memorandum, 13 March 1945, 740.00119 EW/3-1345 Diplomatic Branch, National Archives (in part published in *FRUS* 1945, vol. III, p. 726, Fn 52).

60. Additional memorandum by Bohlen, 13 March 1945, *FRUS*, 1945, vol. III, pp. 726–727.

61. JCS 797, 13 March 1945, *FRUS*, 1945, vol. III, pp. 727–728.

62. *Stimson Diary*, 13 March 1945.

63. WSC to General Ismay and Foreign Secretary, 15 March 1945, *FO* 371/46783/7953, vol. I.

64. CCS 797/1, 15 March 1945, *FRUS* 1945, vol. III, p. 728.

65. WSC to Foreign Secretary, 15 March 1945, *FO* 371/46783/7953, vol. I.

66. Harriman to Secretary of State, 16 March 1945, *FRUS* 1945, vol. III, pp. 731–732.

67. Ibid.

68. Deane and Archer to CCS, 18 March 1945, No. MX23276, *CCS 387 Germany.*

69. Ibid.

70. Ibid.

71. Ibid.

72. *Stimson Diary*, 17 March 1945.

73. General Hull to Mr. Dunn and enclosures, 17 March 1945, 740.00119 EW/3-1745, Diplomatic Branch, National Archives.

74. Ibid.

75. *Stimson Diary*, 17 March 1945.

76. Preparatory version with FDR's initials and Leahy note, dated 17 March 1945, *CCS 387 Germany*. Dispatched version, Grew to Harriman, 20 March 1945, *FRUS*, 1945, vol. III, pp 735–736.

77. *Stimson Diary*, 17 March 1945; Harriman to Secretary of State, 17 March 1945, *FRUS*, 1945, vol. III, pp. 732–733.

78. Ibid. In a second telegram of the same date, Harriman speculated on the reasons for the sharp Soviet reaction. Aside from simple suspicion and the question of prestige mentioned in the cited text, he also thought that the Russians might have some more dark intentions for Germany which could be implemented by *Freies Deutschland*, a Soviet sponsored group of ex-KPD leaders and captured German officers and soldiers. Harriman to Secretary of State, 17 March 1945, 740.00119 EW/3-1745, Diplomatic Branch, National Archives. In his memoirs, Harriman plays down the sharpness of his messages of 16 and 17 March. W. Averell Harriman and Elie Abel, *Special Envoy to Churchill and Stalin, 1941–46* (New York, 1975), p. 433.

79. Clark Kerr to Foreign Office, 17 March 1945, *FO* 371/46783/7953, vol. IV.

80. Eden to Secretary of State, 18 March 1945, 740.00119 EW/3-1845, Diplomatic Branch, National Archives.

81. Ibid.

82. Memorandum by Charles Bohlen, 19 March, and Acting Secretary of State to Harriman, 20 March 1945, *FRUS*, 1945, vol. III, pp. 735–736.

83. The issue of POW treatment has not much concerned historians but it agitated official Washington; see *Stimson Diary*, 2 March 1945f.

84. No. 110 (Dulles) to Glavin, 13 March 1945, *OSS Reports.*

Notes

85. Ibid.
86. See above, Chapter 3, 61f.
87. Glavin to Newhouse, No. 211, 15 March 1945, *OSS Reports*.
88. CCS to Alexander, Fan 506, 12 March 1945, *OSS Reports*.
89. *Crossword*, p. 7.
90. Ibid.
91. *Dulles/Gaevernitz*, p. 11.
92. Ibid.
93. Glavin to Newhouse No. 211, 15 March 1945, *OSS Reports*.
94. *Dulles/Gaevernitz*, p. 11.
95. Ibid.
96. Lemnitzer to Caserta, No. 520, 16 March 1945, *OSS Reports*.
97. CCS to Alexander, 15 March, *OSS Reports*.
98. Glavin to Newhouse, No. 200 (?), 14 March 1945, Lemnitzer to Caserta, No. 520, 16 March 1945, *OSS Reports; Crossword*, p. 11.
99. AFHQ to Dulles, Glavin and Lemnitzer, 19 March 1945 (confirming message of 15 March), *OSS Reports*.
100. Lemnitzer to Caserta, No. 3, 18 March 1945, *OSS Reports*.
101. Lemnitzer to Caserta, No. 540, 20 March 1945, *OSS Reports*.
102. *Dulles Secret*, p. 115.
103. Ibid., p. 123; Lemnitzer to AFHQ, No. 540, 20 March 1945, *OSS Reports*.
104. Airey to AFHQ, 21 March 1945, *OSS Reports*.
105. *Dulles/Gaevernitz*, p. 14.
106. Ibid., p. 16.
107. Ibid., p. 17.
108. Ibid. Airey to AFHQ, 21 March 1945, *OSS Reports*. In the testimony which Gaevernitz gave at Wolff's trial in Hamburg, 1 June 1949, the former OSS man asserted that Wolff had been urged at the 19 March meeting to protect the northern Italian power plants, and had agreed to do so, but there is no sign of this in the contemporary documents. Gero von Gaevernitz File 1-25, Allen Dulles Papers, Princeton, New Jersey.
109. No. 110 (Dulles) to Glavin, 13 March 1945, *OSS Reports*.
110. *Dulles/Gaevernitz*, p. 15.
111. Lemnitzer to Caserta, No. 540, 20 March 1945, *OSS Reports*.
112. Ibid.
113. *Dulles/Gaevernitz*, p. 14.
114. Lemnitzer to Caserta No. 540, 20 March 1945, *OSS Reports*. Gaevernitz apparently even asked the SS man to bring Westphal to Italy, but Wolff though the idea "too risky." Gaevernitz to General E. L. Sibert, G-2, Twelfth Army Group, 10 March 1945, "Chapter 6, Secret Surrender Background Material, etc." Dulles Papers, Princeton, New Jersey.
115. Lemnitzer to Caserta, No. 540, 20 March 1945, *OSS Reports*.
116. Ibid.
117. Ibid.
118. *Dulles/Gaevernitz*, p. 16.
119. Ibid., p. 19; Lemnitzer to Caserta No. 540, 20 March 1945, *OSS Reports*.
120. *Dulles/Gaevernitz*, p. 19.
121. Lemnitzer to Caserta No. 540, 20 March 1945, *OSS Reports*; Later Wolff contended that the Allied representatives "agreed" that he should go to Kesselring but this seems to be a product of the SS man's ex post facto dream world. *Wolff Interrogations*, 1 December 1947, Frame 1173.
122. It was after the Ascona meeting that Wolff wrote the "political precis" which fell into Allied hands at the end of the war but whose present location is unknown. An American official who read it soon after the surrender concluded "that Wolff was fairly aware of the true

Forrest C. Pogue, *George C. Marshall: Organizer of Victory* (New York, 1973), pp. 566–567.

36.   Admiral Leahy to President Roosevelt, 4 April 1945, Admiral Leahy Papers, "Berne Surrender Controversy" File, Joint Chiefs of Staff, RG 218, Modern Military Branch, National Archives.

37.   President Roosevelt to Premier Stalin, 4 April 1945, *FRUS*, 1945, vol. III, pp. 745–746.

38.   Judging from the primary sources one might doubt whether Wolff ever visited Kesselring. Of the German sources only *Dollmann* (p. 229) and *Wolff Interrogations* (1 December 1947, Frames 1173f.) refer to this trip, while Kesselring's own account makes no mention of it. Zimmer gave Dulles information about the trip on 31 March, but the subsequent Allied reports based on this information should be used with great care: Donovan to the Joint Chiefs of Staff, 1 April 1945, *CCS-387, Germany* and Lemnitzer and Airey to AFHQ, 31 March 1945, No. 610, *OSS Reports*.

39.   Donovan to the Joint Chiefs of Staff 1 April 1945, *CCS-387 Germany* and *Wolff Interrogations*, 1 December 1947, Frames 1173–1174.

40.   Ibid., and Lemnitzer and Airey to AFHQ, 31 March 1945, No. 610, *OSS Reports*. The word "advised" was used in the report originating from Dulles, who was nearly always inclined to accept Wolff's tales at face value. Yet Lemnitzer and Airey used the stronger word "authorized." So we are left with the following progression: Zimmer or Wolff may have invented the "advised" tale; Lemnitzer and Airey made it even stronger as "authorized," and this version went to the Combined Chiefs of Staff in a message from Alexander. Naf 907, 1 April 1945, *CCS-387 Germany*.

41.   The most extensive account of Wolff's dealings with the SS chiefs is *Wolff Interrogations*, 1 December 1947, Frames 1176–1179. Two other important sources are the statement of SS Standartenführer Dr. Klaus Huegel, *OSS Reports*, and the uncitable statement made by Wolff in 1948. There are also cryptic references sprinkled through *Selected CSDIC Reports*, especially p. 61. An important brief reference is *Dollmann*, p. 229. On this matter, too, Zimmer gave Dulles some relevant information on 31 March, but this must be used with caution, (Donovan to the Joint Chiefs of Staff, 1 April 1945, *CCS-387, Germany*). There is no mention of the trip in the reports which Lemnitzer and Airey sent to Caserta, presumably either because Dulles did not think it advisable to pass this portion of Zimmer's message on to the generals or because they were reluctant to transmit it to Alexander. Whoever was responsible, it smacks of a cover-up, because even though the Joint Chiefs of Staff received an indication that Wolff was still dealing with Himmler, the Combined Chiefs of Staff did not.

42.   "General von Vietinghoff's Story," in *Dulles/Gaevernitz*, pp. 51–52.

43.   Ibid.

44.   *Selected CSDIC Reports, passim.*

45.   *Crossword*, p. 23; Glavin to No. 110, 21 March 1945, *OSS Reports*.

46.   Parri was not told why he had been released by the Germans, but from Dulles's manner he concluded that it was part of some larger arrangement. Interview with Ferruccio Parri by E. Aga Rossi, 3 June 1977. The Allied debate on what to do with Parri and Usmiani may be followed in *OSS Reports* from 10 to 29 March. Allied concern to use Parri to keep the situation "in hand" at the time of a partisan rising or a German collapse shows up most clearly in Dulles to Glavin, 10 March 1945, Lemnitzer to AFHQ, 24 March 1945 and Dulles to Newhouse, No. 585, 29 March 1945 (all *OSS Reports*).

47.   Lemnitzer to AFHQ, No. 574, 26 March 1945, *OSS Reports*. All the quotations cited in this paragraph were underlined by officers at AFHQ who received the original Lemnitzer message.

48.   Donovan to Joint Chiefs, 29 March 1945, (*CCS-387 Germany*) indicates that Dulles made no reports on Sunrise between 21 and 29 March, or, it he did, the OSS headquarters did not pass them on to the president or the Joint Chiefs of Staff.

49.   Lemnitzer and Airey to AFHQ, 27 and 29 March, No. 575 and No. 588, *OSS Reports*.

50.   Ibid. The message of 29 March raised the possibility that if Army Group C surrendered

intact, it might, after repatriation to Germany, "form [the] nucleus of some future German revival." This point, like the others in the telegrams, however, was simply thrown in at random without further evaluation or comment.

51. AFHQ to General Airey, 2 April 1945, *OSS Reports*.
52. Alexander to the CCS, 28 March 1945, Naf 902, *CCS-387 Germany*.
53. Lemnitzer to AFHQ, 27 March (No. 576) and 30 March 1945, *OSS Reports*.

See also *Rahn*, pp. 285–286; *Dulles/Gaevernitz*, p. 21; *Crossword*, p. 24; and Donovan to the Joint Chiefs, 29 March 1945, *CCS 387 Germany*.

54. Donovan to Joint Chiefs, 1 April 1945, *CCS 387 Germany*; Lemnitzer and Airey to AFHQ, 31 March 1945 No. 610, *OSS Reports*. Considering that the high hopes for a Western surrender entertained by the Anglo-Americans were partly based on the supposed positive influence of General Westphal, and partly on the idea of Wolff's independence from Himmler, it is a tribute to Zimmer's gift of persuasion that in this conversation he discussed Wolff's trip to see Himmler, failed to mention Westphal at all, and still Dulles went away from the meeting without a sense of being manipulated.

55. Ibid. Alexander to CCS, Naf 907, 1 April 1945, *CCS 387 Germany*.
56. Ibid.
57. AFHQ to Lemnitzer and Airey, 31 March 1945, *OSS Reports*.
58. Alexander to CCS, Naf 907, 1 April 1945, *CCS 387 Germany*.
59. Prime Minister to Foreign Secretary, 30 March 1945, *FO 371/46783/7953*, vol. III.
60. Donovan to Joint Chiefs, 4 April 1945, *CCS 387 Germany*.
61. Lemnitzer and Airey to AFHQ, No. 617, 3 April 1945, *OSS Reports*.
62. *Crossword*, p. 32.
63. Donovan to Joint Chiefs, 4 April 1945, *CCS 387 Germany*.
64. Ibid.
65. Ibid.
66. Lemnitzer and Airey to AFHQ, No. 617, 3 April 1945, *OSS Reports*.
67. Donovan to Joint Chiefs, 4 April 1945, *CCS 387 Germany*.
68. Lemnitzer and Airey to AFHQ, 3 April 1945, *OSS Reports*.
69. Ibid. This document together with Alexander's dispatch to Washington (4 April, Naf 911, *CCS 387 Germany*) indicates that the Caserta generals believed they had drawn a sharp line with Wolff. However, the OSS report (see note 67 above) as well as Dulles's published memoir (*Dulles Secret*, pp. 129–132) and the account originating with Parrilli (*Lanfranchi*, pp. 221–222) suggest that no such line was drawn. The clincher in favor of the view that something close to an ultimatum was issued appears in *Dulles/Gaevernitz*, p. 24. It shows that in May, 1945, Dulles thought that the line was sharp, and that twenty-one years later he softened it while preparing *Secret Surrender*.

70. Alexander to the CCS, 4 April 1945, Naf 911, *CCS 387 Germany*.
71. Harrison Minutes, 3 April 1945, *FO 371/46783/7953/* vol, IV.
72. Harrison Minutes, 4 April 1945, *FO 371/46783/7953*, vol. IV.
73. Prime Minister to Foreign Secretary and Lord Ismay, 3 April 1945, *FO 371/46783/7953*, vol. IV.
74. As Forrest Pogue has indicated in *George C. Marshall: Organizer of Victory* (New York, 1973), p. 666, footnote 14, Churchill was badly fooled about who was the author of the "Roosevelt" letters to Stalin. When he finally learned that Marshall had played a part in their preparation, he still did not know of Leahy's critical role and attributed phrases that Marshall had written to the president, while the portions Leahy had composed he credited to Marshall. If a man as sensitive to language and FDR's personality as Churchill could be so completely wrong, one ought to be very careful about reading Franklin Roosevelt's intentions into these messages. See *Churchill*, pp. 446–449.
75. Prime Minister to Marshal Stalin, draft, 6 April 1945, *CAB 21/1602/7953*, Public Records Office, London.

76. Extract from Lord Beaverbrook's letter to the prime minister, 6 April 1945, PREM 3/198/2/7990, Public Records Office, London.

77. WM(45) 40th Conclusions, Confidential Annex, 4 April 1945, PREM 3/198/2/7990, Public Records Office, London. The OSS from the beginning had decided not to inform British intelligence in Switzerland of Operation Sunrise. See AFHQ note, 12 March 1945, *OSS Reports.*

78. *Churchill,* pp. 449–451.

79. Prime Minister to President Roosevelt, 5 April 1945, *FRUS,* 1945, vol. III, pp. 746–747.

80. President Roosevelt to Prime Minister, 6 April 1945, "Franklin D. Roosevelt—W. Churchill Messages," Box 7, Map Room, Franklin Roosevelt Library, Hyde Park, New York. See also *Roosevelt and Churchill,* p. 705.

81. See Stephen E. Ambrose, *Eisenhower and Berlin, 1945* (Garden City, New York, 1967).

82. Deane to Marshall, No. M23664, 4 April 1945, Admiral Leahy Files, "Berne Surrender Controversy" File, RG 218, Modern Military Branch, National Archives.

83. Ibid.

84. Ibid., and Deane to Marshall, No. M23662, 4 April 1945, "Europe File," Interservice Agencies, U.S. Military Mission, Moscow, RG 334, Modern Military Branch, National Archives. No reference to this conversation between Molotov and Harriman appears in *FRUS.*

85. Grew Memorandum for the President, 4 April 1945, Map Room, 370 Germany, Box 35, Franklin D. Roosevelt Library, Hyde Park, New York.

86. William Leahy, *I Was There* (New York, 1950), p. 335.

87. Premier Stalin to President Roosevelt, 7 April 1945, *FRUS,* vol. III, pp. 749–751.

88. *Churchill,* p. 453.

89. Prime Minister to Foreign Secretary, 8 April 1945, *CAB 21 Crossword.*

90. Prime Minister to President Roosevelt, 11 April 1945, *FRUS,* 1945, vol, III, p. 752.

91. "Notes, Roosevelt-Stalin Messages," Box 9, Map Room, Franklin D. Roosevelt Library, Hyde Park, New York.

92. Brown Memorandum to Admiral Leahy, 9 April 1945, Box 35, 370 Germany, Map Room, Franklin D. Roosevelt Library, Hyde Park, New York.

93. Roosevelt to Stalin, 12 April 1945, *FRUS,* 1945, vol. III, p. 756. On 10 April, when the question arose of a possible cease-fire in the Netherlands, Roosevelt tentatively agreed to talks but informed Churchill that in light of Stalin's reaction to Sunrise the Russians had to be informed before any discussion occurred with the Germans. See *Roosevelt and Churchill,* p. 707.

94. Harriman to President Roosevelt, 12 April 1945, *FRUS,* 1945, vol. III, p. 756.

95. President Roosevelt to Ambassador Harriman, 12 April 1945, *FRUS,* 1945, vol. III, p. 757.

Chapter 6: The Long Mile to Caserta

1. George Elsey to Admiral Brown, 16 April 1945, German Surrender Negotiations, Historical Reports and Notes, Box 3, Papers of George M. Elsey, Harry S. Truman Library, Independence, Missouri.

2. *Dulles/Gaevernitz,* pp. 26 and 51–52; *Stuhlpfarer,* pp. 125–126.

3. *Dulles/Gaevernitz,* pp. 26–27. The memorandum did question whether German naval forces would obey a surrender order.

4. *Dulles/Gaevernitz,* pp. 26–27; Alexander to Joint Chiefs, 12 April 1945, Naf 916, CCS 387 Germany; 110 (Dulles) to Glavin, 9 April 1945, Nos. 646 and 647, *OSS Reports.*

5. Ibid.

6. *Lanfranchi,* pp. 223–228.

7. 110 (Dulles) to Glavin, 9 April 1945, No. 647, *OSS Reports.*

Notes

8. Buxton to Joint Chiefs, 10 April 1945, *CCS 387 Germany.*

9. BAF to SACMED 5 April (No. 693), 7 April (No. 699), 11 April (No. 711), and 13 April 1945 (No. FX59427), German Surrender Files, *Post and Counselor Files.*

10. Kirk to Secretary of State, 12 April No. 1491, 740.00119 Control (Italy) 4-1245, Diplomatic Branch, National Archives. Kirk's effort, in the same period, to persuade the military to take more account of the law-and-order issue in their operational planning for the north also seems to have had no significant impact on Caserta (Kirk to AFHQ, 11 April 1945, No. 34, 820.02 Italy Resistance, Box 639, *Post and Counselor Files)* nor were any Anglo-American authorities willing to touch the Vatican's belated peace efforts of April, 1945. See p. 138; *Deakin,* p. 297f, and the President to Ambassador Taylor, 6 April 1945, No. 36, *FRUS,* vol. III, p. 747.

11. *Crossword,* p. 32.

12. Lemnitzer to 110 (Dulles), 9 April 1945, No. 612, *OSS Reports.*

13. Ibid.

14. 110 (Dulles) to Lemnitzer, 10 April 1945, No. 662, *OSS Reports.*

15. Alexander to CCS, 12 April 1945, No. 916, *CCS 387 Germany.*

16. Aide Memoir, British Embassy to the Department of State, 14 April 1945, *FRUS,* 1945, vol. III, pp. 757–758, and fn. 14.

17. Prime Minister to President Truman, April 15 1945, CAB 21/1602/7953, Public Records Office London.

18. Ibid.

19. 110 (Dulles) to Lemnitzer, 13 April 1945, No. 684, *OSS Reports.*

20. 110 (Dulles) to Lemnitzer, 15 April 1945, No. 693, *OSS Reports.*

21. *Kesselring,* p. 406.

22. *Dulles/Gaevernitz,* p. 52.

23. Ibid.

24. 110 (Dulles) to Lemnitzer, 15 April (No. 693), 17 April (No. 699), 24 April (No. 758), *OSS Reports.*

25. *Wolff Interrogations,* 16 December 1947, Frame 1186f; 110 (Dulles) to Lemnitzer, 24 April 1945, No. 758, OSS Reports. The records of the postsurrender monitoring of Wolff's cell indicate that Kaltenbrunner knew of Wolff's trips to Switzerland and that Wolff had tried to get Kaltenbrunner to participate in the Sunrise operation. *Selected CSDIC Reports,* pp. 21 and 51.

26. Ibid. Hitler was in Berlin at this time, but Wolff told the Allies that he had met him in a bunker "outside Berlin." This was probably a feeble attempt to mislead Allied intelligence even at this late date.

27. Ibid.

28. Ibid.

29. *Selected CSDIC Reports,* p. 62.

30. Compare 110 (Dulles) to Lemnitzer 15 April and 16 April 1945 (No. 679 and No. 693) *OSS Reports* with Cheston to Joint Chiefs, 19 April 1945, *CCS 387 Germany.* Wolff claimed that Vietinghoff was fearful of Sunrise chiefly because of the alleged activities of an agent provocateur. This story also grew with the telling and by the cold war period Gaevernitz and others flatly asserted that the agent provocateur existed and was a Russian agent. Gaevernitz to Toland, 25 July 1963, *Toland; Kimche,* pp. 140–141 (see also *Dulles Secret,* pp. 153–154). No confirming evidence regarding this incident has come to light, but at the time the Caserta authorities believed that the Germans had probably invented the story. See Lemnitzer to 110 (Dulles), no I.D. number, 18 April 1945, *OSS Reports.*

31. Buxton to Joint Chiefs, 13 April 1945, *CCS 387 Germany.*

32. 110 (Dulles) to Glavin, 16 April 1945 No. 696, *OSS Reports.*

33. Cheston to Joint Chiefs, 19 April 1945, *CCS 387 Germany.* For the failure of the Allied authorities to get the point, see p. 154.

34. 679 to 110 (Dulles), 15 April 1945, No. 693, *OSS Reports.*

35. Ibid.

36. 110 (Dulles) to Glavin, 17 April 1945, No. 699, *OSS Reports.*

37. Lemnitzer to 110 (Dulles), 11 April 1945, No. 626, *OSS Reports.*

38. Ibid.

39. Airey to 110 (Dulles), 14 April 1945, No. 640, *OSS Reports.*

40. Lemnitzer to 110 (Dulles), 13 April 1945, No. 633, *OSS Reports.*

41. Lemnitzer to 110 (Dulles), 18 April 1945 (no I.D. number), *OSS Reports; Crossword,* p. 40.

42. 110 (Dulles) to Glavin, 17 April 1945, No. 699, *OSS Reports.*

43. 110 (Dulles) to Glavin, 18 April 1945, *OSS Reports.*

44. Ibid.

45. Ibid.

46. Lemnitzer to 110 (Dulles), 19 April 1945, No. 667, *OSS Reports.*

47. This chapter and chapter 4 contain a number of examples of this contrast. See the *OSS Reports* for more instances.

48. Lemnitzer to 110 (Dulles), 21 April 1945, No. 681, *OSS Reports.* On 22 April Deane reported to Alexander that the Soviets had been informed of the cut-off order. Deane to Alexander, 22 April 1945, No. M-24003, *OSS Reports.*

49. *Cox Race,* p. 102f. Directive on Partisan Operations, 14 April 1945, WO 204/7299/X/L03413, Public Records Office London, and Charles F. Delzell, *Mussolini's Enemies* (Princeton, New Jersey, 1961), p. 511.

50. Lemnitzer to 110, 23, and 24 April 1945 (No. 692 and No. 698), *OSS Reports.* For Partisan actions see Roberto Battaglia, *Storia della Resistenza Italiana* (Turin, 1964), p. 539f and Charles F. Delzell, *Mussolini's Enemies* (Princeton, New Jersey, 1961), p. 511f.

51. *Rahn,* p. 289f; *Stuhlpfarer,* p. 127f.

52. *Stuhlpfarer,* p. 127.

53. Ibid., p. 128.

54. A copy of Vietinghoff's instructions is attached to the surrender documents: C.C.S. Memorandum for Information No. 277, 7 June 1945, *CCS 387 Germany.*

55. *Dulles/Gaevernitz* (Short selections from Vietinghoff's "Diary"), p. 53.

56. Vietinghoff to Alexander, 23 May 1945, *OSS Reports.*

57. *Dulles/Gaevernitz,* p. 53.

58. Ibid.

59. *Selected CSDIC Reports,* p. 70.

60. Ibid.

61. *Deakin,* p. 297f.

62. *Selected CSDIC Reports,* p. 69.

63. Ibid.

64. Ibid.; See also *Dollmann,* p. 237f.

65. *Selected CSDIC Reports,* p. 69; *Dulles/Gaevernitz* (Wolff Statement), p. 47. Once again we are faced with the question whether Wolff's postwar statements, indicating Kesselring knew what was going on, were more exaggerated than Kesselring's subsequent protestations that he had been left in the dark. After the war, Ambassador Rahn characterized Wolff's belief that he could cooperate with Kesselring in engineering a surrender as "wishful thinking." (Statement by Rahn, no date, Secret Surrender Files, Dulles Papers, Princeton, New Jersey.) It would seem then that even if Kesselring knew more than he outwardly indicated, he was never a serious participant in a surrender plan.

66. *Selected CSDIC Reports,* p. 69; *Kesselring,* p. 407.

67. 110 (Dulles) to Lemnitzer, 23 April 1945, No. 744, *OSS Reports.*

68. Ibid., No. 741.

69. Ibid., No. 744.

70. Ibid.

71. Ibid., No. 747.

72. Ibid., No. 749.

73. Ibid., No. 747.

Notes

74. Ibid., No. 749, plus the other Dulles dispatches, 23–25 April in this file.
75. Lemnitzer to 110 (Dulles) 23 and 24 (?) April 1945, Nos. 691, 692, 698, *OSS Reports*.
76. Ibid.
77. 110 (Dulles) to Lemnitzer, 23 April 1945, No. 756, *OSS Reports*.
78. *Dulles/Gaevernitz*, p. 36.
79. *Toland Last 100*, p. 538.
80. Lemnitzer to 110 (Dulles), 25 April 1945, No. 702, *OSS Reports*.
81. *Toland Last 100*, p. 537.
82. 110 (Dulles) to Lemnitzer, 25 April 1945, No. 761, *OSS Reports*.
83. 110 (Dulles) to Lemnitzer, 23 April 1945, No. 756, *OSS Reports*.
84. 110 (Dulles) to Lemnitzer, 25 April 1945, No. 762, *OSS Reports*.
85. Ibid.
86. Ibid.
87. Ibid. No. 761, 110 (Dulles) to Lemnitzer, 23 April 1945, No. 756, *OSS Reports*.
88. 110 (Dulles) to Lemnitzer, 25 April 1945, No. 761, *OSS Reports*.
89. Ibid. No. 762.
90. Ibid. 110 (Dulles) to Lemnitzer, 26 April 1945, No. 769, *OSS Reports*.
91. Ibid.
92. *Toland Last 100*, pp. 541–542; Statement by SS Sturmbannführer Dr. Klaus Huegel, *OSS Reports*.
93. *Deakin*, p. 304f. That Mussolini was not just playacting in his claim that the Germans had deceived him is indicated by A. Mellini Ponce de Leon, *Guerra Diplomatica a Salò ottobre 1943–aprile 1945* (Bologna, 1950), pp. 148–149.
94. *Deakin*, p. 308; Statement by SS Sturmbannführer Dr. Klaus Huegel, *OSS Reports*.
95. *Toland Last 100*, p. 537; *Kimche*, p. 145f.
96. *Dulles/Gaevernitz*, p. 38; *Dulles Secret*, p. 186f; *Toland Last 100*, p. 541f.
97. Ibid. A copy of Jones's report is in *Dulles/Gaevernitz*, p. 39.
98. Ibid.
99. *Selected CSDIC Reports*, p. 64.
100. *Dulles/Gaevernitz*, pp. 39–40; *Dulles Secret*, pp. 192–193.
101. MOI Reports of 26/27 April. *FO* 371/49802/2446 and Charles to FO, 27 April, 1945, No. 681, *FO* 371/49802/2406.
102. Dulles claims the telegram arrived on the morning of the twenty-seventh, after he was at work (*Dulles Secret*, p. 197) but the message is clearly dated 26 April (Lemnitzer to 110, No. 710, *OSS Reports*) and other such messages arrived in Bern immediately.
103. In addition to all the earlier troubles, the Joint Chiefs suspected that Dulles had disobeyed orders, and an investigation of his conduct—which seems not to have censured him—was made. (See Cheston to Joint Chiefs of Staff, 25 April and Cheston to General A. J. McFarland, 26 April 1945, *CCS 387 Germany*.)
104. Caserta's request for a reversal of the cut-off order (Naf 929, 23 April 1945) said "Presume you have seen OSS message 920 (9) and 922 (9) from Berne" (misspelled "Berge"). Leahy wrote next to this passage, "*Not Seen*." Admiral Leahy Files, "Berne Surrender Controversy" File, RG 218, Modern Military Branch, National Archives.
105. *Stimson Diary*, 23 April.
106. 110 (Dulles) to Lemnitzer, 26 April 1945, no. 770, *OSS Reports*.
107. 110 (Dulles) to Lemnitzer, 27 April 1945, no. 773, *OSS Reports*.
108. Ibid., *Dulles/Gaevernitz*, p. 40.
109. *Dulles/Gaevernitz*, p. 41.
110. 110 (Dulles) to Lemnitzer, 27 April 1945, No. 773 and Lemnitzer to 110 (Dulles) 28 April 1945, No. 717, *OSS Reports*.
111. Lemnitzer to 110 (Dulles), 27 April 1945, No. 711, *OSS Reports*.
112. *Crossword*, p. 56.

113. Ibid., pp. 56–57; Lemnitzer to 110 (Dulles), 28 April 1945, No. 772, *OSS Reports*. The former source puts the arrival at 4:15 P.M.,the latter at 3:15 P.M.

114. The surrender document is filed as CCS Memorandum for Information no. 277, 7 June 1945 in *CCS 387 Germany*. Another copy showing handwritten corrections is included in *OSS Reports*. Material on the preparation of the surrender instrument is sprinkled through various files and collections, but the most important items are in German Armistice File, *Post and Counselor Files*.

115. *Crossword*, p. 57; "Arrangements for the Reception, etc." *OSS Reports*.

116. Combined Chiefs to Alexander, 21 April 1945, Fan 528, *OSS Reports*.

117. Deane to Alexander, 25 April 1945, No. MX 24054, *OSS Reports*.

118. Churchill to Stalin, 26 April 1945, No. 2176, CAB 21/1602/7953, Public Records Office, London; Archer to Alexander, 27 April 1945, No. MX 24091, *OSS Reports*.

119. Lemnitzer to Admiral Stone, 27 April 1945, No. F66485, *OSS Reports*.

120. Ltnt. Col. Count de Salis to Col. W. M. Cunningham, 27 April 1945, *OSS Reports*.

121. "Arrangements for the reception, etc." 27 April 1945, *OSS Reports*.

122. An AFHQ Joint Planning Staff memorandum shows that the whole scenario was arranged so the Soviets could make "no claim to previous consultation." Arrangements for Acceptance of Surrender, etc., 12 April 1945, Joint Planning Staff Files, Box 624, *Post and Counselor Files*. Twenty years later, General Morgan told John Toland that the Soviets were shown the surrender terms "just after" they were shown to the Germans. Box 9, *Toland*.

123. CCS 861, initially dated 23 May 1945, developed into a fat file. See *CCS 387 Germany*.

124. The notes for this session, and subsequent sessions, are attached to the surrender document (see note 114 above).

125. Ibid., p. 28. The following account of the session comes from this source.

126. Gaevernitz Report, p. 33, Box 9. *Toland*.

127. As in other areas—especially following the civil war in Greece—the Allies were leery of anything that would leave arms in the hands of Italian resistance groups. The draft surrender, which had been prepared in the early stages of the Sunrise dealings, envisioned large German units remaining intact within partisan areas until their eventual disarmament by Western forces. Such a procedure indicated the intensity of Anglo-American civil war fears as well as the prevailing cavalier attitude toward the resistance. In fact, when the surrender instrument went into force in early May, the Allied offensive had smashed through the German lines, and aside from SS and army units in the Tyrol and Venezia Guilia, as well as a few pockets in the western portions of the country, only tattered fragments remained in partisan-controlled territory.

128. See above, p. 133.

129. The Surrender Document (as cited in note 114, this chapter), p. 6.

130. Ibid., p. 5.

131. As with the first session, all material for the second session comes from the notes attached to the surrender document, see note 114, this chapter.

132. These issues crop up repeatedly in the Henry Morgenthau Jr. Diary (Hyde Park, New York) as well as the Charles Fahy Papers (RG 59) in the same repository. Indications of the planning in Italy may be found in Kirk to Secretary of State, 26 March 1945, No. 1175, 740.00119 EW/3-2645 and Kirk to Secretary of State, 16 May 1945, No. 1308, 740.00119 Control (Italy)/5-1645, Diplomatic Branch, National Archives.

133. Surrender Document, see note 114, this chapter.

134. Gaevernitz Report, Box 9, *Toland*.

135. The Surrender Document, see 114, this chapter.

136. *Dulles Secret*, pp. 205–206.

137. Ibid.

138. Lemnitzer to 110 (Dulles), 29 April 1945, *OSS Reports*.

139. *Dulles Secret*, pp. 206–207.

140. Ibid. p. 206.
141. Ibid.
142. The Surrender Document, see note 114, this chapter.
143. Alexander to the Combined Chiefs, 29 April 1945, No. 935, *CCS 387 Germany.*
144. Ibid.

Chapter 7: Somewhere Between Sunrise and Sunset

1. *Stuhlpfarer*, p. 129.
2. Ibid. A number of accounts by Sunrise personalities date this event as 28 April (see *Dulles/Gaevernitz*, pp. 47 and 54), but this seems to have been merely the day on which it was publicly announced. Dulles hints at the true state of affairs when, in his effort to paint Kesselring as the villain in the latter stages of Sunrise, he says that those favoring surrender had "feared" subordination to the field marshal. Obviously, every German in a responsible position knew this was coming. *Dulles Secret*, p. 228.
3. For the Innsbruck meeting see: *Rahn*, p. 225; *Dollmann*, p. 242; *Dulles/Gaevernitz*, p. 53; *Kesselring*, p. 407; and *Dulles Secret*, p. 225.
4. *Kesselring*, p. 406.
5. For the Meran meeting see *Rahn*, p. 225; *Dollmann*, p. 243; *Dulles Secret*, p. 226; and *Stuhlpfarer*, p. 129.
6. In addition to the sources indicated in the preceding note, see *Dulles/Gaevernitz*, pp. 46 and 53 and *Selected CSDIC Reports*, pp. 68–69. The primary source materials for much of what happened between 28 April and 2 May rest on a number of statements made by Wolff, and all of these require caution. Wolff relished any opportunity to recount these events in later years so that he could stress that it was the army, and not the SS, which had opposed implementing the capitulation. The tone of these statements, plus what we now know of Wolff's motives from the *CSDIC Reports*, as well as other sources, are sufficient to indicate that the Obergruppenführer was doing a good bit of purposeful special pleading with the Allies. If anyone has doubts on this matter they should be removed by a letter which Wenner wrote to Dollmann on 7 May in which Wolff's adjutant explained that the Obergruppenführer was spinning the old "political threads" and had told an American colonel the story of the last phase in "complete openness." Wenner added that he believed that Dollmann would see the "effects" of Wolff's revelations to the Americans in a "short time." Wenner to Dollmann, 7 May 1945, T-175, RFSS u. Chef d. Deutschen Polizei, Roll 225, EAP 170-b-10-18/2, Frame 2763803, Modern Military Branch, National Archives.
7. *Selected CSDIC Reports*, p. 69.
8. For the De Angelis affair, see ibid. pp. 68–70, plus *Dulles/Gaevernitz*, pp. 47 and 53–54; Wolff to Toland, 25 July 1963, Box 9, *Toland*; *Stuhlpfarer*, p. 131f; Smith to Glavin, 1 May 1945, No. 1552, *OSS Reports*; *Kimche*, p. 148f; and *Lanfranchi*, p. 344f.
9. *Dulles/Gaevernitz*, p. 53; *Stuhlpfarer*, p. 132; *Lanfranchi*, p. 344f.
10. *Selected CSDIC Reports*, p. 69.
11. Basing his conclusion on the German police records, Stuhlpfarer (p. 133) concluded that tales of the incident were exaggerated and that no civilians were killed, but other sources, especially an OSS report, point strongly in the other direction. See *Kimche*, p. 149; *Lanfranchi*, p. 347; and Smith to Glavin, 1 May 1945, No. 1552, *OSS Reports*.
12. *Stuhlpfarer*, p. 132. Wolff used the word "secrets" in regard to Hofer's report to Kesselring, but the gist of both reports was presumably the same. *Selected CSDIC Reports*, p. 69.
13. *Kesselring*, p. 407.
14. *Stuhlpfarer*, p. 132; *Dulles Secret*, pp. 228–229; and *Selected CSDIC Reports*, p. 70.
15. Ibid. and *Dulles/Gaevernitz*, p. 54, plus the statement of General Friedrich Schulz, MS

No. B-813, RG 338, Foreign Military Studies, Modern Military Branch, National Archives. Wolff's contention that Vietinghoff promised to resist any effort to arrest him—a contention that has slipped into virtually every account by Sunrise supporters—is impossible to substantiate.

16. *Dulles/Gaevernitz*, p. 48 and OSS message 30 April 1945 (Fairbury series, no number), *OSS Reports*.

17. *Selected CSDIC Reports*, p. 70.

18. Summary of Wolff statements made by Major H. W. Evans, 12 May 1945, *OSS Reports*. It should be noted that Wolff relayed a message to Dulles as early as 14 April in which he contended that the chief army commanders were "with him" whatever the commander of Army Group C might do. *Dulles/Gaevernitz*, p. 33.

19. For this episode, see especially *Dulles Secret*, p. 230f; *Dulles/Gaevernitz*, pp. 48–49; *Selected CSDIC Reports*, p. 70–71; and *Kimche*, p. 149.

20. Ibid. The quotation comes from *Selected CSDIC Reports*, p. 71.

21. The most important sources for this meeting are: *Selected CSDIC Reports*, pp. 71–72 and *Dulles/Gaevernitz*, p. 49. Caution on the use of Wolff's assertions applies with great force here.

22. The name is garbled but must be Blaskowitz, *Selected CSDIC Reports*, p. 72.

23. Alexander's "Fairbury" message, 30 April 1945, *OSS Reports*. Ambassador Kirk was so entranced that he reported to the State Department that General Clark would probably announce the end of resistance before the surrender went into effect. Kirk to Secretary of State, 30 April 1945, No. 1826, 740.0011EW/4-3045, Diplomatic Branch, National Archives.

24. Fairbury messages, 1 May 1945, Nos. 14 and 15, *OSS Reports*. In the first transmission, the word "centers" appeared as "cities," and this apparently caused some confusion in Caserta.

25. *Dulles/Gaevernitz*, p. 48. An unnumbered message from the radio operator secreted in Wolff's headquarters suggests that some of his crystals were broken and that this may have been the basis of the trouble. Fairbury message, 30 April 1945, *OSS Reports*.

26. Fairbury message, 1 May, No. 17, *OSS Reports*.

27. *Dulles/Gaevernitz*, p. 49; *Dulles Secret*, p. 232; *Selected CSDIC Reports*, pp. 72–73.

28. *Dulles/Gaevernitz*, p. 49.

29. *Toland Last 100*, p. 604; *Dulles/Secret*, p. 233; *Dulles/Gaevernitz*, p. 49; and Erich Winhold, "Kapitulation in Italien," *Sammeldokumentation, Das Dritte Reich/Zeiter Weltkrieg*, No. 51, p. 504.

30. *Selected CSDIC Reports*, p. 73. The timing of all this is important in determining the causal relationships. Doenitz made his announcement at 10:20 P.M., and Wolff claims in all of his statements that the orders to ground arms had gone out before this news reached the Bolzano group at 11:00 or 11:15.

31. Frido von Senger und Etterlin, *Krieg in Europa* (Cologne and Berlin, 1960), pp. 389 and 391. In his many statements Wolff contended that Schulz still refused to go along and threw the others out of his office (see *Dulles/Gaevernitz*, p. 50). But this contention was intertwined with his belief that he was subsequently threatened by a mass arrest order from Schulz and Kesselring, and as can be seen from the following note, this belief was probably false. Senger von Etterlin's version, which depends on his own experience, as well as subsequent talks with his commanders, generals Lemelsen and Schulz, fits the course of events much better.

32. *Dulles/Gaevernitz*, p. 50 and *Dulles Secret*, p. 234. Kesselring's cryptic account seems to indicate that he was reacting to the earlier developments—the Sunrise plot, the arrest of Schulz, and the cutting of communications with Italy, *Kesselring*, p. 408. The omission of Lemelsen and Herr from the arrest order, together with the inclusion of Kempf and Schweinitz, indicates strongly that the earlier developments, not any midnight initiative by Schulz, were the cause.

33. Fairbury message, 2 May 1945, No. 18, *OSS Reports*.

34. *Selected CSDIC Reports*, p. 73; *Dulles Secret*, pp. 235–236; *Dulles/Gaevernitz*, p. 50; Summary of Wolff statements made by Major H. W. Evans, 12 May 1945, *OSS Reports*.

Notes

Significantly, Kesselring uses the argument of the need to avoid another incident of Germans breaking their word—the proposition stressed by Wolff—to explain his course of action. *Kesselring*, p. 409.

35. Ibid. Statement of General Friedrich Schulz, MS No. B-813, RG 338, Modern Military Branch, National Archives.

36. Fairbury message, 2 May 1945, no. 20, *OSS Reports*.

37. *Ibid*. no. 21.

38. Alexander to CCS, 2 May 1945, Naf 941, *CCS 387 Germany*.

39. *Crossword*, p. 69.

40. *Stimson Diary*, 2 May 1945.

41. In his book, *Secret Surrender*, Dulles did not stress the importance of Operation Sunrise for the acquisition of Trieste, but he and Gaevernitz considered it one of their major achievements. See *Dulles/Gaevernitz*, p. 1 and Gaevernitz's comment to Dulles (19 September 1966) regarding a critical review of *Secret Surrender* in the *New York Review of Books*: "I understand that this review is controlled by a group of leftists. Obviously they are not too pleased that we kept the Russians out of Trieste." "The Secret Surrender, Gero von Gaevernitz in Germany" File, Dulles Papers, Princeton, New Jersey.

42. Alexander to the Fifteenth Army Group (probably 29 April 1945), AFHQ, Reel 132, RG 331, Federal Records Center, Suitland, Maryland.

43. Kirk to Acting Secretary of State, 27 April 1945, 740.0011EW/4-2745, Kirk to Acting Secretary, 28 April 1945, 740.0011 EW/4-2845, Diplomatic Branch, National Archives.

44. This decision was made at the second Quebec conference during a conversation between Roosevelt and Churchill. See Memorandum, W. Leahy for Freeman Matthews, 19 September 1944, in *Coles and Weinberg* (p. 591), and Memorandum for Harry Hopkins from Freeman Matthews, 16 September 1944, *FRUS, The Conference at Quebec, 1944*, pp. 485–486. In a memorandum dated 4 May 1945, Acting Secretary of State Joseph Grew briefed President Truman on the background of the situation in Venezia Giulia and Roosevelt's stand thereon. Papers of Harry S. Truman, President's Secretary Files, Harry S. Truman Library, Independence, Missouri.

45. Memorandum of Middleton (British Embassy) and Jones (State Department), 24 February 1945, Office of Western European Affairs, Box 3, RG 59, Diplomatic Branch, National Archives.

46. For British-Yugoslav relations in this period see E. Llewellyn-Woodward, *British Foreign Policy in the Second World War*, vol. III (London, 1971), p. 336f.

47. For the text of Eden's note (10 February 1945), see *FRUS, the Conferences at Malta and Yalta, 1945*, pp. 888–889. For the background of this proposal see the extensive material in the papers of the British Post Hostilities Planning Staff of the War Cabinet (CAB 81, 46/8267), Public Records Office, London.

48. For this decision, see Woodward, *British Foreign Policy in the Second World War*, vol. III, p. 367, plus the minutes of the meeting held at the British Embassy in Athens on 15 February 1945 between Eden, Alexander, Cadogan, Airey, and others. PREM 3 495/5 7990, Public Records Office, London and the report by Kirk to the Secretary of State (20 February 1945) of Alexander's political meeting in Caserta, *FRUS, 1945*, vol. IV, pp. 1103–1106.

49. The minutes of the Alexander-Tito meeting have never been published; they are in *FO* 371/48810/4632/8228.

50. Ibid.

51. Interview with General Morgan, Box 9 *Toland*.

52. Kirk to the Secretary of State, 2 March 1945, *FRUS, 1945*, vol. IV, p. 1113. See also other reports to Washington of the same period published therein for a critical appraisal of Alexander's attitude. For Macmillan's views see *Cox Race*, p. 18. The opposition of Kirk and Macmillan was probably decisive in preventing Alexander from committing himself more formally with Tito on the question of the administration of Venezia Giulia.

53. Prime Minister to Foreign Secretary, 11 March 1945, PREM 3/495/5 7990, Public Records Office, London.

54. Eden to Prime Minister, 15 March 1945, PREM 3 495/5 7990, Public Records Office, London. On the eighteenth, Eden wrote another long note to Churchill related to British long-term policy toward Yugoslavia, stating that it was more important than ever to maintain British influence in Yugoslavia to protect the Western positions in Greece and Italy and to counterbalance Russian influence. See Woodward, *British Foreign Policy in the Second World War*, vol. III, pp. 364–365.

55. Secretary of State to Kirk, 12 April 1945, *FRUS, 1945*, vol. IV, pp. 1120–1121. Since it was assumed that the Yugoslavs would control Zara, it was excluded from the planned Allied Military Government.

56. Supreme Allied Commander's Conference, note by Deputy Chief of Staff on Allied Military Control in Venezia Giulia, 24 April 1945, *Allied Control*, 10000/136/262; Kirk to Secretary of State, 25 April 1945, *FRUS, 1945*, vol. IV, pp. 1123–1125.

57. Alexander to CCS, 26 April 1945, Naf 932, PREM 3, 495/6 7990, Public Records Office, London.

58. Churchill to President Truman, 27 April 1945, *FRUS, 1945*, vol. IV, p. 1125. Ironically, the only known instance in which Roosevelt had taken up the problem of Trieste with the prime minister was to strongly rebuke him in July, 1941, for rumors that the British government was promising Trieste to Yugoslavia, *Roosevelt and Churchill*, pp. 149–151.

59. Churchill to President Truman, 27 April 1945, *FRUS, 1945*, vol. IV, p. 1125. Cox oversimplifies the conflicts, *Cox Race*, pp. 150–152.

60. *Stimson Diary*, 27–29 April.

61. CCS to Alexander, 28 April 1945, Fan 536, PREM 3, 495/6 7990, Public Records Office, London.

62. Alexander to Clark, 30 April 1945, *Allied Control* 10000/105/497. Published in part in *Coles and Weinberg*, p. 595.

63. Churchill to President Truman, 30 April 1945, *FRUS, 1945*, vol. IV, pp. 1130–1132.

64. Ibid. Here again, Cox makes Churchill out to have been more in possession of a clear and realistic policy than the evidence warrants. *Cox Race*, p. 154.

65. Churchill to Alexander, 1 May 1945, Guard 2765, PREM 3 495/6 7990, Public Records Office, London, and *Cox Race*, p. 193f.

66. Ibid.

67. President Truman to Prime Minister, 29 April 1945, *FRUS, 1945*, vol. IV, p. 1127.

68. *Stimson Diary*, 30 April 1945.

69. Memorandum by the Acting Secretary, 30 April 1945, *FRUS, 1945*, vol. IV, pp. 1129–1139; *Stimson Diary*, 30 April 1945.

70. President Truman was torn between the need to stand firm against the Soviets, as the State Department suggested—his famous scene with Molotov was the clearest example of this "get-tough attitude"—and the belief, which he shared with the War Department, that it was vital to get the Soviet Union into the war against Japan, and that therefore it was important to avoid further tension. Since all the top American officials believed that Tito was backed by the Soviet Union, an involvement in the Balkans could have prejudiced an early entry into the Pacific war by the Soviet Union.

71. Memorandum by the Director of the Office of European Affairs on a Conference with the President, Grew, Leahy, Phillips, and Matthews. *FRUS, 1945*, vol. IV, pp. 1128–1129.

72. Truman to Churchill, 30 April 1945, ibid. p. 1132; *Cox Race*, pp. 154–155.

73. *Stimson Diary*, 2 May 1945.

74. Ibid., 7 May 1945.

75. Ibid., 2 May 1945.

76. Field Marshal Alexander to Churchill, 1 May 1945. *Churchill*, p. 553. Churchill did not publish his answer, which, according to Alexander's biographer, was the "sharpest rebuke" that

Notes

he ever addressed to the field marshal. See Nigel Nicholson, *The Life of Field Marshal Alexander of Tunis* (New York, 1973), p. 279.

77. The following description of the Allied entrance into Trieste comes mainly from Geoffrey Cox, *Road to Trieste* (London, 1947), pp. 1–7 and 193f, and the same author's *Cox Race*, pp. 9f and 156f. Cox was the intelligence officer of the second New Zealand Division. The information on the dual occupation of Venezia Giulia is taken from the following additional sources: Bogdan C. Novack, *Trieste, 1941–1945* (Chicago, 1970); Diego De Castro, *Il Problema di Trieste* (Bologna, 1953); C.R.S. Harris, *Allied Military Administration of Italy, 1943–1945* (London, 1957); Robin Kay, *Official History of New Zealand in the Second World War, Italy*, vol. II (Wellington, New Zealand, 1967); Jacsic Paule, *The Liberation of the Julian March by the Yugoslav Army* (no date, no place); and Intelligence reports on the events in Trieste from 26 April to 2 May, OWI Records, E: Italy, Trieste 1/6/c, RG 208, Federal Records Center, Suitland, Maryland.

78. Some units surrendered to the Yugoslavs and joint Yugoslav-New Zealand assault overcame others. *Cox Race*, p. 15.

79. *Stimson Diary*, 4 May 1945.

80. The best account of the Yugoslav advance in English is *Cox Race*, p. 170f, which makes extensive use of Yugoslav sources.

81. The diplomatic documents in *FRUS, 1945*, vol. IV, p. 1146f, and the *Stimson Diary* from 8 to 11 May, testify to this reversal of policy in Washington, and to Stimson's loss of influence on the president in favor of Grew. On the twelfth, Truman wrote to Churchill advocating a firm stand on Trieste. See also *Churchill*, p. 554f.

Chapter 8: Conclusion

1. Kurt W. Böhme, *Die deutschen Kriegsgefangenen in amerikanischer Hände* (Bielefeld, Germany, 1973).

2. For the Italian area see materials in: *FRUS, 1945*, vol. V, pp. 1103–1104; "German Armistice File" *Post and Counselor Files; CCS-387 Germany*. For the general question see Julius Epstein, *Operation Keelhaul* (Greenwich, Connecticut, 1973); and Nikolai Tolstoy, *The Victims of Yalta* (London, 1977).

3. See Les K. Adler and Thomas Paterson, "The Merger of Nazi Germany and Soviet Russia in the American Image of Totalitarianism, 1930s–1950s," American Historical Review, vol. LXXV, No. 4 (April, 1970), pp. 1046–1064.

4. See *Dulles/Gaevernitz*, pp. 1 and 32.

5. Hedrick Smith, *The Russians* (New York, 1978), pp. 432–433.

6. This is even true of mildly revisionist works like John Lewis Gaddis, *The United States and the Origins of the Cold War* (New York, 1972), pp. 92–94.

7. Gabriel Kolko, *The Politics of War: The World and United States Foreign Policy, 1943–1945* (New York, 1968), p. 375f.

8. For the general situation see Gaddis, *The United States and the Origins of the Cold War*; Yergin, *Shattered Peace;* and Robert J. Donovan, *Conflict and Crisis: The Presidency of Harry S. Truman 1945–1948* (New York, 1977). For Trieste, which has not been seriously studied as a cold war issue, the best course is probably to consult *Cox Race*, and to follow out the document references included in notes 43 through 80 of chapter 7.

9. See *Dulles Secret* and Leonard Mosley, *Dulles*, p. 101f.

10. See Mosley, *Dulles*, for the general development of this trend.

11. Wenner to Dollmann, 7 May 1945, T-175, *RFSS u. Chef d. deutschen Polizei*, Roll 225, EAP 170-b-10-18/2, Frame 2763803, Modern Military Branch, National Archives; Fairbury messages, 4 May and following, *OSS Reports*.

12. See the reports and telegrams of 4–6 May 1945, *OSS Reports*.

13. See the messages on Gaevernitz's trip to Bolzano and the measures for the families of Wolff and Parrilli, etc., 9–26 May, *OSS Reports*.

14. John P. Delany, *The Blue Devils in Italy* (Washington, 1947), p. 225f, and *Dollmann*, p. 252f.

15. Record of the Meeting of the Four Chief Prosecutors, 24 August 1945, *FO* 371/50486/U6602.

16. *Wolff Interrogations*, 14 December 1946, Frames 943–944 and 973; Letter from General Telford Taylor to the authors, 1 June 1978.

17. Ibid., plus *Wolff Interrogations*, 25 February 1947, Frame 979.

18. See Box 9 *Toland*, and Gero von Gaevernitz File 1-25, Dulles Papers, Princeton, New Jersey.

19. Nuremberg Document NO-2207.

20. Interrogation Report on Rudolf Rahn, 8 July 1948, Freedom of Information Center, U.S. Army Intelligence Agency Records, Fort Meade, Maryland.

21. *Selected CSDIC Reports*, p. 52.

Bibliography*

ARCHIVES AND MANUSCRIPT COLLECTIONS

United States
A. National Archives, Diplomatic Branch:
   Department of State Files, 1943–1945, RG 59
   H. Freeman Matthews File, RG 59
B. National Archives, Dwight D. Eisenhower Library, Abilene, Kansas:
   W. Bedell Smith Collection of World War II Documents
C. National Archives, Federal Record Center, Suitland, Maryland:
   Allied Control Commission Records, RG 331
   Allied Forces Headquarters Mediterranean, Records, RG 331
   Office of War Information Records, RG 208
   Post and Counselor Files, Caserta, RG 84
D. National Archives, Modern Military Branch:
   Records of the Army Staff, RG 319
   Records of the Combined Chiefs of Staff, RG 218
   Foreign Military Studies, RG 338
   Records of the U.S. Joint Chiefs of Staff, RG 218
   Leahy Papers, RG 218
   Interservice Agencies, "Military Mission Moscow," RG 334
   Nuremberg Interrogations, RG 1019, RG 80
   Operations Division Files, RG 165
   Records of the OSS, Research and Analysis Branch, RG 59
   Records of the Office of the Secretary of War, RG 107
   Records of the War Department, General and Special Staff, RG 165
   Micro Copy T–175, Reichsführer SS
E. National Archives, Franklin Delano Roosevelt Library, Hyde Park, New York:
   Charles Fahy Papers, RG 59
   Map Room File, Allied Control Commission for Italy
   Henry Morgenthau Jr. Diary
   Naval Aides Files, Germany, Warfare
   President's Secretary's File, OSS
F. National Archives, Harry S. Truman Library, Independence, Missouri:
   George Elsey Papers
G. Freedom of Information Center, United States Army Intelligence Agency, Fort Meade, Maryland:
   Interrogation of Ambassador Rudolf Rahn
H. Hoover Institution, Stanford University, Stanford, California:
   M. Preston Goodfellow Papers
I. Library of Congress:
   Cordell Hull Papers
   John Toland Collection
J. Princeton University, Princeton, New Jersey:
   Allen Dulles Papers

* The following bibliography is restricted to works cited in the text.

222

K. University of Virginia, Charlottesville, Virginia:
   Edward Stettinius Papers
L. Yale University, New Haven, Connecticut:
   Henry L. Stimson Papers

Germany
Berlin Document Center:
   Personnel Files, SS Obergruppenführer Karl Wolff

Great Britain
Public Records Office, London:
   CAB 122, British Joint Staff Mission
   CAB 21, Cabinet Offices
   CAB 79, Chiefs of Staff
   CAB 80, Chiefs of Staff
   Foreign Office, General Correspondence, FO 371
   PREM 3 Prime Minister
   War Office Papers, WO 204

Interviews
Elena Agarossi with Ferruccio Parri, June 1977
Bradley F. Smith with John Toland, September 1977
Personal communication from General Telford Taylor, 1 June 1978

OFFICIAL PUBLISHED DOCUMENTS

Coles, H. L., and A. K. Weinberg, *Civil Affairs, Soldiers Become Governors, The U.S. Army in World War II*. Washington, D.C., 1964.
The Morgenthau Diaries (Germany), 2 vols. Washington, D.C., 1967.
OSS War Report, 2 vols., Manuscript, Modern Military Branch National Archives. Washington, D.C., 1949.
U.S. Department of State, *Foreign Relations of the United States:*
   Annual volumes, 1943–1945. Washington, D.C., 1963–1968.
   The Conferences of Washington, 1941–1942 and Casablanca, 1943. Washington, D.C., 1968.
   The Conference at Quebec 1944. Washington, D.C., 1972.
   The Conferences at Malta and Yalta. Washington, D.C., 1955.

BOOKS

Agarossi, Elena. "La Politica degli alleati verso l'Italia nel 1943," in R. De Felice, ed. *L'Italia tra tedeschi e alleati* (Bologna, 1973), pp. 171–219.
Ambrose, Stephen E. *Eisenhower and Berlin, 1945: The Decision to Stop at the Elbe*. Garden City, New York, 1967.
Battaglia, Roberto. *Storia della resistenza italiana*. Torno, Italy, 1964.
Bocca, Giorgio. *Storia dell'Italia partigiana*. Bari, Italy, 1966.
Böhme, Kurt W. *Die Deutschen Kriegsgefangenen in Amerikanischer Hände*. Bielefeld, Germany, 1973.
Brown, Anthony Cave, ed. *The Secret War Report of the OSS*. New York, 1976.
Catalano, Franco. *Storia del CLNAI*. Bari, Italy, 1956.
Churchill, Winston S. *Triumph and Tragedy*. Boston, Massachusetts, 1953.

Bibliography

Collotti, Enzo. *L'amministrazione tedesca dell'Italia occupata, 1943–1945*. Milan, 1965.

Cornia, Carlo. *Monterosa, Storia della divisione alpina Monterosa della RSI*. Udine, Italy, 1971.

Corson, William R. *The Armies of Ignorance*. New York, 1977.

Cox, Geoffrey. *The Race for Trieste*. London, 1977.

———. *The Road to Trieste*. London, 1947.

De Castro, Diego. *Il problema di Trieste*. Bologna, 1953.

Delaney, John P. *The Blue Devils in Italy*. Washington, D.C., 1947.

Delzell, Charles F. *Mussolini's Enemies: The Italian Antifascist Resistance*. Princeton, New Jersey, 1961.

Dollmann, Eugen. *Dolmetscher der Diktatoren*. Bamberg, Germany, 1963.

Donovan, Robert J. *Conflict and Crisis: The Presidency of Harry S Truman 1945–1948*. New York, 1977.

Dulles, Allen. *Secret Surrender*. New York, 1966.

———. *Germany's Underground*. New York, 1947.

Dulles, Allen, and Hamilton Fish Armstrong. *Can We Be Neutral?* New York, 1936.

Ehrman, John. *Grand Strategy*, vols. 5–6, History of the Second World War, United Kingdom Series. London, 1956.

Eisenhower, Dwight D. *Crusade in Europe*. New York, 1948.

Epstein, Julius. *Operation Keelhaul*. Greenwich, Connecticut, 1973.

Gaddis, John Lewis. *The United States and the Origins of the Cold War, 1941–1947*. New York, 1972.

Hagen, Walter. *Unternehmen Bernard*. Wels and Starnberg, 1955.

Harriman, Averell W., and Elie Abel. *Special Envoy to Churchill and Stalin, 1941–1946*. New York, 1975.

Harris, C. R. S. *Allied Military Administration of Italy, 1943–1945*. London, 1957.

Hesse, Fritz. *Das Spiel um Deutschland*. Munich, 1953.

Hoffmann, Peter. *The History of the German Resistance, 1933–1945*. Cambridge, Massachusetts, 1977.

Höhne, Heinz. *The Order of the Death's Head*. New York, 1970.

Hymoff, Edward. *The OSS in World War II*. New York, 1972.

Irving, David. *The Destruction of Dresden*. New York, 1963.

Jacsic, Paule. *The Liberation of the Julian March by the Yugoslav Army*. No place, No date.

Kay, Robin. *Official History of New Zealand in the Second World War—Italy*, vol. 2. Wellington, New Zealand, 1967.

Kennan, George F. *Russia and the West under Lenin and Stalin*. New York, 1962.

Kesselring, Albert. *Soldat bis zum letzten Tag*. Bonn, 1953.

Kimche, Jon. *Spying for Peace*. London, 1961.

Kolko, Gabriel. *The Politics of War: The World and United States Foreign Policy, 1943–1945*. New York, 1968.

Lanfranchi, Ferruccio. *La resa degli ottocentomila*. Milan, 1948.

Leahy, William D. *I Was There*. New York, 1950.

Loewenheim, Francis L, Harold D. Langlen, and Manfred Jonas, eds. *Roosevelt and Churchill, Their Secret Wartime Correspondence*. New York, 1976.

Mellini Ponce de Leon, Alberto. *Guerra diplomatica a Salò, ottobre 1943–aprile 1945*. Bologna, 1950.

Moelhausen, Eitel Federico. *La carta perdente*. Rome, 1948.

Mosley, Leonard. *Dulles: A Biography of Eleanor, Allen, John Foster Dulles, and Their Family Network*. New York, 1978.

Nicholson, Nigel. *The Life of Field Marshal Alexander of Tunis*. New York, 1975.

Novack, Bogdan C. *Trieste, 1941–1945*. Chicago, 1970.

Plehwe, Friedrich Karl von. *The End of an Alliance*. London, 1971.

Pogue, Forrest C. *George C. Marshall: Organizer of Victory, 1943–1945*. New York, 1973.

Rahn, Rudolf. *Ruheloses Leben*. Düsseldorf, 1949.

Salvadori, Massimo, *Resistenza e Azione*. Bari, Italy, 1951.

Schlabrendorff, Fabian von. *They Almost Killed Hitler*. New York, 1947.

Schuster, Ildefonso. *Gli ultimi tempi di un regime*. Milan, 1946.

Secchia, Pietro, and Filippo Frassati. *La resistenza e gli alleati*. Milan, 1967.

Senger und Etterlin, Frido von. *Krieg in Europa*. Cologne and Berlin, 1960.

Shtemenko, S. M. *The Last Six Months*. Garden City, New York, 1977.

Smith, Bradley F. *Reaching Judgment at Nuremberg*. New York, 1977.

Smith, Bradley F., and Agnes F. Peterson, eds. *Himmler Geheimreden*. Frankfurt, 1974.

Smith, Harris. *The OSS, the Secret History of America's First Central Intelligence Agency*. New York, 1972.

Smith, Hedrick. *The Russians*. New York, 1978.

Speer, Albert. *Inside the Third Reich*. New York, 1970.

Stimson, Henry L., and McGeorge Bundy. *On Active Service in Peace and War*. New York, 1947.

Stuhlpfarer, Karl. *Die Operationszonen "Alpenvorland und Adriatisches Küstenland,"* 1940–1945. Vienna, 1969.

Toland, John. *Adolf Hitler*. New York, 1976.

———. *The Last 100 Days*. New York, 1967.

Tolstoy, Nikolai. *The Victims of Yalta*. London, 1977.

Warner, Geoffrey. "Italy and the Powers," in Stuart J. Woolf, ed. *The Rebirth of Italy, 1943–1945*. London, 1972, pp. 30–56.

Woodward, E. L. *British Foreign Policy in the Second World War*, vols. 3–5. London, 1962–1976.

Wright, Gordon. *The Ordeal of Total War*, New York, 1968.

Yergin, Daniel. *Shattered Peace, The Origins of the Cold War and the National Security State*. Boston, Massachusetts, 1977.

Zhukov, Georgi K. *The Memoirs of Marshal Zhukov*. New York, 1971.

ARTICLES

Adler, Les K., and Thomas Paterson. "The Merger of Nazi Germany and Soviet Russia in the American Image of Totalitarianism, 1930s–1950s," *The American Historical Review* LXXV (1970): 1046–1064.

Agarossi, Elena. "La situazione politica ed economica dell'Italia nel periodo 1944–1945: i governi Bonomi," *Quaderni dell'Istituto Romano per la storia d'Italia del fascismo alla Resistenza* no. 2 (1971): 5–151.

Di Nolfo, Ennio. "L'operazione 'Sunrise': spunti e documenti," *Storia e Politica* XIV (1975), no. 3: 345–376 and no. 4: 501–522.

Illardi, Massimo. "Nuovi Documenti sugli interventi tedeschi nell'industria italiana tra il 1943 e il 1945." *Il Movimento di Liberazione in Italia* XXIV (1972): 77–92.

Maurizio (Ferruccio Parri). "Il movimento di liberazione e gli alleati," *Il Movimento di Liberazione in Italia* I (1949): 7–27.

Scalpelli, Adolfo. "La formazione delle forze armata di Salo attraverso i documenti dello Stato Maffiore della RSI," *Il Movimento di Liberazione in Italia* XV (1963): 19–70.

Villa, Brian L. "The U.S. Army, Unconditional Surrender, and the Potsdam Proclamation," *The Journal of American History* LXIII (1976): 66–92.

Winhold, Erich. "Kapitulation in Italien," *Sammeldokumentation, Das Dritte Reich/Zweiter Weltkrieg* no. 51: 499–504.

Wolff, Karl. "Ecco la verità," *Tempo* XIII (1951): nos. 5–11.

Index

Index

Index